In this fascinating book, textile artist, writer and educator Katerina Knight presents unique techniques for incorporating dried flora and plant materials into your practice. With tips for growing plants and creative ideas for how to include them in your textile art, you will learn how to find inspiration in nature's transitions, growing and gathering all year long.

The book begins with a look into Katerina's personal journey to stitching with nature, before sharing practical tips on sowing seeds and the tools and methods needed. This section offers fascinating insight into which flowers are best for use in textile art, and explores Katerina's four favourite plants to work with: lavender, cornflower, dahlia and statice. The next section contains information on foraging, harvesting, drying and storing plant materials, with tips on when to harvest and how to forage sustainably. Finally, a section on stitching techniques contains a step-by-step guide to eight different stitches that can be used to create beautiful pieces of art.

This practical and inspirational guide combines the meditative effects of spending time in nature and practising handicrafts, prioritising mental wellbeing and helping you to calm your mind, creatively. Packed with advice and inspiration, this book is a must-have for anyone inspired by the beauty of nature.

Stitching *with* Nature

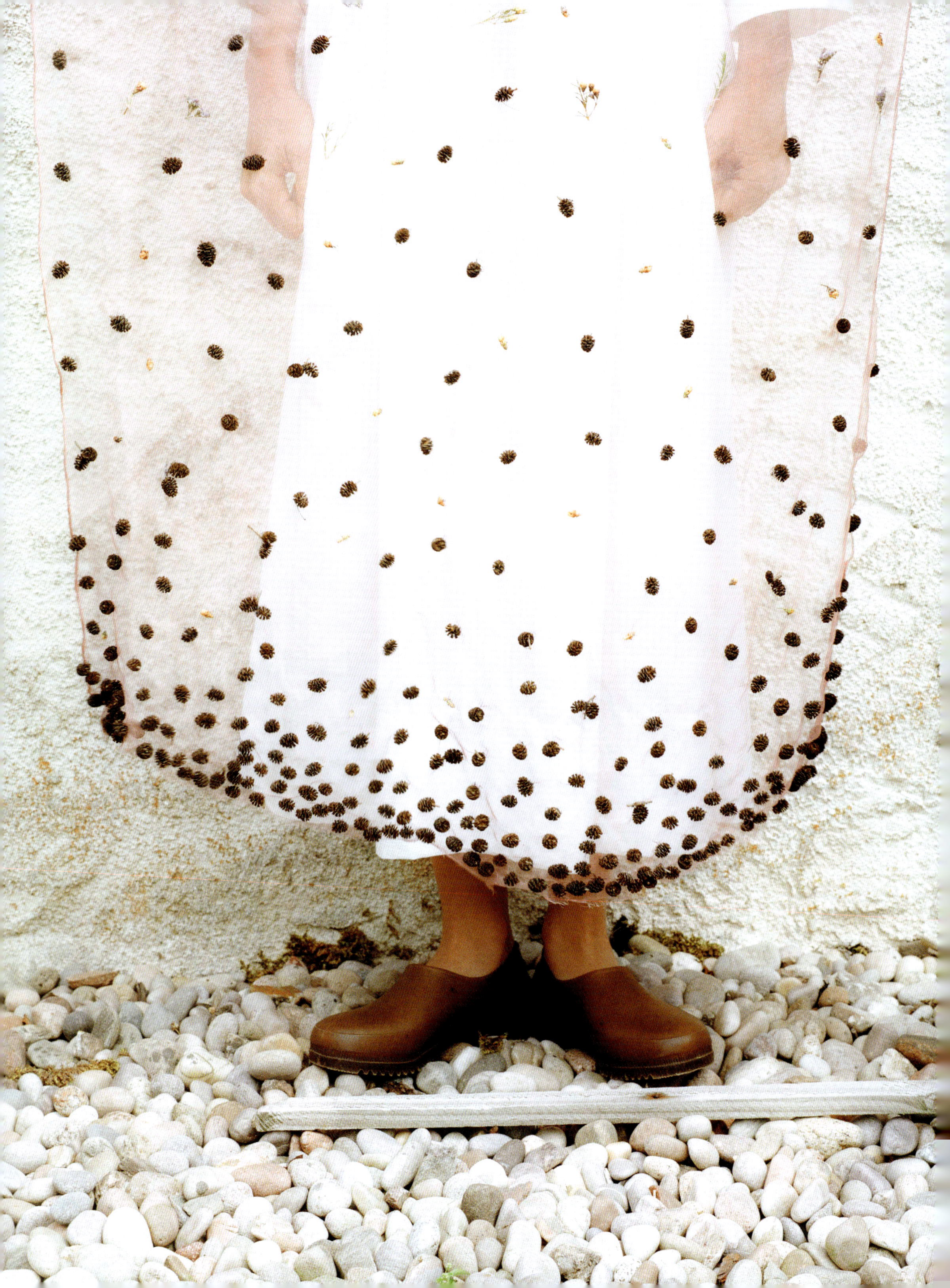

KATERINA KNIGHT

CREATING MATERIAL MAGIC WITH THE NATURAL WORLD

Stitching *with* Nature

BATSFORD

First published in the United Kingdom
in 2026 by
Batsford
43 Great Ormond Street
London
WC1N 3HZ

An imprint of B. T. Batsford Holdings Limited

ISBN 978 1 83733 062 1

A CIP catalogue record for this book is available from the British Library.

10 9 8 7 6 5 4 3 2 1

Reproduction by Rival Colour Ltd, UK
Printed by Toppan Leefung Printing International Ltd, China

This book can be ordered direct from the publisher at www.batsfordbooks.com, or try your local bookshop

Distributed throughout the UK and Europe by Abrams & Chronicle Books, 1st Floor, 22–24 Ely Place, London EC1N 6TE and 57 rue Gaston Tessier, 75166 Paris, France

www.abramsandchronicle.co.uk
info@abramsandchronicle.co.uk

FSC www.fsc.org
MIX
Paper | Supporting responsible forestry
FSC® C104723

Contents

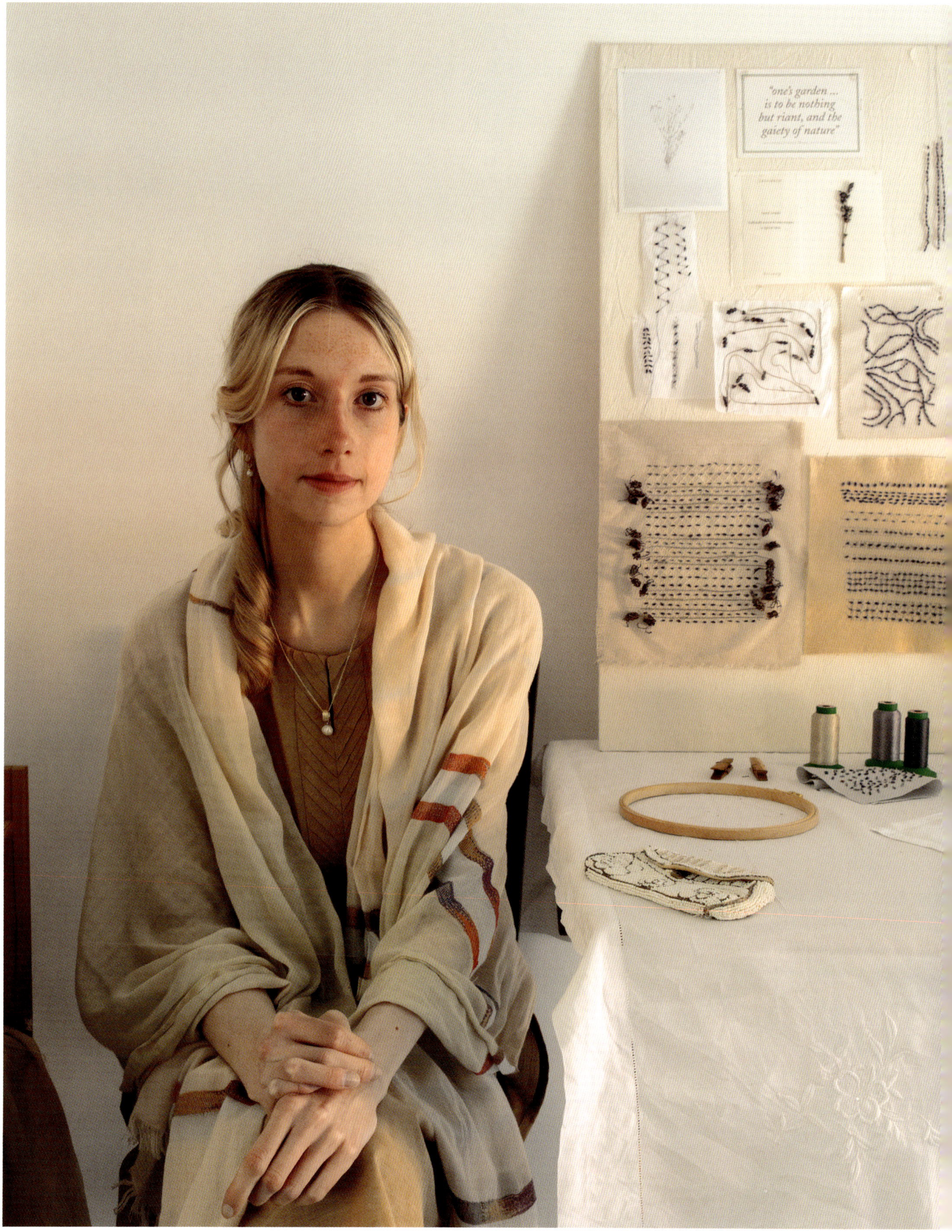
"one's garden ... is to be nothing but riant, and the gaiety of nature"

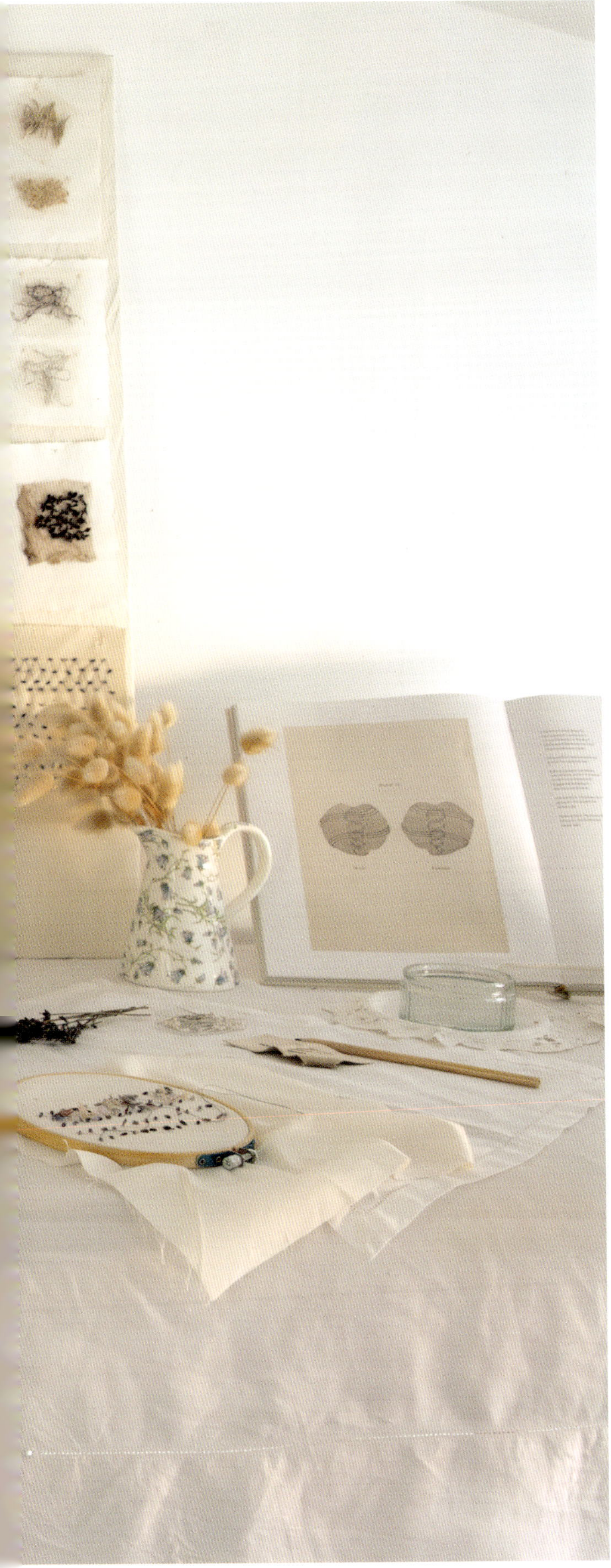

Introduction

As I sit to write this book, my life is immeasurably different from what it was just four years ago. Then, immersed in the fast-paced world of fashion, I couldn't have imagined leaving a city like London behind, and fleeing for a quiet life in the countryside, to live in a rural setting where I knew not a single person and had no ties. Yet, now, living in the Malvern Hills in the heart of the Worcestershire countryside, I've discovered something that has defined my artistic practice: an enduring connection with nature. My connection is with the land, the trees, the forests, the hills; with the flowers that I grow, and the wild ones that I forage.

This bond has transformed both my creative work and my inner world to flourish into something that is rooted in authenticity, shaped by the seasons and guided by a deep awareness of how we, as makers, consume and contribute to our planet.

The transition from the intensity of fashion and city life, to days spent walking, writing, gardening, hand-stitching and simply being, has taught me the quiet power of presence. I've come to understand the beauty in impermanence; how every living thing with its fleeting nature holds something sacred; something worth cherishing rather than resisting.

Gardening and slow textile craft have renewed a sense of meaning and purpose in my life. I've found a new definition of beauty: one that is wild, cyclical and curious. With each passing season, my creative appetite deepens – ever flowing and ever evolving.

If you are longing to slow down, to reconnect and to move with the rhythm of the Earth, this book may offer you the invitation you've been seeking.

The Joy of Slow Processes

In this book I will share with you the place where horticulture and textiles meet. I introduce beginner horticulture techniques – sowing seeds, growing flowers, harvesting and drying – then move into traditional hand-embroidery stitches with plant embellishments.

All of the techniques in this book rely on repetitive and cyclical patterns. None of the processes are groundbreaking or difficult to master. What I believe may be most challenging, in our fast and instant world, is the patience that these processes require; the skill of slowing down.

When working by hand, you can only move at the speed at which your fingertips can take you. In the garden you might spend hours diligently weeding to find that you have only a small but well-cleared patch to show for it. Similarly, to hand-stitch an intricate embellished design can take even the most skillful embroiderer months to complete, no matter how experienced. In both instances, a slow hand that moves with a consistent, steady flow is needed.

My process is chemical-free and machine-free. I work with processes that require only my hands and a simple toolkit. I bring horticultural practices together with handcraft, working with intricate embroidery processes and reimagining the possibilities of embroidery embellishments utilizing my homegrown dried flora.

Some of my larger pieces might take four months to complete, and one of the most common things people say when they encounter my work is: 'I don't know how you have the patience to make this.' But for me, this slow dedication becomes a ritual. It's my greatest form of meditation. I stop noticing the passage of time and fall softly into the stitching.

Whether your interest lies in textiles, gardening, mindful practices or simple curiosity, I hope these pages offer you inspiration. I extend to you an invitation to deepen your connection with nature and to embrace a gentler, more deliberate pace of living and making.

This book is an offering to slowness. Let the shifting seasons move through you. Let it be a reminder that we do not need to live life in acceleration in order to grow, to learn or to thrive.

You may wish to take your time turning each page, allowing the techniques and reflections to unfold at your own rhythm. Or perhaps you'll skip the practices entirely, and instead find joy and inspiration in simply observing the delicate details you can discover in nature.

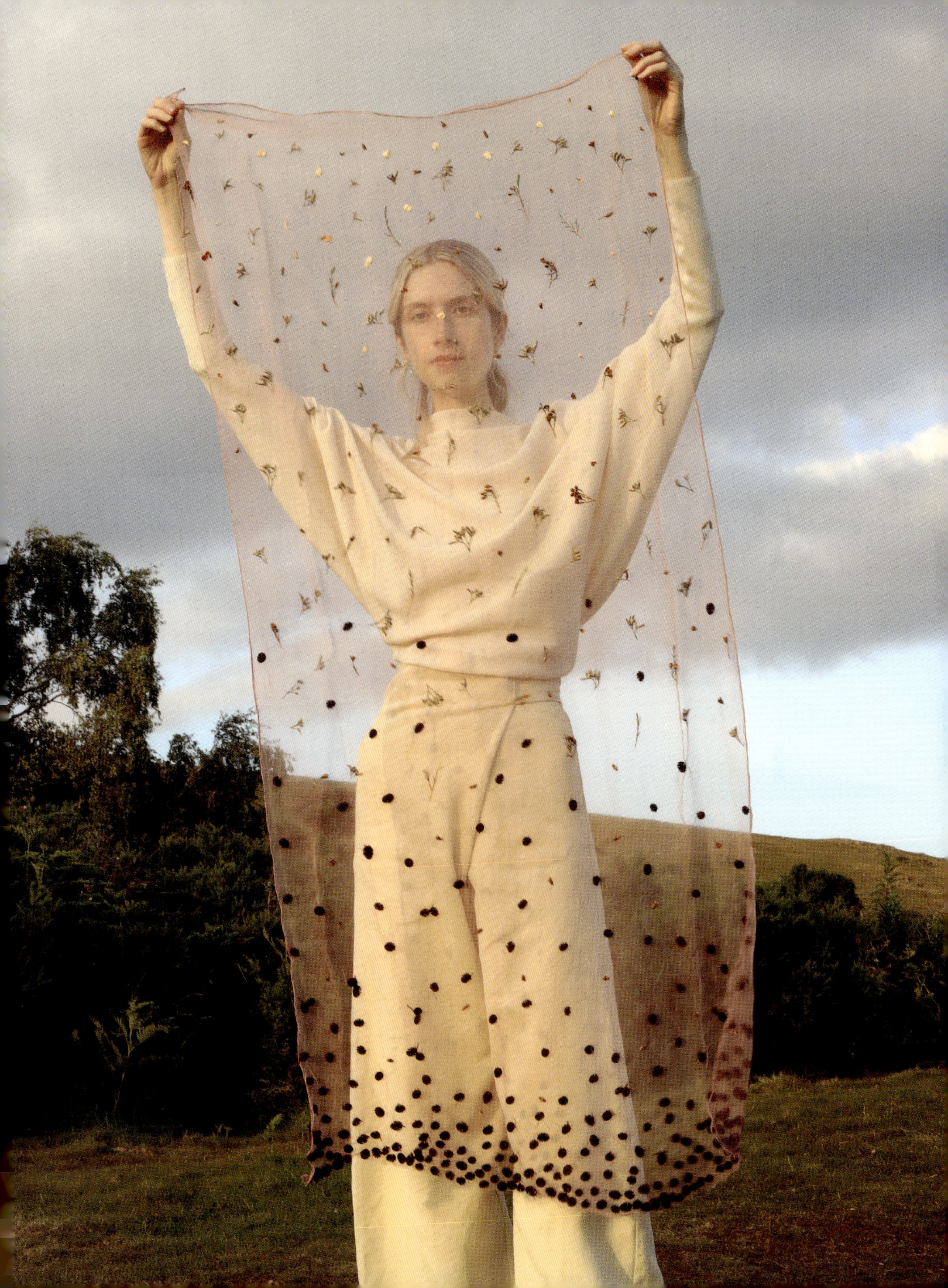

'Knowing that you love the earth changes you, activates you to defend and protect and celebrate. But when you feel that the earth loves you in return, that feeling transforms the relationship from a one-way street, into a sacred bond.'

ROBIN WALL KIMMERER

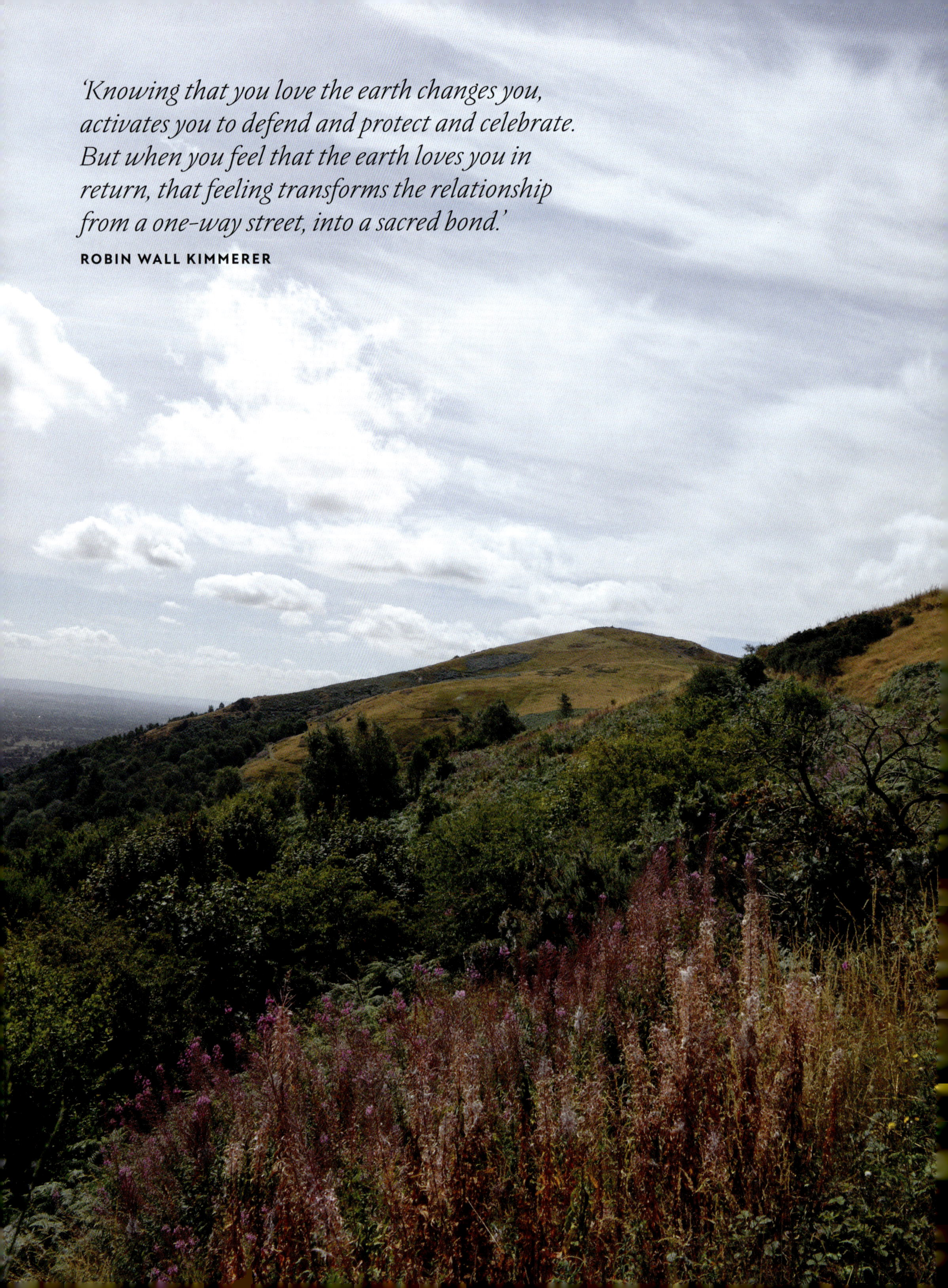

My Journey to Stitching with Nature

CONNECTING TO CLOTH

Through studying and shaping my career in textiles, I've developed a deep bond with materials. Textiles often carry negative connotations – it is an industry that has had detrimental effects for our ecosystem, from synthetic dyes to overconsumption. In many spiritual teachings, materialism is seen as something to reject. It is believed that one who frees themselves from attachment to material goods will unlock the true path to happiness.

But to me, being materialistic means forming a respectful, emotional relationship with the things we create and use, and honouring their value in our lives. If all my materials were taken from me, I'd feel I had lost something vital. This bond teaches care and reverence. When we value materials deeply, we consume with intention, make with intention and respect our materials.

In a world that can often feel saturated by destruction and devastation, the ability to be able to create something of great beauty with your hands that adds inspiration, joy and wonder to the world holds great power. Nature too invites beauty into our lives. When nature and textiles come together, I believe it creates a kind of magic.

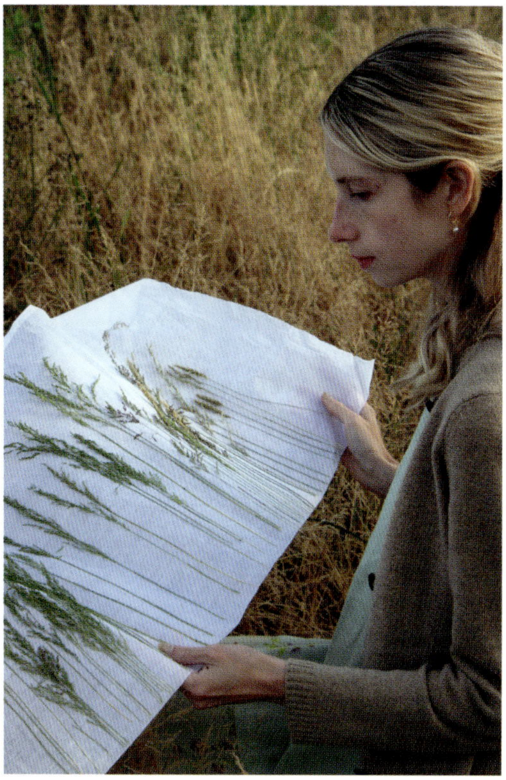

CONNECTING TO THE EARTH

I discovered gardening during a period of mental and physical burnout and illness. When I returned to my parents' home in the Worcestershire countryside for a necessary period of pause, they had recently taken on an allotment. However, with full-time jobs, they had little time to tend to it. I adopted a small section of the plot and I ventured there alone each day and would spend hours there, alone with my thoughts, weeding the ground. In late winter, I started sowing my own seeds too, and as they slowly grew from delicate seedlings into young plants I learned how to listen to their needs and care for them.

When I reflect back now on this period of time, I see how essential this plot of land was as a place of healing. The earth needed tending, and in that act of nurture, it began to tend to me too. When I was incapable of caring for myself, I was able to care for the soil, and the soil, in return, healed me.

The botanist and author Robin Wall Kimmerer speaks of the deep emotional bond that forms when you raise a plant from seed, and I have come to understand that connection intimately.

That same connection can be found in textiles – when you craft something by hand and watch your materials slowly develop into a work of art, you develop a deep emotional connection to that piece of cloth too.

OPPOSITE The Malvern Hills, Worcestershire.

ABOVE Katerina in the process of working on *Lay with Me in the Long Grass* (2025).

WHERE CLOTH AND THE EARTH MEET

British gardener Carol Klein once said, 'gardening is a process, not a product.' When I first heard those words, everything made sense: they hold the true essence of my entire practice.

There are a number of correlations I draw between gardening and hand-embroidery – the act of weeding, for me, is akin to stitching, as it requires a repetition of the hands. Similarly the act of sowing seeds in soil is parallel to stitching individual seed stitches into cloth – both offering a quiet meditation and intimate moments alone with your material.

Learning to garden has allowed me to re-learn textiles, finding a new way of working that feels kind to myself and to our planet. Since starting my workshop series *Stitching with Nature* in 2024 and sharing my craft, I have found that others find healing in this practice too.

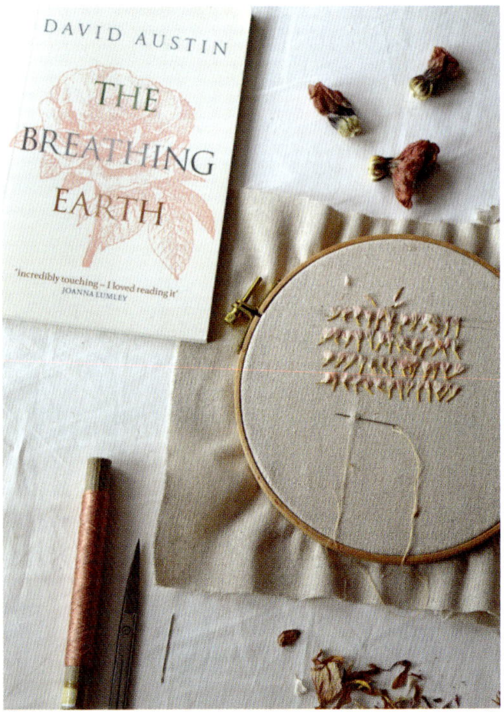

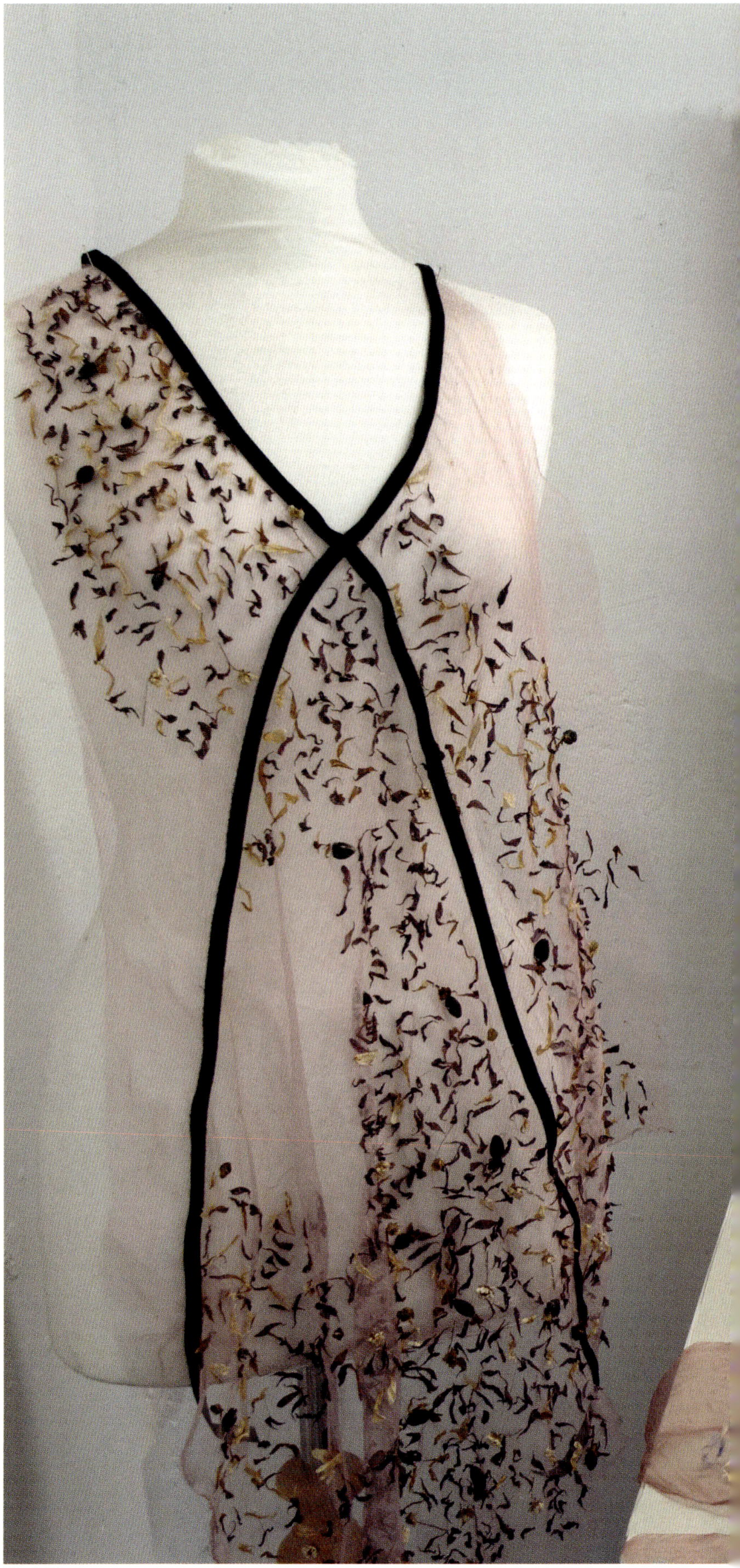

ABOVE Detail of Katerina's embroidery desk at her home in Malvern.

RIGHT Katerina's studio space while completing her Masters at the Royal College of Art, London.

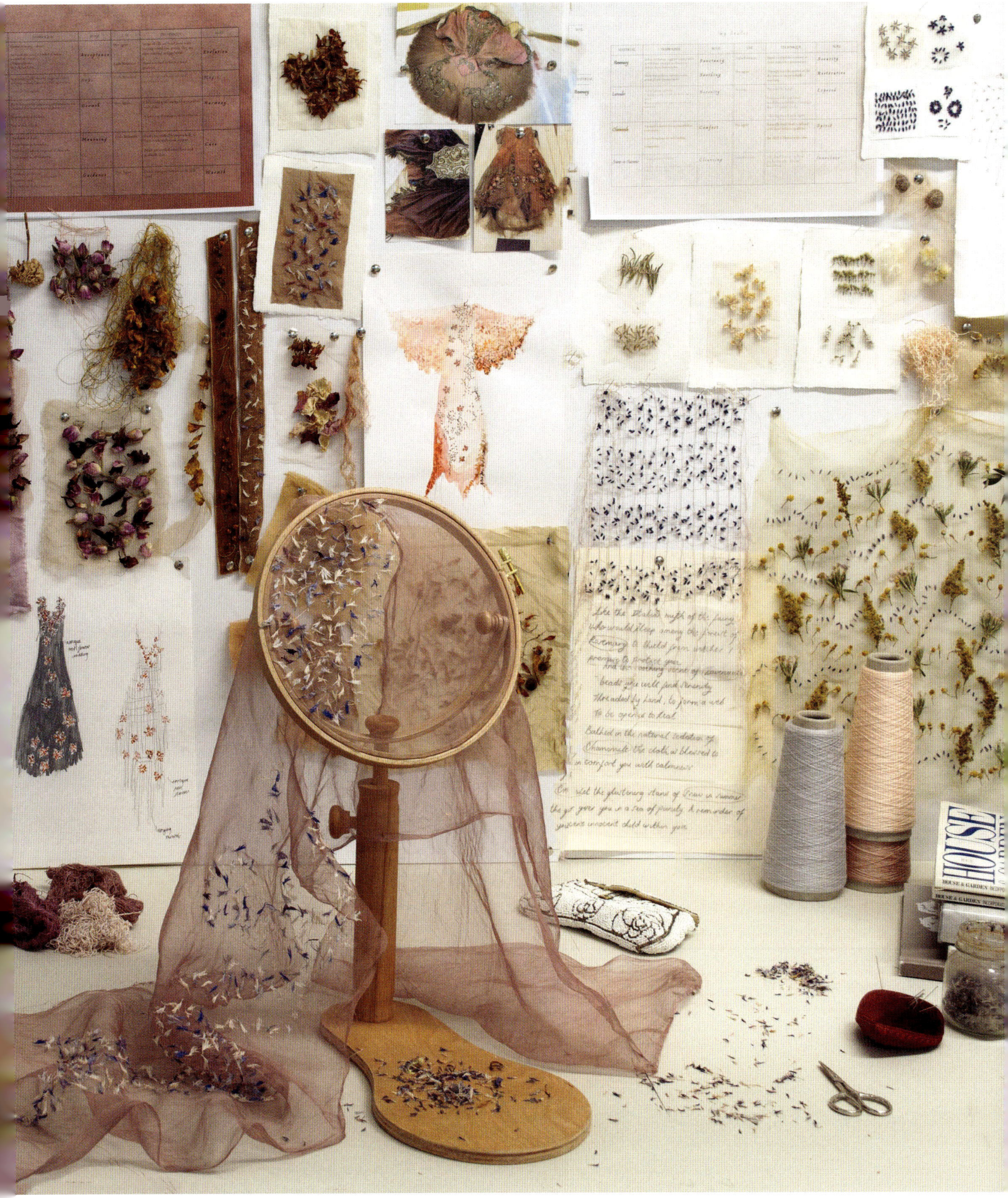

INSPIRATION FROM GARDENING

The garden offers an endless stream of inspiration for a textile designer or artist. Flora and fauna have long influenced my practice; I can't quite pinpoint where this devotion began, it just feels instinctive. Perhaps it began in my childhood, when my mother would bring new fresh flowers into the house each week. An empty vase still makes her home feel incomplete.

Many of us might remember studying flowers in school art class, carefully observing their form, texture and colour through still life painting. For me, that early practice left a lasting impression. Even now, I find myself pausing in gardens to examine each bloom with the same attentive gaze. In this book, we will take that inspiration one step further, working with flowers not as objects to admire, standing still in a vase, but as active materials that will bring life and texture to the pieces we create.

You will also be introduced to fundamental gardening techniques, so you can grow the plants you will later stitch with. My own gardening knowledge has been self-taught and sought out, reading my way through the horticulture shelves of libraries, listening to *Gardeners' Question Time*, spending my weekends visiting gardens for inspiration, and wandering nurseries with quiet excitement (and often, great restraint). Gardening also connects me to my father, a landscape designer whose garden has shaped much of my own understanding.

Throughout my twenties, my life has been in flux, moving from one small rental flat to the next. Yet, in every space I've called home, I've found a way to grow flowers. From window boxes to small balconies, any inch of outdoor space became a place for planting. Now, outside my apartment, I have created a container garden – a modest patch brimming with pots. It's a perfect, sun-drenched spot, ideal for growing flora.

I also grow my flowers in a small patch at the local Pure Land Buddhist temple, where I worship. The spot is shaded, not ideal for flower growing, but in our tradition, we follow Amida Buddha, whose name means limitless light and life. With little sun but much care, patience and faith, my flowers bloom each year, providing the floral materials that I harvest and dry to use in my textile works and teaching for the year ahead.

I share this as encouragement: you don't need a large garden to grow your own floral materials. Even if you live in a tower block amid a concrete skyline, a few pots on a balcony or windowsill can yield enough petals, leaves and seeds with which to explore the following embroidery techniques.

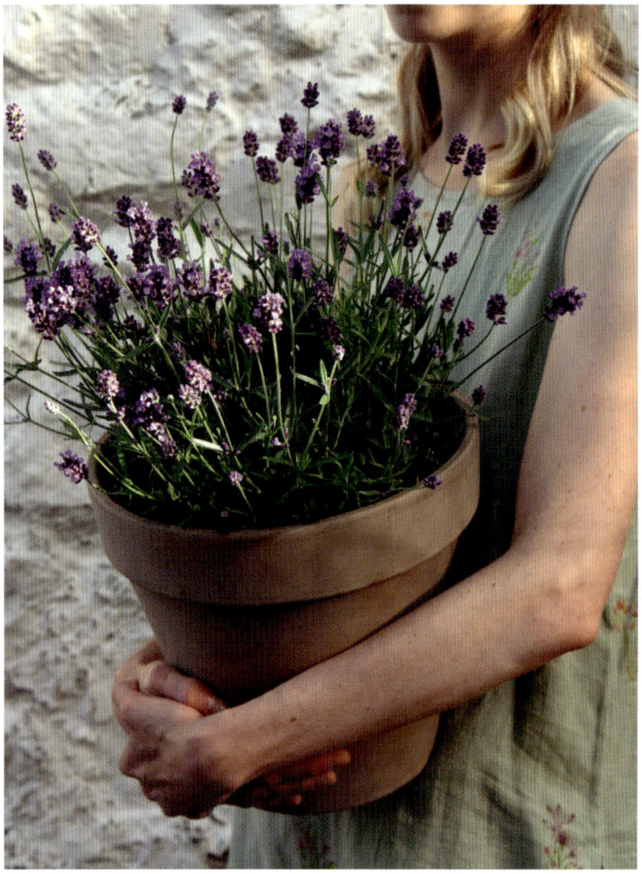

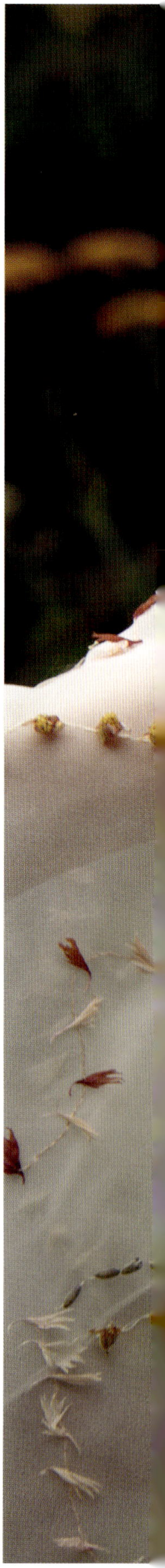

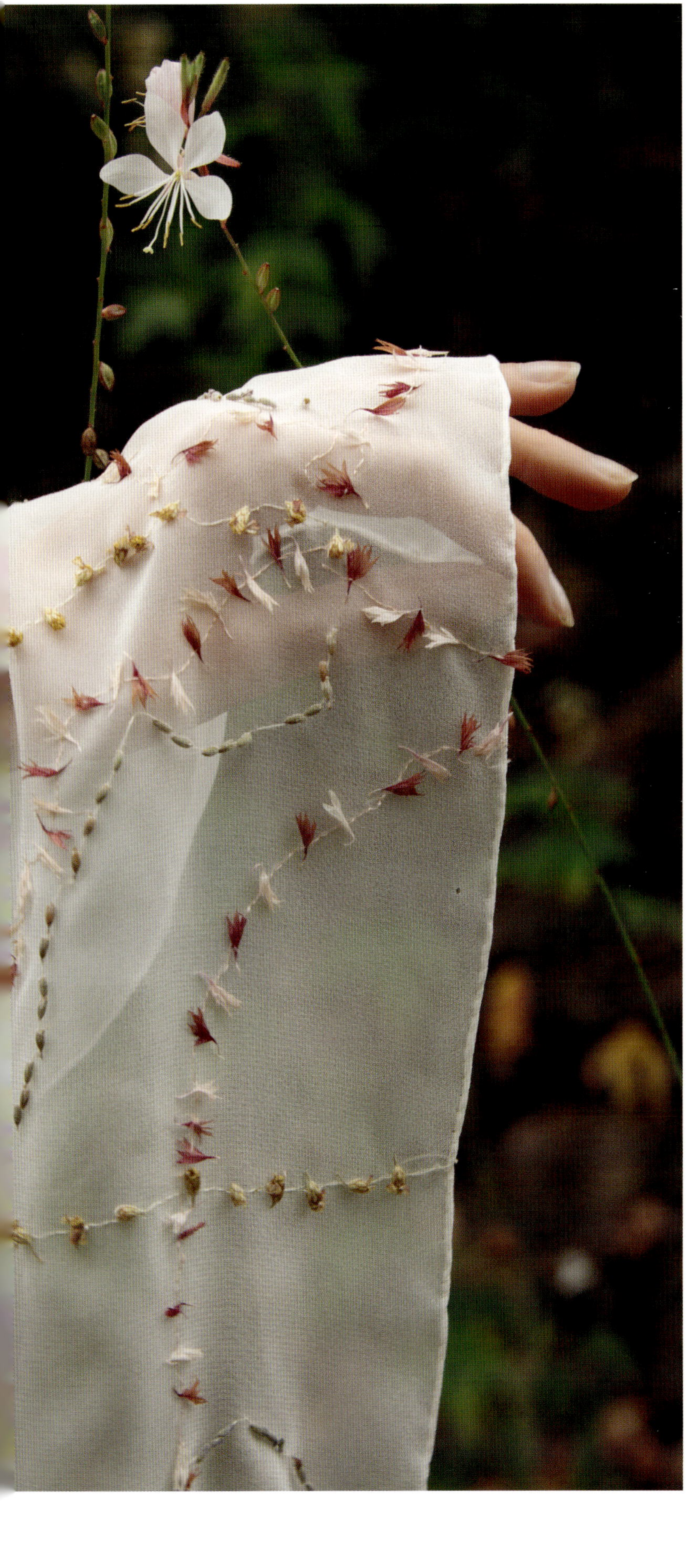

LEFT Detail of *Summer Days Won't Last Forever* (2025). Lavender, cornflowers and achillea hand-embroidered with silk thread on silk georgette.

One of the joys of working with plant materials in embroidery is just how far a single bloom can go. Just one marigold flower can offer more than 20 stitchable petals, and from one healthy plant you can harvest dozens of flowerheads over a season. I'm still using petals from marigolds I grew back in 2021 – proof of their abundance and longevity.

The garden we are responsible for extends far beyond the private land that we own – it is the living, breathing world around us. I live at the foot of the hills in Malvern, with forests behind me and, in front, open common land that becomes a tapestry of wild flora in spring. If growing simply isn't possible for you, the foraging section of this book (pages 62–65) will guide you in finding materials out in the wild. Nature is generous if you go looking.

NATURE AS TEACHER

In this practice, nature will be your greatest teacher – the contents of this book will simply provide you with additional support, but nature will be guiding you. From the practice of *Stitching with Nature*, I have learned to appreciate the rich colours and details in offerings from Earth, be that flowers, leaves or seeds.

Plant materials are deeply intelligent: they provide us with natural, medicinal and healing benefits, so when you are stitching with a seed of lavender, for example, you will breathe in a sweet aroma and remedy to calm your mind.

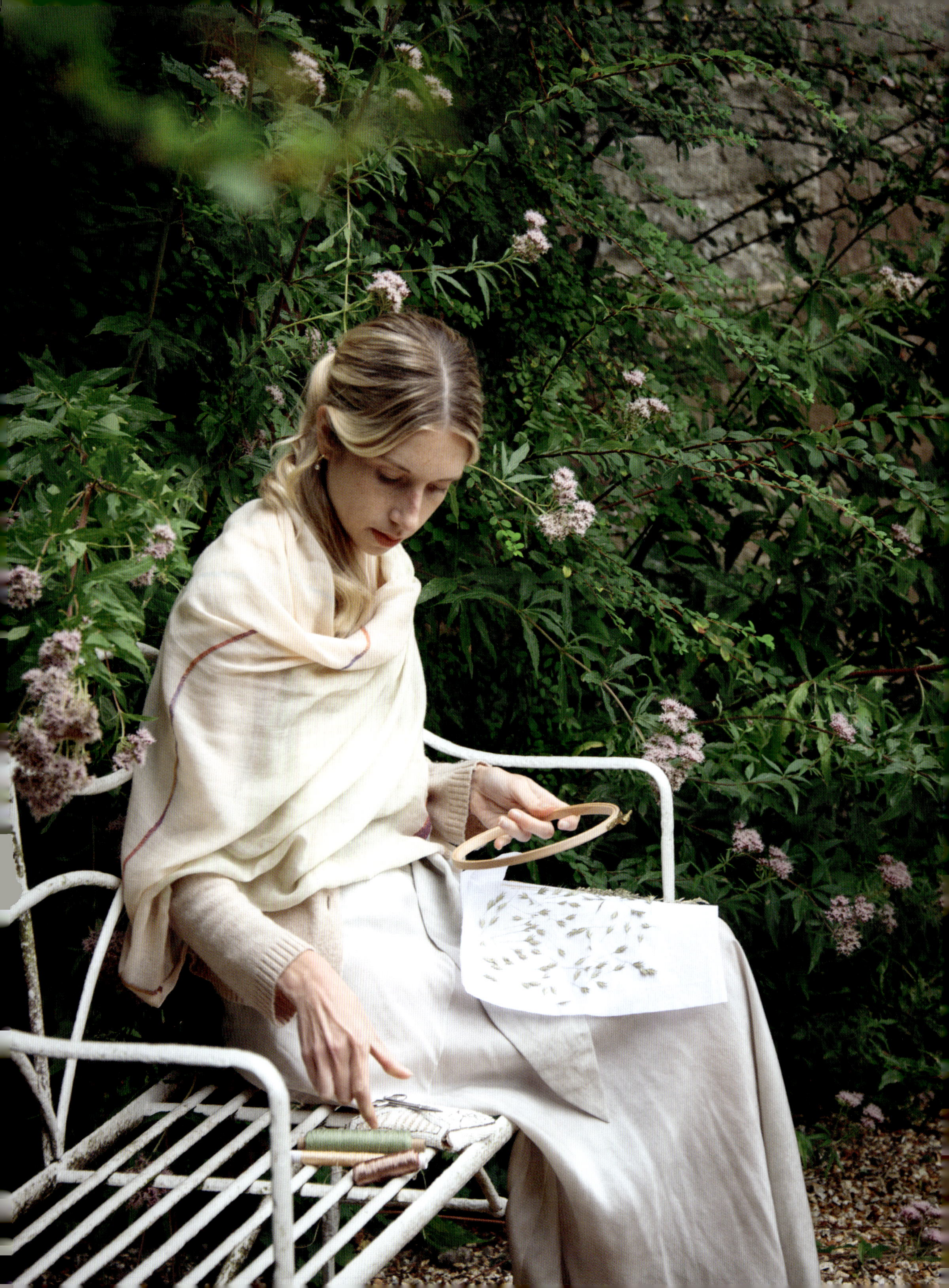

Through the process of learning how to grow your own materials, you will learn to listen to nature and respond to its needs. To help give it water, light and kindness. We need to guide it towards a healthy life, so that its flowers bloom brightly. When humans and nature come together, we can make things of great beauty. We can make a beautiful world.

After one growing season, sowing, growing and finally harvesting, you will learn that nothing in nature is fixed: flowers fade and seasons change. Working with plants teaches you to embrace impermanence. You might wonder how long the textiles you will create using plant embellishments will last. Honestly, I don't know. Even dried flowers, preserved with care, will shift in colour, form and strength over time. But there is something I find freeing in that. As a Buddhist, I've come to understand that impermanence is not something to fear, it's something to honour – it teaches us to treasure the moment.

Through the practices in this book, I invite you to experience the joy of being present and to notice the tiny details in the moment: a dried petal, a single seed, a single stitch.

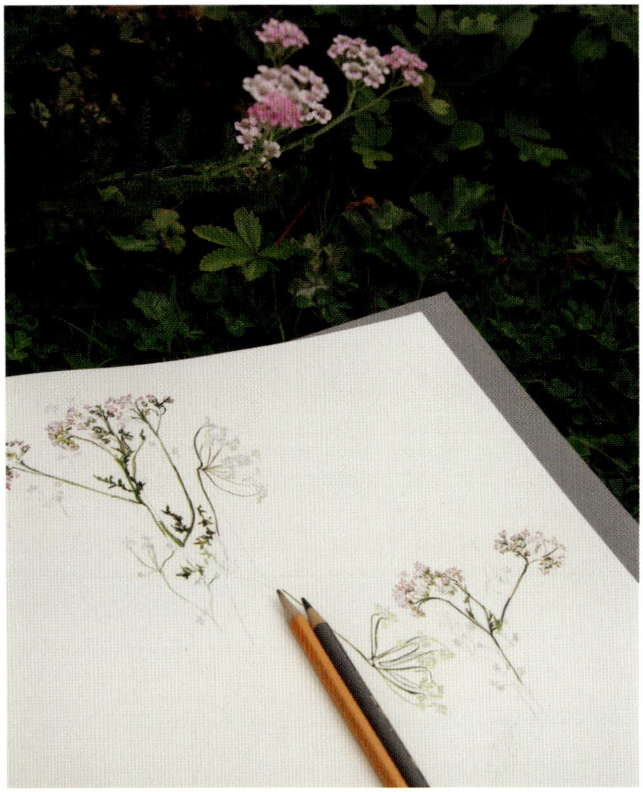

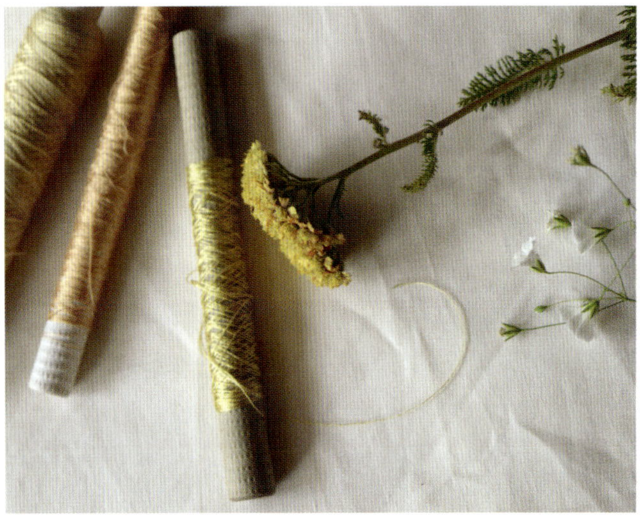

SEASONS OF MAKING

Through blending horticulture and textiles, I have found my most organic rhythm, both in life and in my artistic practice. If you follow these techniques, you can find a natural rhythm too. In the summer I grow, harvest, forage, walk, observe, think and gather – but make very little. As summer transitions to autumn, the final harvest, I am still foraging, and there is lots of drying, storing and preserving my materials, while I'm beginning to think through making, trying new ideas, new techniques, and exploring new materials. Then in winter, as the cold and wet English weather sets in, I find solace inside. I spend hours making. There is no foraging now; no growing – but still I'm thinking, what will I grow next year? Then, once we have made it through the darkest of days and spring starts to reveal itself again, I begin to sow seeds. Thus the cycle of gathering starts again.

So let us begin, with sowing the seeds.

OPPOSITE Katerina stitching in the dye garden at Hellens Manor in Herefordshire.

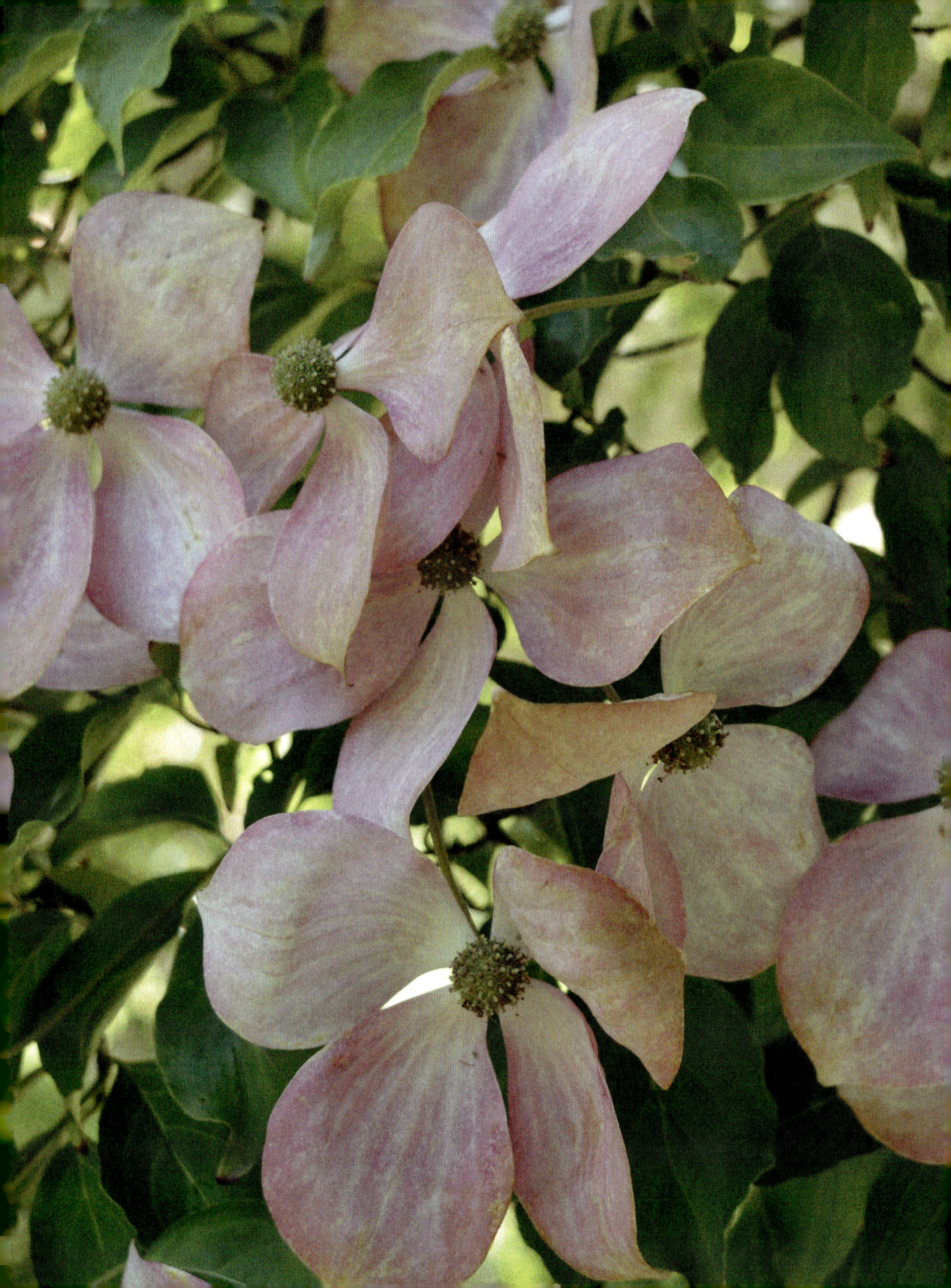

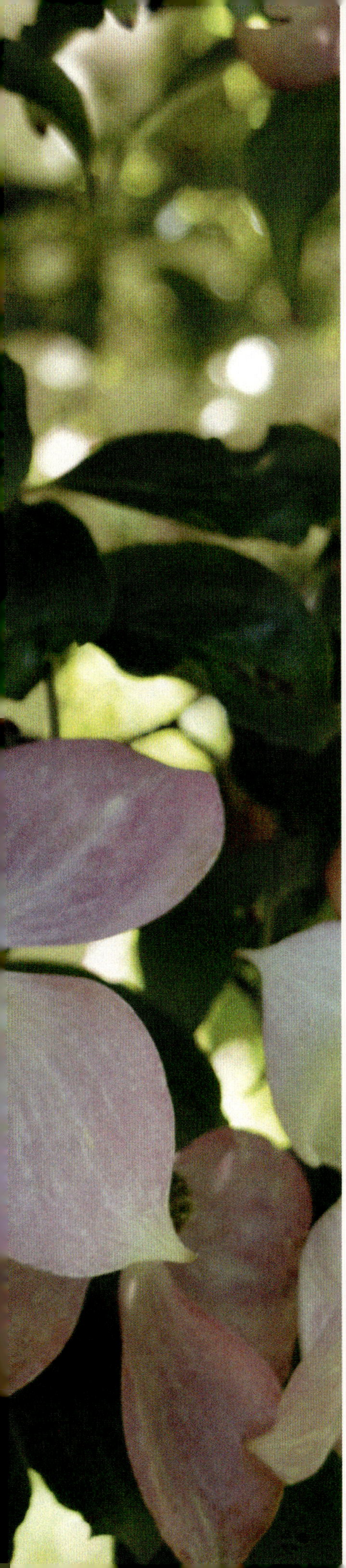

SOWING SEEDS

'We depend on the gifts of nature, but these gifts must be received with gratitude and not exploited or abused.'

SATISH KUMAR

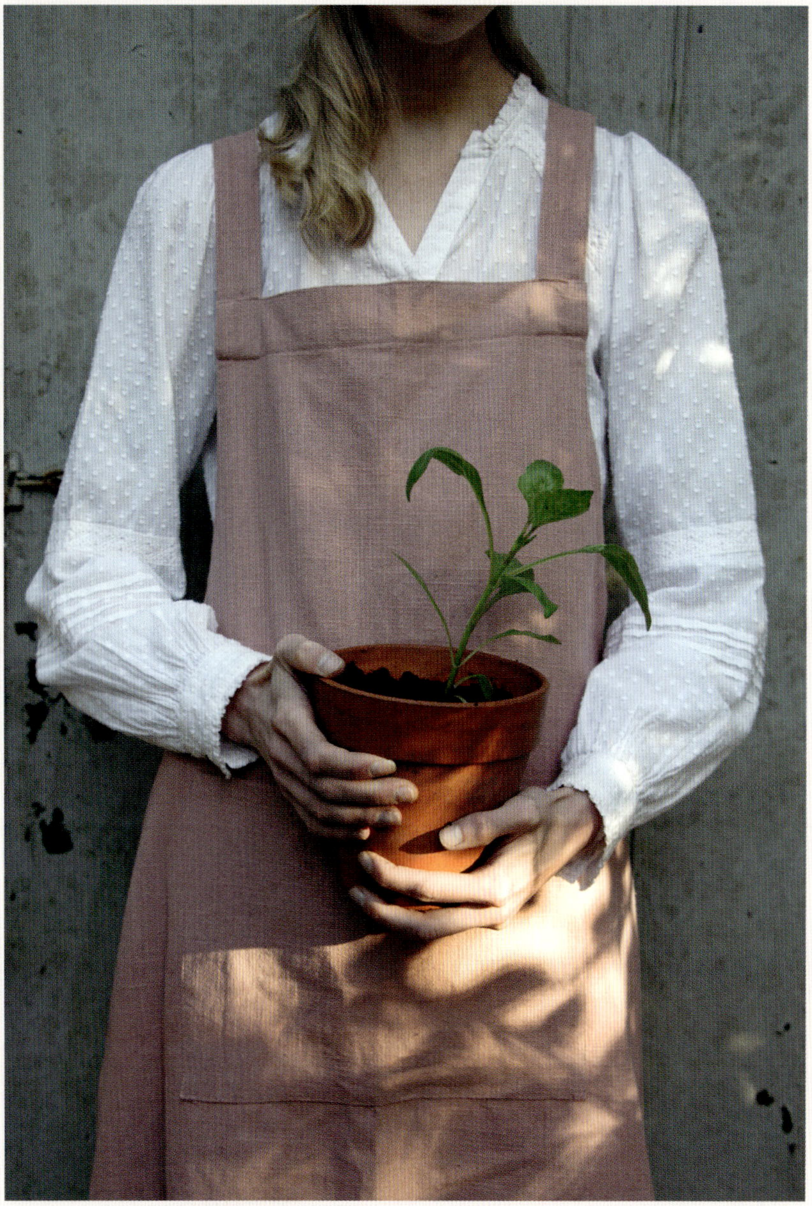

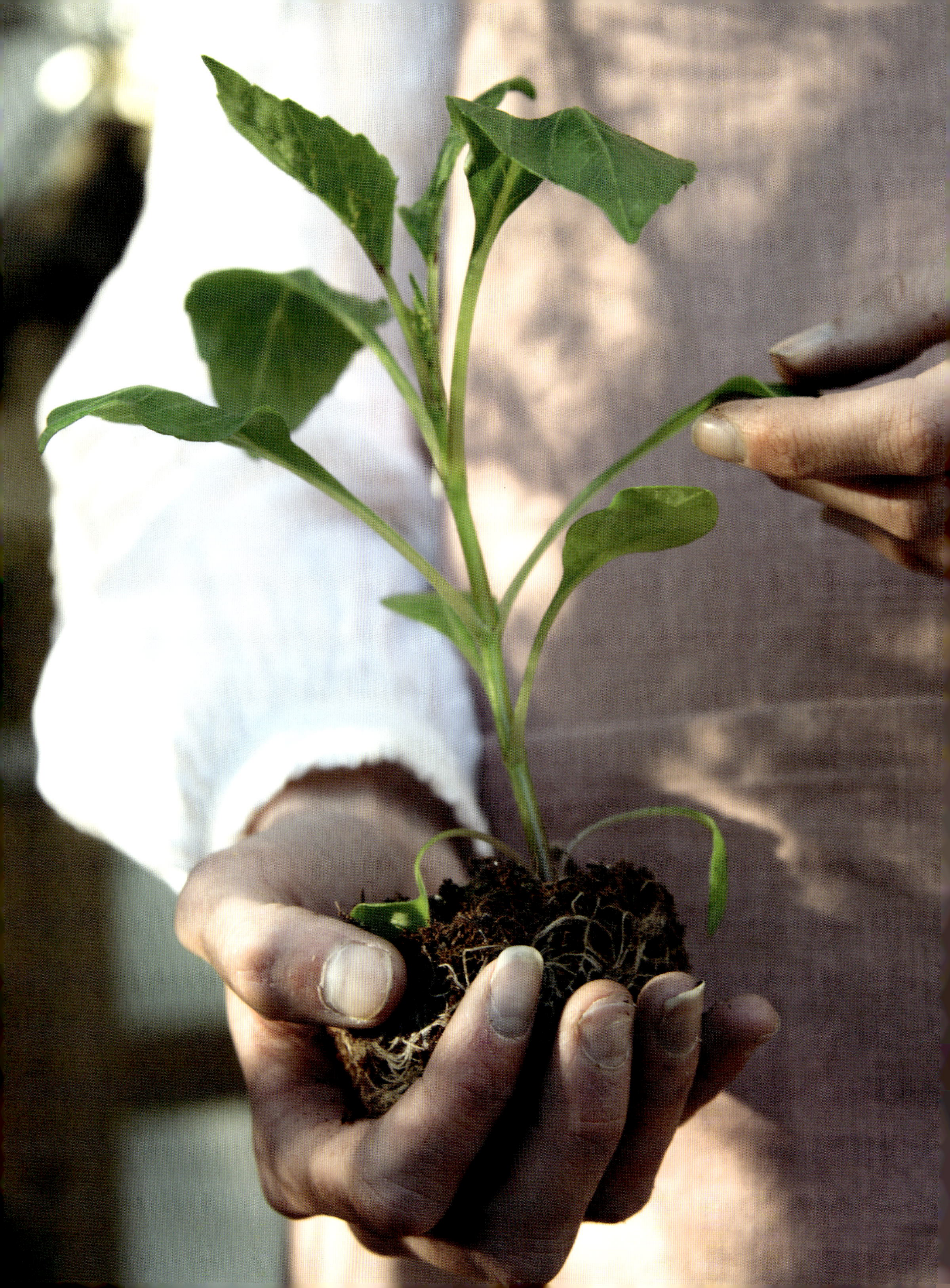

Sowing Seeds

Selecting the right flowers to be used for your embroidery embellishments is an important step, and one that invites a bit of personal exploration. Over time, I have found the flowers that I enjoy growing most are: lavender (page 32), cornflowers (page 35), dahlias (page 38) and statice (page 41). Through practice, these flowers have proven strong enough for my needle to pass through them, while offering longevity and retaining their form and colour. There are many other plant materials that might suit this practice too, and part of the joy lies in discovering which ones you enjoy growing both as a gardener and embroiderer.

Many gardeners say when you are beginning to grow vegetables that you should start with those you like to eat. That same idea could be applied to this practice: consider what colour palette you like to work with. If you like a bold mix of colours you might opt for statice, which offers a variety of bright colours ranging from purple and pink to yellow in one seed mix. If you prefer softer, muted tones try chamomile – their flowerheads provide delicate white petals and a soft yellow centre.

When choosing what seeds to sow, you should also consider the space you have available. If you are limited to a few pots on your balcony, lavender or rosemary, which offer a dual culinary purpose, would be an excellent place to start. Most importantly, start by selecting a couple of plants to begin your embroidery garden. This is something you can grow and evolve each year. It is easy to get carried away when sowing seeds, but learning how to nurture a few plants successfully and then exploring the art of embroidering with them is the best place to begin.

A packet of seeds can cost less than a cup of coffee and in return can gift you an abundance of cut flowers to decorate your home all summer. When you watch a seed grow into a tiny seedling, then develop into a small plant ready to be planted outside to grow into a beautiful flower, the deep emotional connection you create with it is indescribable.

When planting out my seeds I always worry at first: are they strong enough to withstand the world and all its elements? Yet it always amazes me how plants find their own way in the world, with their resilience and their ability to withstand and adapt. Growing plants from seeds, much like hand-sewing, can take practice and a lot of patience. Each gardening year, I learn new things. Some seeds work successfully year after year for me, but sometimes things don't go quite as you expect. That is okay. Sowing seeds is a slow process.

You, too, will find your own way of doing things, whether you grow seeds in a professional seed tray or a toilet paper tube, in a greenhouse, on your kitchen windowsill or next to the radiator in your living room, and whether you are an accurate and meticulous sower or take a try-it-and-find-out approach. There really is no right way of doing things. It is a process that should be enjoyable and fulfilling for you. A time to take a moment away from the hustle and bustle of daily life, away from a screen, a quiet moment to just do something simple.

There is a lot to learn with gardening. It can be easy to make mistakes – overwater, underwater, plant in the wrong position, plant at the wrong time – but I have found that nature is forgiving of our errors while on the path of learning. It is natural to make these mistakes, so be kind to yourself, listen and be guided by the signals that the plants are giving you, and each season you will get that little bit better.

Here is a guide to how I do things, to help you get started.

Sowing Tools

WHAT YOU WILL NEED . . .

- **Modules** – You do not need to spend a lot, if anything at all. Most garden centres have recycling points for pots and seed trays where you can pick up containers for free to use for sowing your seeds. I prefer to sow seeds in individual plugs/cells. You can try making your own modules from cardboard egg cartons or toilet roll inserts. Whatever you choose, it is essential to ensure that there are drainage holes in the base.
- **Shallow tray** – Using a shallow tray follows a 'bottom watering' approach. This causes less disturbance to delicate seedlings. You place your seed tray on top of a shallow tray filled with 3cm (1¼in) of water, and the soil will absorb the water from the bottom up.
- **Watering can** – Once your seedlings are less delicate, you can begin watering gently with a watering can.
- **Wooden marker sticks** – When sowing many varieties of plants it can be easy to get them mixed up, so marker sticks allow you to identify each pot or tray.
- **Gardening gloves** – Avoid selecting a pair that are too thick. You want to be able to easily move your hands and fingers, to feel the ground. However, I would invite you to take off your gloves as much as you can and feel the earth between your fingertips. Get to know your soil: what does it feel like? Smell like? What texture does it have?
- **A trowel** – You will need this small hand tool for digging holes when ready to plant out your seedlings.
- **A hand hoe** – This is an essential tool for keeping on top of weeds. Weed maintenance in your cut flower beds is important.
- **Seed storage envelopes** – Use small brown paper envelopes to collect seeds at the end of the season to store and use the following year or swap at your local seed swap.
- **Compost** – For sowing seeds it is best to use a specialist seed compost. Then, when planting out, you can use a peat-free multi-purpose compost. Seeds thrive best when you sow in a specialist seed compost as they require fewer nutrients in their early developmental stages.
- **Water** – Water is precious, so try to collect rainwater if you can.
- **Terracotta pots** – Ensure that you use frost-proof terracotta pots with drainage holes. These are available from any good garden centre, or look out for them at second-hand stores or reclamation yards.

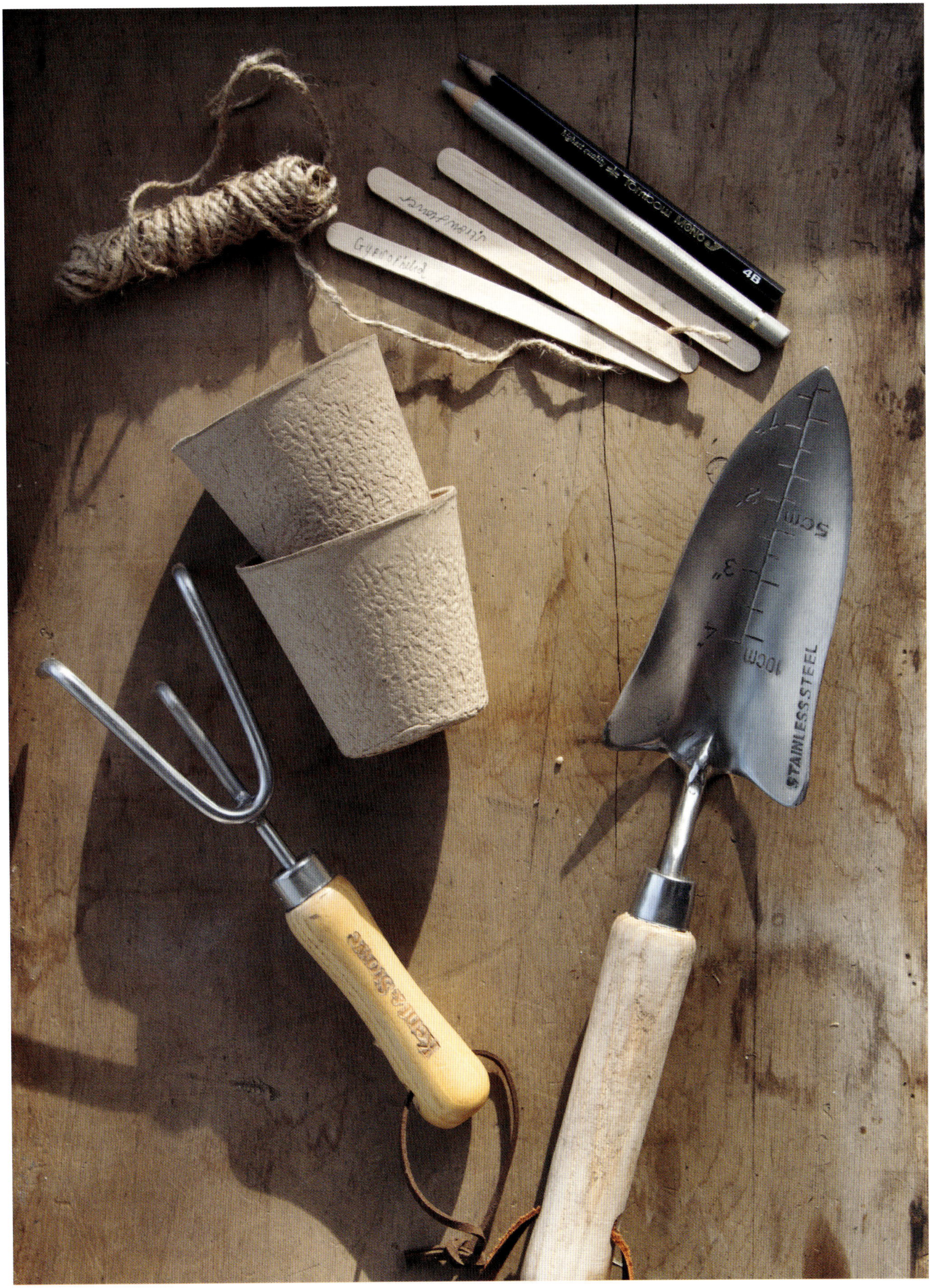
STAINLESS STEEL
4B

How to Sow Seeds

SOWING STEPS . . .

1 Fill your chosen module with seed-potting compost until they are approximately three-quarters full.

2 Sprinkle your seeds evenly over the surface of the compost. For most seeds, leave a 3cm (1¼in) gap between each seed. For larger seeds, sow only one seed per module.

3 Cover your seeds with a thin layer of compost, taking care not to disrupt the placement of seeds.

4 Water gently and then place your seeds on a windowsill with good natural light or inside a greenhouse if you have one. Keeping your seeds in a warm, well-ventilated space will encourage germination.

5 Once your seedlings have germinated, check every couple of days that your compost is moist. You should then water them by placing the modules in a shallow tray of water and leaving for ten minutes to absorb the water – this avoids disturbing delicate seedlings.

6 Once your seeds have developed into young plants, if there are multiple seedlings in one module they will be ready to be pricked out. Gently lift one seedling at a time, by their leaf, separating their roots from other seedlings. You can then transplant the seedling into an individual small pot.

7 Once they begin to outgrow a small pot, you will need to pot them into a bigger pot again, to allow their root development.

8 Once the last frost has passed and when the young plants are approximately 10cm (4in) tall, they will be large enough to be planted outside. Begin by hardening off: placing your plants outside during the day and bringing them back inside at night. Repeat this every day for one week and they will then be ready to plant out.

9 Plant out in the ground in well-weeded soil or in larger pots.

**In the next chapter I provide specific growing guidance for my favourite plants, if selecting others do check the advice on the seed packet.*

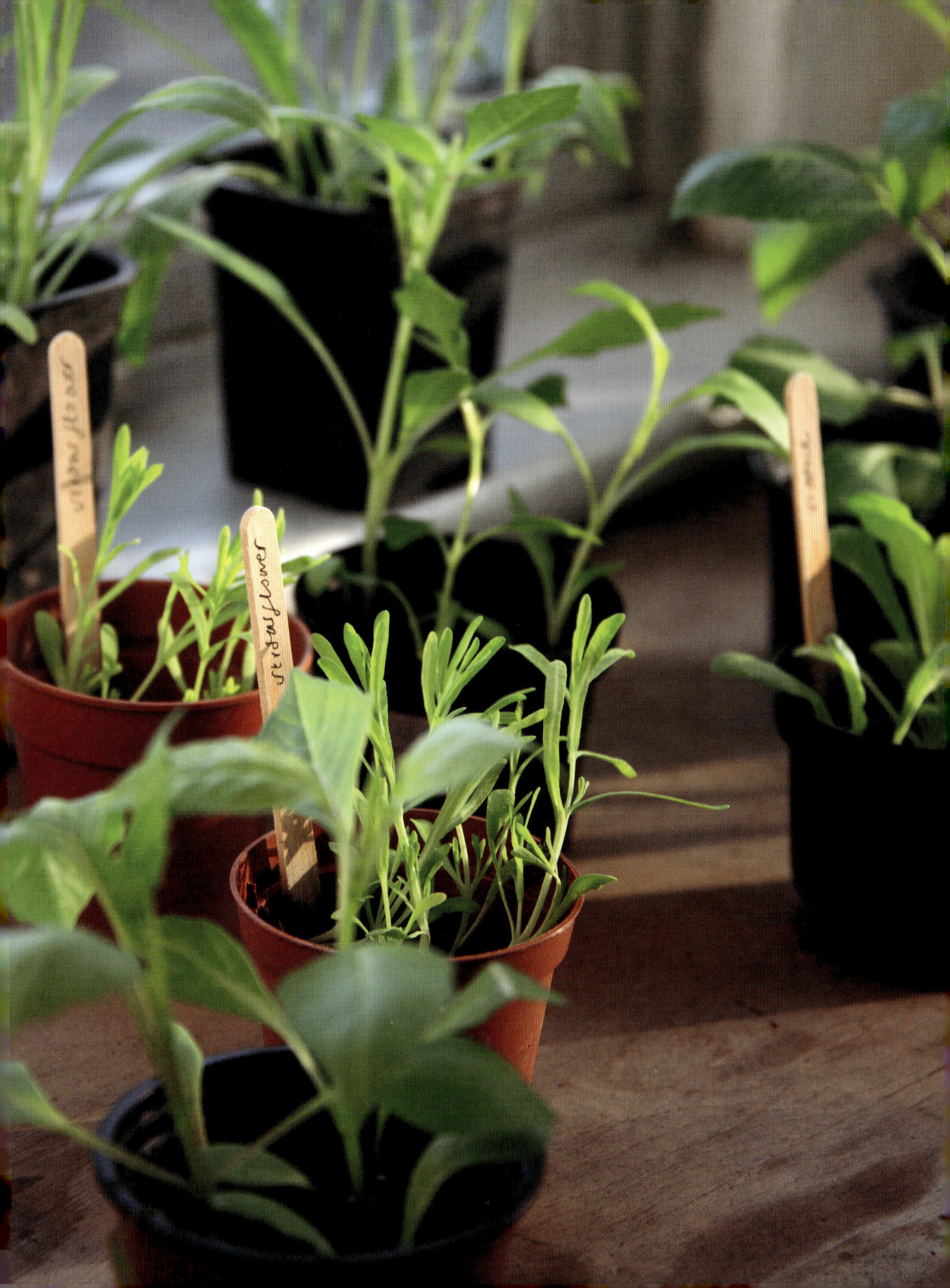

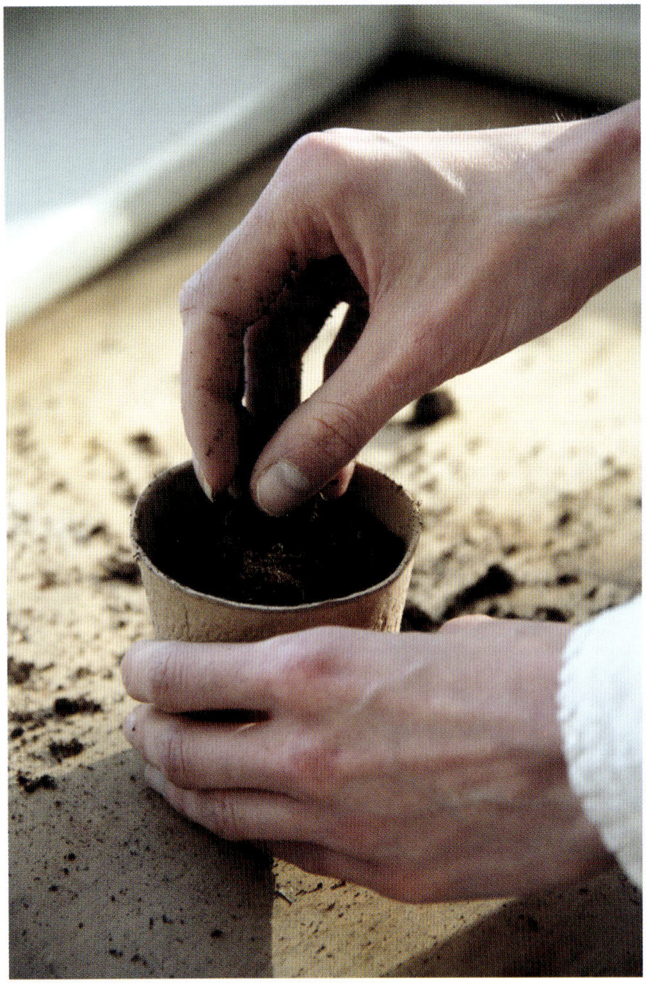

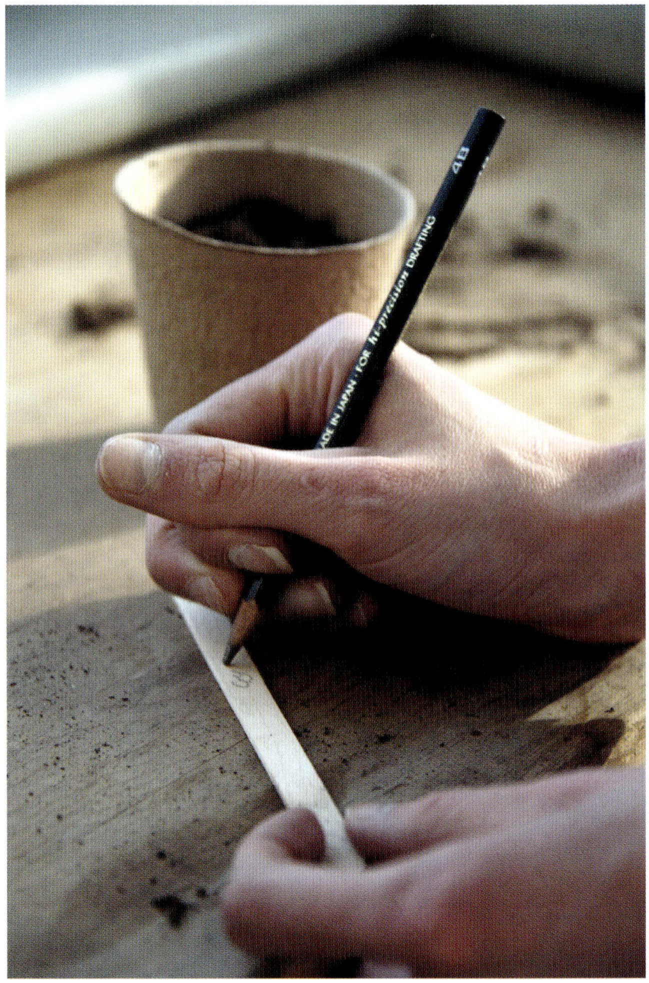

WHEN TO START SOWING . . .

When sowing under cover (see opposite), seeds can be sown indoors at any time of year, so you can enjoy the process and anticipation of watching your seedlings grow all year round. I begin sowing my seeds at the end of February and early March. However, the late winter period, from New Year through to 1 February, is when I begin to get excited, as the days start to get longer and flowers such as snowdrops and crocuses start to shine through. I am excited because I know that we have made it through the hardest days of darkness, and it is almost time to start sowing seeds again for the year ahead.

WHERE TO BUY SEEDS . . .

Start by making a list of plants you would like to grow. Seed catalogues and seed shelves at garden centres can overwhelm you with choice, so having a specific list of the seeds you are looking for will help focus your search. There are many suppliers who specialize in certain varieties, while companies such as Chiltern Seeds, Crocus and Sarah Raven offer an excellent range of flower seeds. If you can, try to buy locally from organic nurseries. These seeds can often be found at local nurseries, independent garden centres, or organic fruit, vegetable and wholefood shops – and always avoid Genetically Modified Organisms (GMOs). Supporting these smaller, ethical suppliers not only ensures higher-quality seeds, but also helps to sustain more environmentally conscious growing practices.

THE TWO WAYS OF GROWING FROM SEED . . .

Sowing under cover means sowing seeds indoors, in a greenhouse or your home. Then, once they have developed into seedlings, you will transplant them into the ground. Most seeds are best sown under cover, as this method allows you to have a little more control and will produce more consistent results. Starting seeds under cover in warm conditions speeds up the germination process.

Sowing direct means that you plant your seeds directly into the ground. You should ensure that you plant into well-drained soil that is free from weeds. The soil should be warm and moist; therefore the best time to do this is in April or early May. This works best for plants that are quick to germinate and tolerant of a range of weather conditions; for example, wild flowers such as love-in-a-mist and cornflowers. You should ensure that seeds are sown thinly and spaced out evenly, following the specific guidance on the seed packet. Otherwise, you can take a packet of wildflower seeds, scatter them freely and watch a beautiful wildflower meadow bloom.

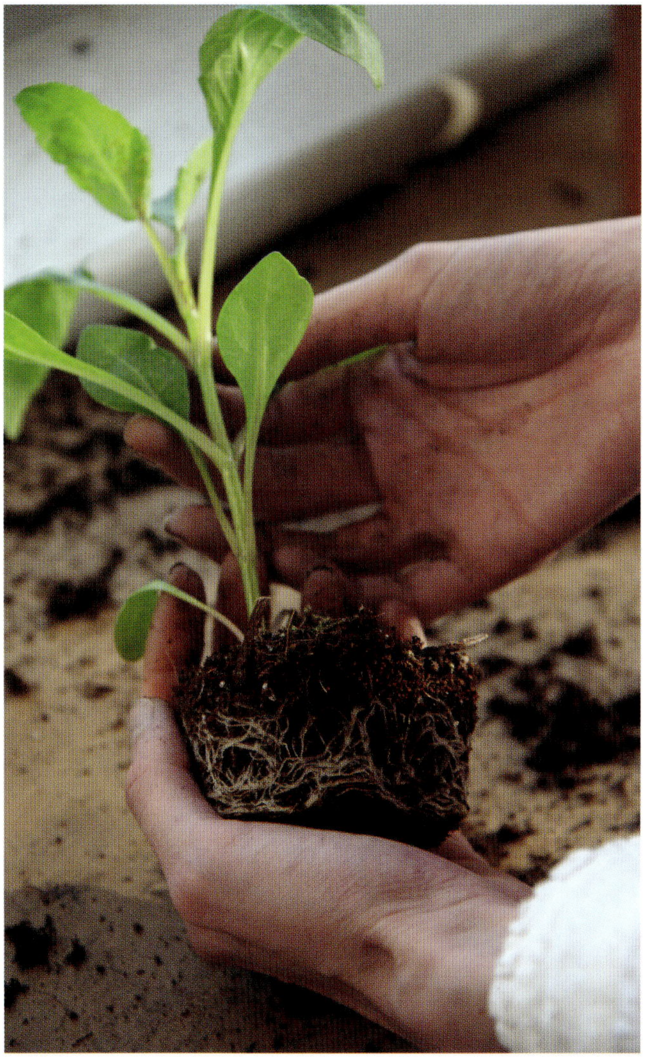

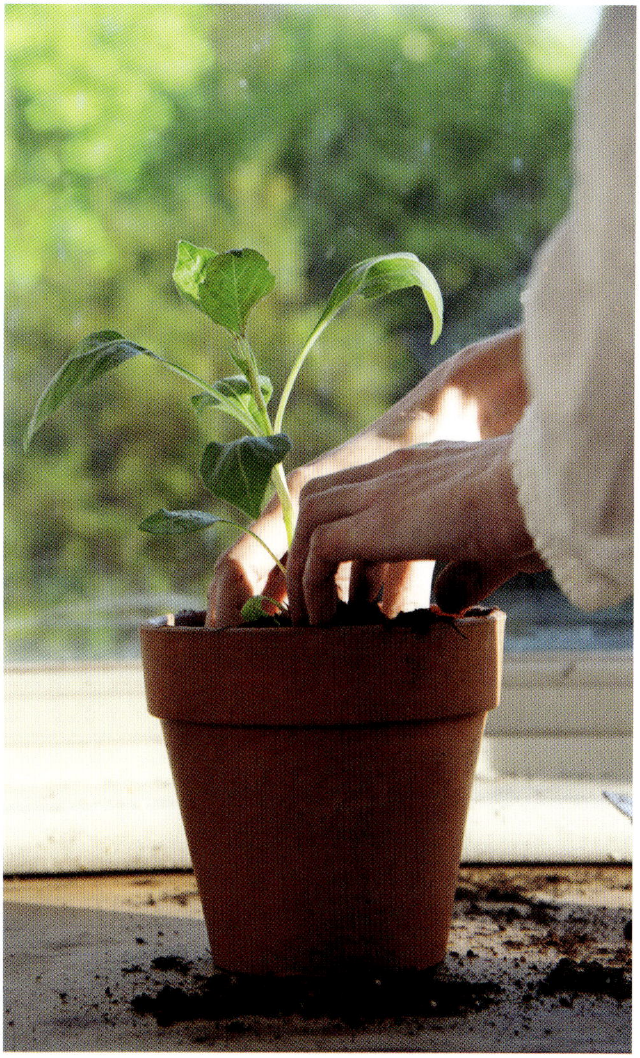

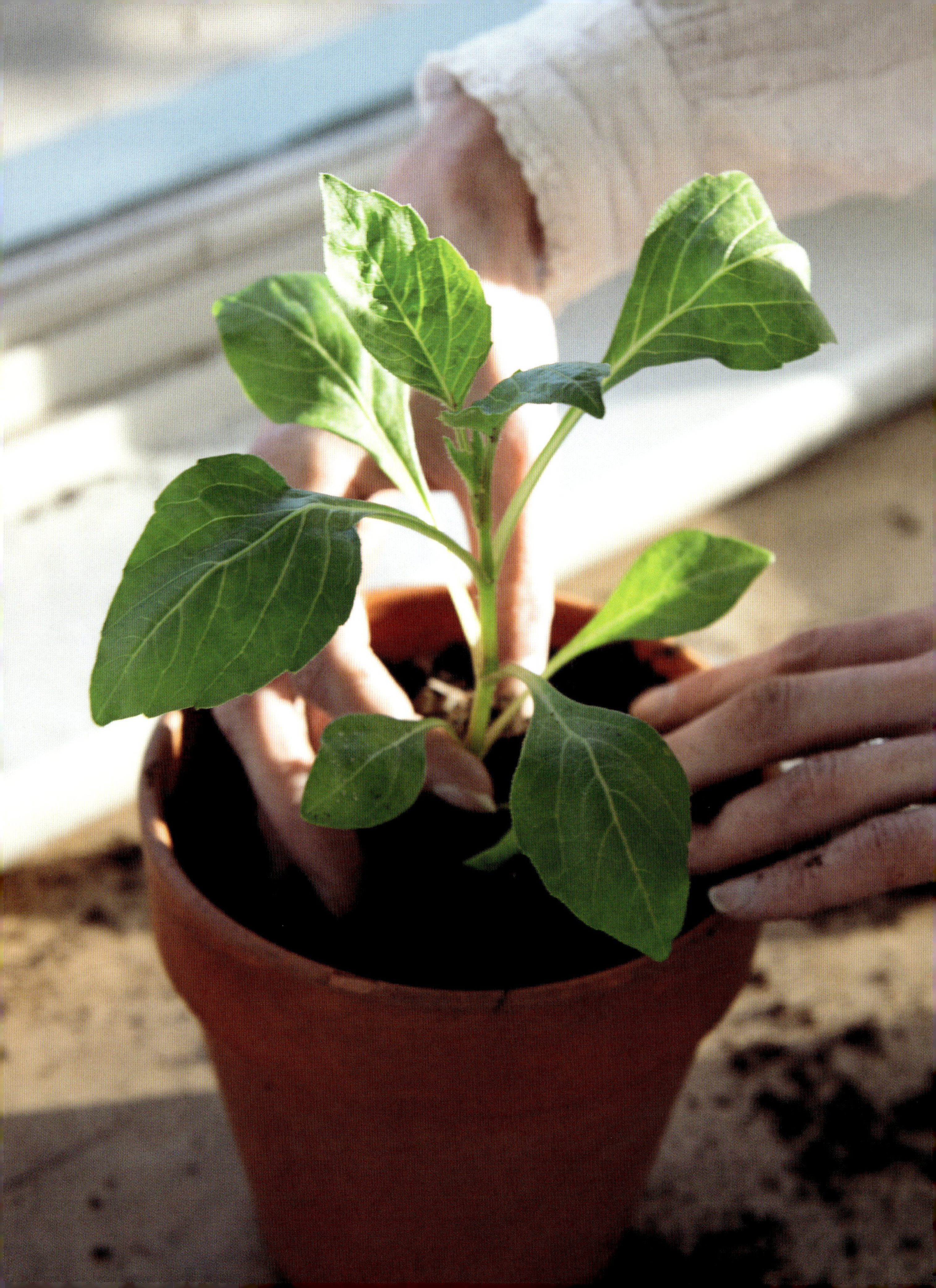

Gardening Glossary

When you enter into the world of gardening you will find a whole new language to discover and words to learn.

- **Annual** – A plant that lives only for one year and flowering season.
- **Biennial** – A biennial plant in its first year will only form roots and leaves; in its second year it will produce a flower. Once the flowering season is over, the plant will set seed and die. E.g., poppy (*Papaver* spp.).
- **Bolting** – When a plant is finishing its life cycle and will not produce another year of flowering.
- **Companion planting** – Planting several plants together in the same area because they benefit each other's ability to grow successfully.
- **Deadheading** – To remove dead or dying flowerheads from a plant in order for it to put its energy into cultivating new blooms.
- **Germination** – When a seed starts to sprout and grow.
- **GMO** – Genetically Modified Organism; this refers to types of seeds that have been altered in a laboratory or sprayed with fertilizers and chemicals.
- **Half-hardy annual** – A half-hardy annual will not survive outside during a frost when conditions are wet and cold. E.g., marigold (*Tagetes* spp.).
- **Hardening off** – Allowing a plant to transition from a protected indoor or greenhouse environment to the harsher outdoor conditions.
- **Hardy annual** – A hardy annual can withstand cold and wet climates, surviving outside through frosts. E.g., love-in-a-mist (*Nigella damascena*).
- **Perennial** – Any plant that can live longer than two years is categorized as a perennial. E.g., lavender (*Lavandula* spp.).
- **Self-seeding** – Plants that drop their seeds so once they die back they will then germinate once again on their own the following year.

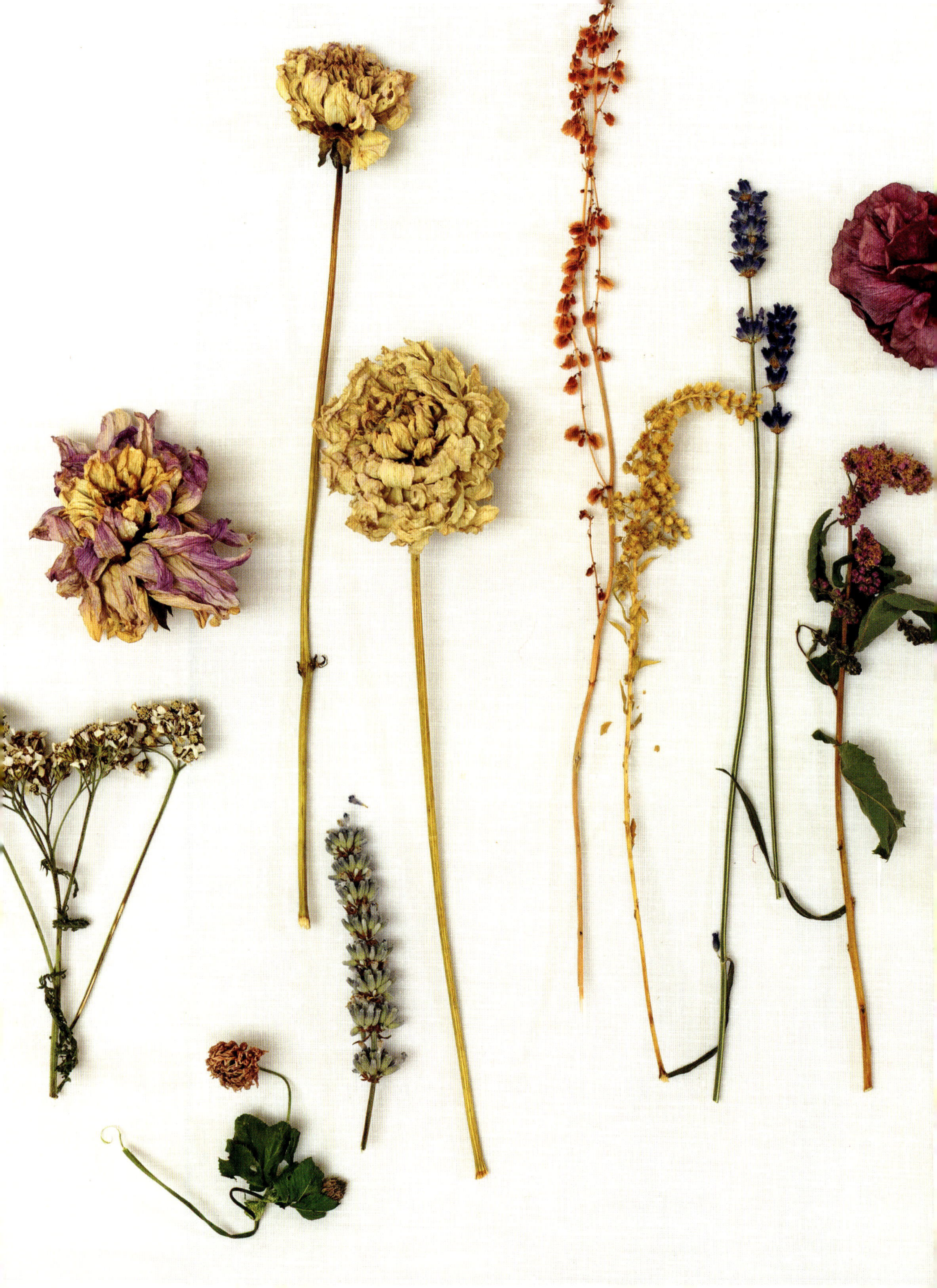

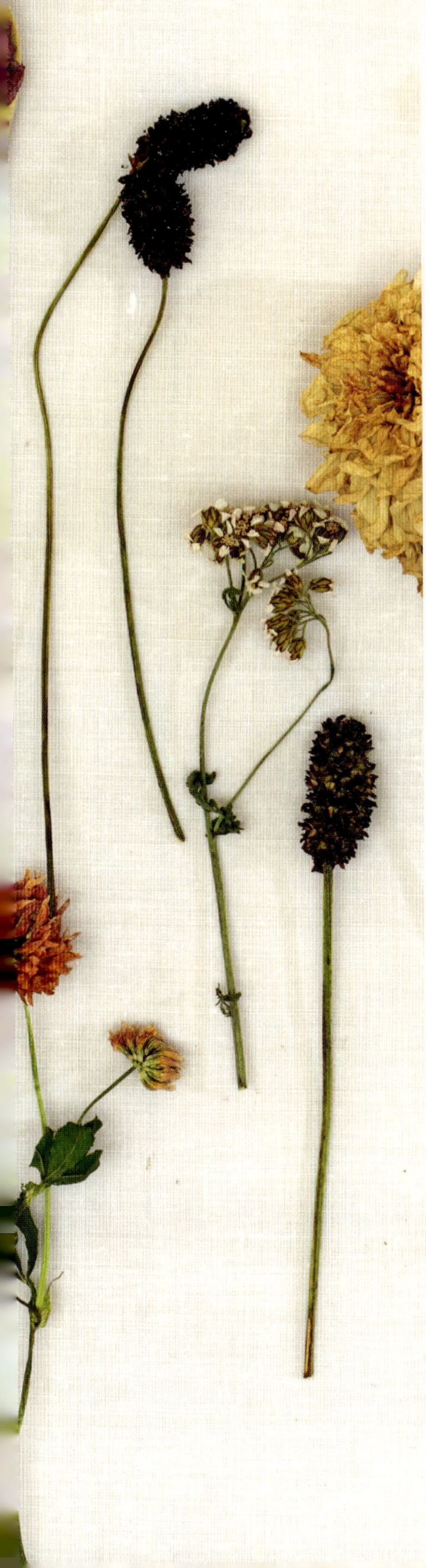

FLOWERS FOR USE IN TEXTILES

In this chapter, I share some of my favourite flowers that I grow year after year for my artworks. I will share my tips and tricks to help you cultivate them successfully. These blooms will provide the perfect petals and seeds to use as materials for the techniques we'll explore in the next section of this book.

'Wherever nature works there will be beauty.'

WILLIAM MORRIS

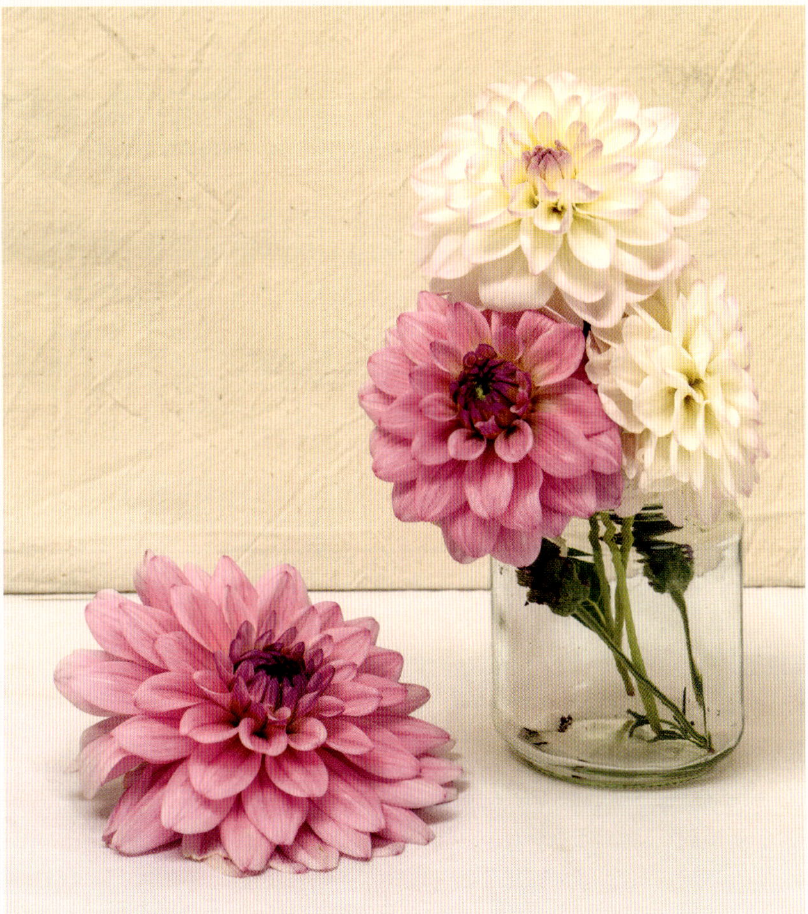

Lavender

Lavender is a perennial flowering plant that grows best in a dry Mediterranean climate. It produces silvery grey-green, dense spiky leaves and small purple seeds. During its flowering period, from late spring through summer, its flowers can vary from pink to subtle lilacs to deep blue-purple tones, depending on the variety. Its stems can grow to around 60cm (24in).

BOTANICAL NAME: *Lavandula*

FAMILY: Lamiaceae (Mint family)

ETYMOLOGY: Derived from the Italian word *lavare*, 'to wash'. Literature from the 14th century suggests that women would wash their clothing in water with sprigs of lavender to transfer the aroma to the fibres of their textiles. Lavender-based soaps and detergents are still popular today.

ORIGIN: Lavender is native to the Mediterranean and spread through northern Europe in the Middle Ages.

PLANT KNOWLEDGE: Lavender offers natural calming qualities; it can help to reduce anxiety, aid sleep, heal wounds and support skin health.

FOLKLORE: The medicinal uses of lavender can be traced back more than 2,500 years in Mediterranean countries and there are many tales that link lavender to stories of love and protection. In Spain and Portugal, lavender was an integral plant used in bonfire rituals on St John's Day to help ward off evil spirits. On St Luke's Day in the 1400s and 1500s, young women would sip on water infused with lavender in the hope that they would see their true love in their dreams that night.

WHY I GROW LAVENDER . . .

Lavender has always been a favourite plant of mine. Its strong, sensorial aroma transports me to a space of calm and serenity. However, I find it to be one of the more challenging plants to grow. Although I do have some success, I have yet to master cultivating a thriving crop of happy lavender plants. Each year I hope to learn a little more about how I can tend to its needs. I want to develop a relationship with this plant where I nurture it as much as its soothing scent nurtures me, and that provides me with the encouragement to keep on trying.

When I visited FARMERS' Welsh Lavender, a farm set 335m (1,100ft) up on a wild windswept hill in the middle of Wales, I was given hope by FARMERS' founder Nancy Durham: if she could grow 2.5 acres of lavender on the wet and exposed Welsh land, then a garden with a rich array of lavender on the Malvern Hills might be possible for me one day too.

OPPOSITE Harvested and dried English and French lavender.

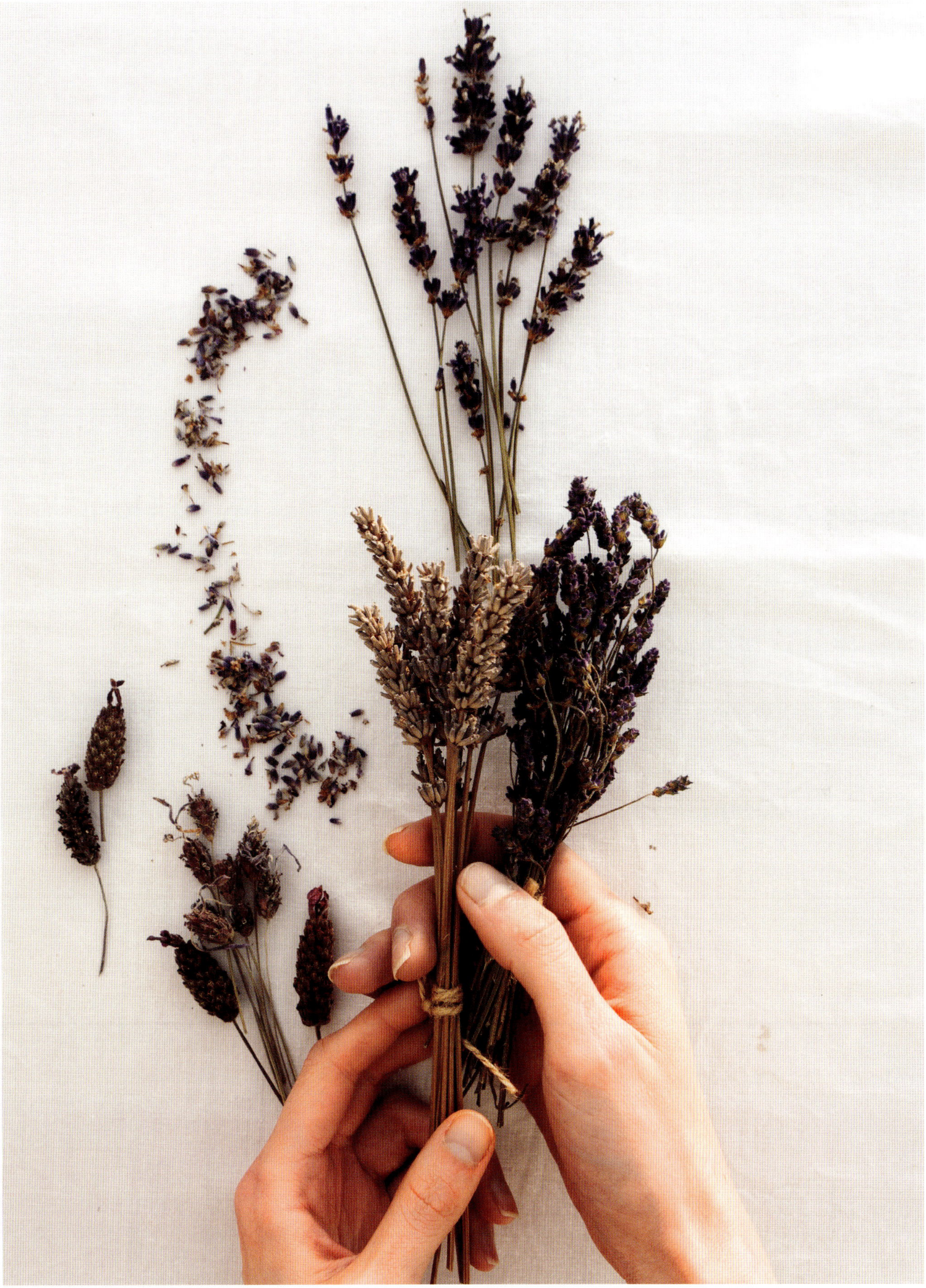

A GUIDE FOR GROWING . . .

- To thrive best, lavender requires a sheltered spot in the garden in full sun, planted in free-draining soil. Heavy soil, overwatering or excessive rain will result in a stressed lavender plant.

- It can be tricky to grow lavender from seed, so you may find that buying small plants from a local plant nursery is best. Planting lavender outside should be done in April and May.

- When growing lavender in a container, fill a terracotta pot with horticultural grit to improve drainage, then top up with peat-free compost. Leave a hole in the centre the depth and size of your plant, add in your plant, and fill in with compost where it is needed, ensuring that the plant is firm and supported. Finish with a few handfuls of horticultural grit on top and water well.

- If you are planting directly into the ground, adding horticultural grit to your hole and finishing with a thin layer of grit on the surface will help improve drainage.

- To stimulate new growth, so that you can keep on harvesting throughout the summer, you should cut back the stems by one-third their length every 2–3 weeks.

- After September, when the plant has finished flowering, you can prune well by removing any remaining flower stalks. However, don't cut into the woody stems, as they will struggle to grow back.

- If cared for and pruned correctly, well-established lavender plants of hardy varieties can keep on flowering year after year for around 15 years. More tender varieties might live for around five years.

- Together, rosemary and lavender make perfect companion plants and create aromatic harmony.

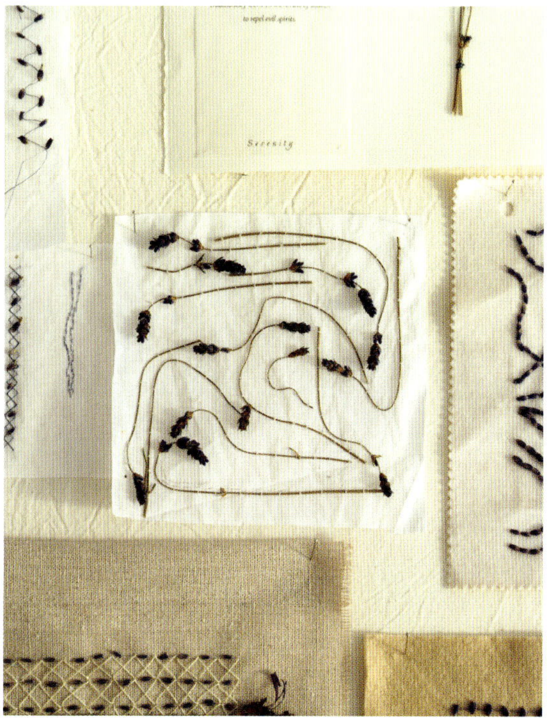

BELOW Detail from Katerina's desk with various samples hand-embroidered with lavender.

USING LAVENDER AS AN EMBELLISHMENT

Lavender seeds make perfect alternative beads: they are hardy and durable, retain their colour, and are far less delicate to work with than some of the other materials explored in this book. Although different varieties are available, I have found that traditional English lavender works best (my variety of choice is *Lavandula angustifolia* 'Munstead') because you can harvest many vibrant purple seeds from one stem. French lavender varieties (*Lavandula stoechas*) also produce interesting seeds, though they are a muted green colour and less hardy.

Cornflower

This quintessential British wild flower was introduced to the UK from the Mediterranean thousands of years ago. This hardy annual can give up to three months of beautiful blooms, with delicate, multi-coloured and pointed petals that range from white, to pink, to deep purple, to a striking blue. They are especially popular with pollinators, so expect bees and butterflies to flock to your garden in the summer months if you plant a bed of cornflowers.

WHY I GROW CORNFLOWERS . . .

I spent most of my twenties living in London, which is where my love for cornflowers first began. To escape the city's bustle, I would seek out quiet wildflower meadows – small pockets of calm where I could bask in the beauty of the flora. One vivid memory stays with me: in the summer of 2022, a year after the Covid lockdowns, I was cycling with my friend Maisy through the Olympic Park in Stratford, East London. The evening was warm, the sky awash with the colours of a setting sun, and all around us bloomed a sea of blue cornflowers. It felt magical; a moment of peace and beauty in a world still heavy with uncertainty. Now, year after year, I continue to grow cornflowers. The way they catch the light, glistening like tiny stars in the evening sun, always fills me with nostalgic warmth.

BOTANICAL NAME: *Centaurea cyanus*

FAMILY: Asteraceae (Daisy family)

ETYMOLOGY: The botanical name *Centaurea* is derived from the story of Chiron, a centaur who used cornflowers to heal a wound caused from an arrow poisoned by the blood of the hydra. The Latin word *cyanus* is derived from the goddess Flora (Cyanus), whose favourite flower was the cornflower. Cyanus spent a lot of time gathering cornflowers in the fields, and it is believed that when he died he was found lying in a field of cornflowers. Thus, the goddess Flora transformed him into a flower.

ORIGIN: Native to Europe.

PLANT KNOWLEDGE: The medicinal qualities of the cornflower are documented in the 12th-century writings of Hildegard of Bingen, a saint, composer and poet. They are considered to have antibacterial, anti-inflammatory, antiseptic and astringent properties used to remedy fever, digestion and eye strain.

FOLKLORE: The cornflower was once considered an invasive weed, often found growing wild among fields of corn – hence its name. It's also known as 'bachelor's button', a nod to an old tradition when young men in love would pin the vivid blue bloom to their jackets as a symbol of affection. If the flower faded quickly, it was believed to be a sign that their love was unrequited.

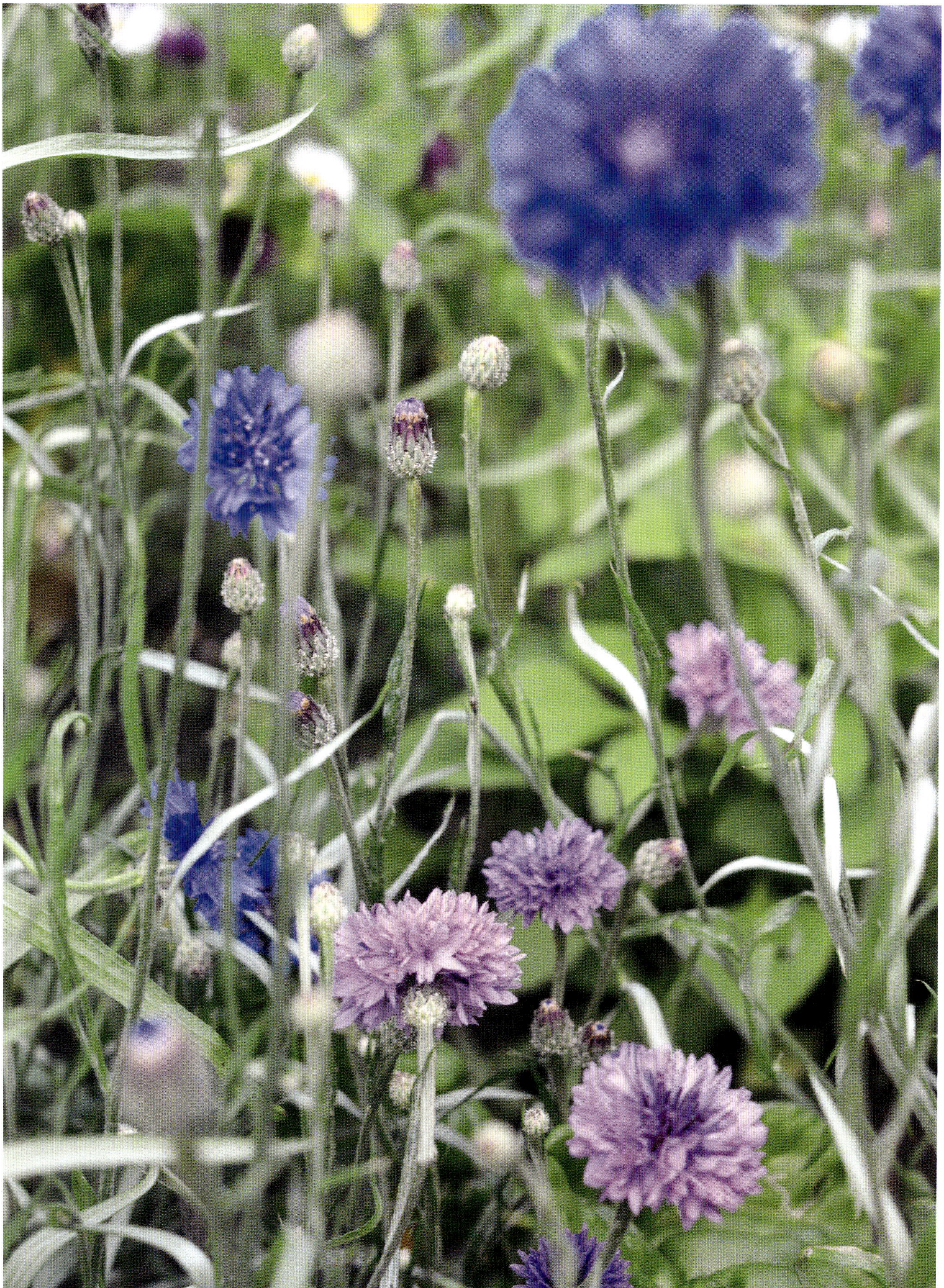

A GUIDE FOR GROWING . . .

- Cornflowers can be sown indoors or sown directly outside. To sow directly in your garden, scatter seeds directly into the ground. However, it is best to ensure that your ground is weed-free. If not, do not worry: cornflowers are a wild flower so will still happily flower among weeds.

- I prefer sowing cornflowers indoors so I can then plant them out in my desired position. I sow seeds in late March.

- Once the seedlings are ready to plant out and the last frost has passed, plant your seedlings 30cm (12in) apart and water well.

- Cornflowers respond best to well-drained soil in full sun.

- As a wild flower, cornflowers are not demanding of your attention; they are easy to grow when exposed to enough sunlight.

- They will grow up to a height of 75cm (30in).

- Cornflowers grow prolifically; during the flowering season, you should be able to harvest the flowers several times a week.

- As a hardy annual, cornflowers will produce flowers for one growing season only. Collect seeds and store these to give you a supply for the next year.

- Once the flowering season is complete, pull up your plants and add them to your compost heap.

USING CORNFLOWERS AS AN EMBELLISHMENT

Cornflowers come in a wide range of colours, offering a rich palette of embellishments to work with. Once dried, their petals retain their vibrant hues beautifully. You can find seeds in single colours or mixed varieties. I personally enjoy growing mixed varieties for the diversity they offer, though my favourite tones remain 'Black Ball', a deep crimson, and the soft, romantic pinks. Dried cornflower petals have a paper-like quality that makes them ideal for use as embroidery embellishments. They preserve well, lasting a long time until you're ready to stitch with them.

OPPOSITE Cornflowers in bloom in the community garden at Bright Earth Temple, Malvern.

RIGHT Harvested and dried cornflowers ready to be stored.

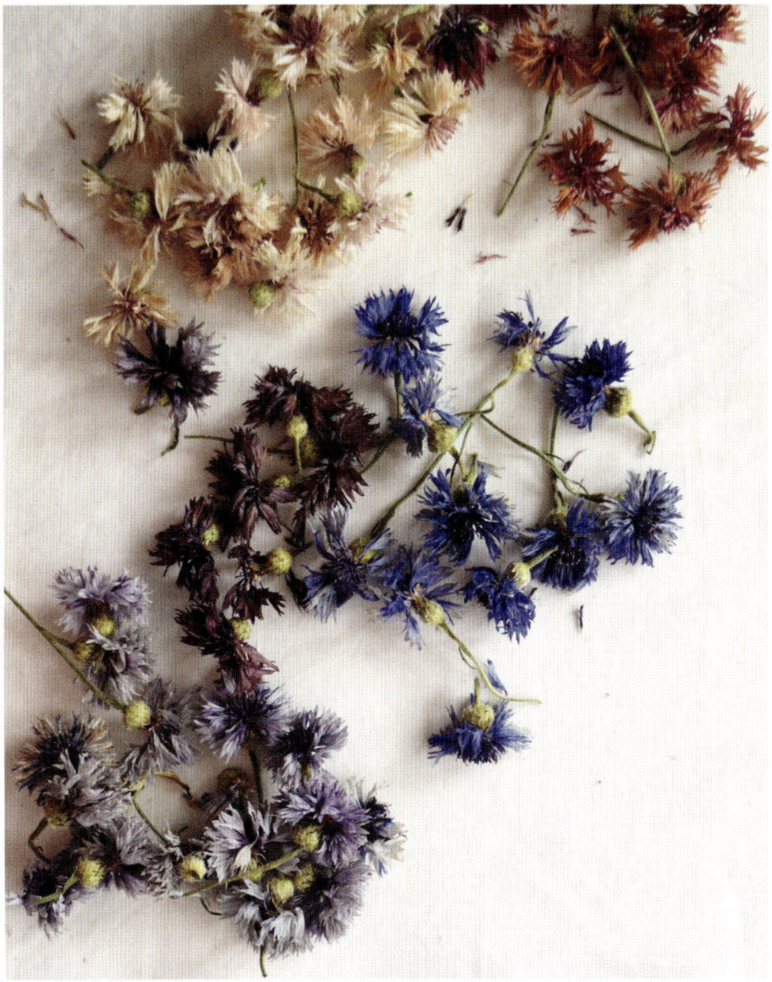

Dahlia

A popular cut flower with origins in Central America and Mexico, the dahlia was first cultivated in Europe in the 18th century as a simple, open-centred bloom. Since then, its diversity has flourished. Today, more than 51,000 dahlia varieties are registered with the Royal Horticultural Society (RHS), falling into 15 distinct classifications based on shape and form. These range from the elegant water lily dahlia to the tightly packed pompon, the single-headed types and the anemone-flowered dahlias.

WHY I GROW DAHLIAS . . .

Dahlias are tender perennials and extremely sustainable to grow. If stored correctly they will come back again year after year. Dahlias aren't one of my personal favourites, but I grow them because they make me think of my mother. They are her favourite cut flower, and we began growing them together three years ago. I have cherished memories of walking up the country lane to our allotment on a hot summer evening, where I would harvest cornflowers and my mother her dahlias. We would always smile in amazement at how big the blooms were and how fast they would replenish themselves. Now, I can never look at a dahlia without thinking of my mother, and growing them provides with me a comforting feeling that she is always there beside me.

BOTANICAL NAME: Dahlia

FAMILY: Asteraceae (Daisy family)

ETYMOLOGY: Dahlias were named in 1971 by the Director of the Royal Gardens of Madrid, Antonio Jose Cavanilles, after Anders Dahl, the 18th-century naturalist.

ORIGIN: Native to Central America.

PLANT KNOWLEDGE: Dahlias were an important medicinal plant among the pre-Columbian cultures. Dahlia tubers were valued for the inulin stored inside of them. Inulin is a plant-based nutrient that can help the body manage its glucose levels and aid digestion. More modern research highlights that dahlia petals have the ability to calm inflammation of the brain.

FOLKLORE: There is an ancient Aztec myth, as told by the 16th-century Spanish botanist Francisco Hernández, that an earth serpent goddess was ordered by the sky gods to stab a dahlia flower on the sharp point of a maguey leaf and to hold both to her heart all night. When she woke the next morning she gave birth to Huitzilopochtli. He was the powerful Aztec god of the sun and war, and the patron deity of the Aztecs, with a thirst for blood from the dahlia.

OPPOSITE Harvested and drying dahlias, 'Espacio' and 'Snowstorm' varieties.

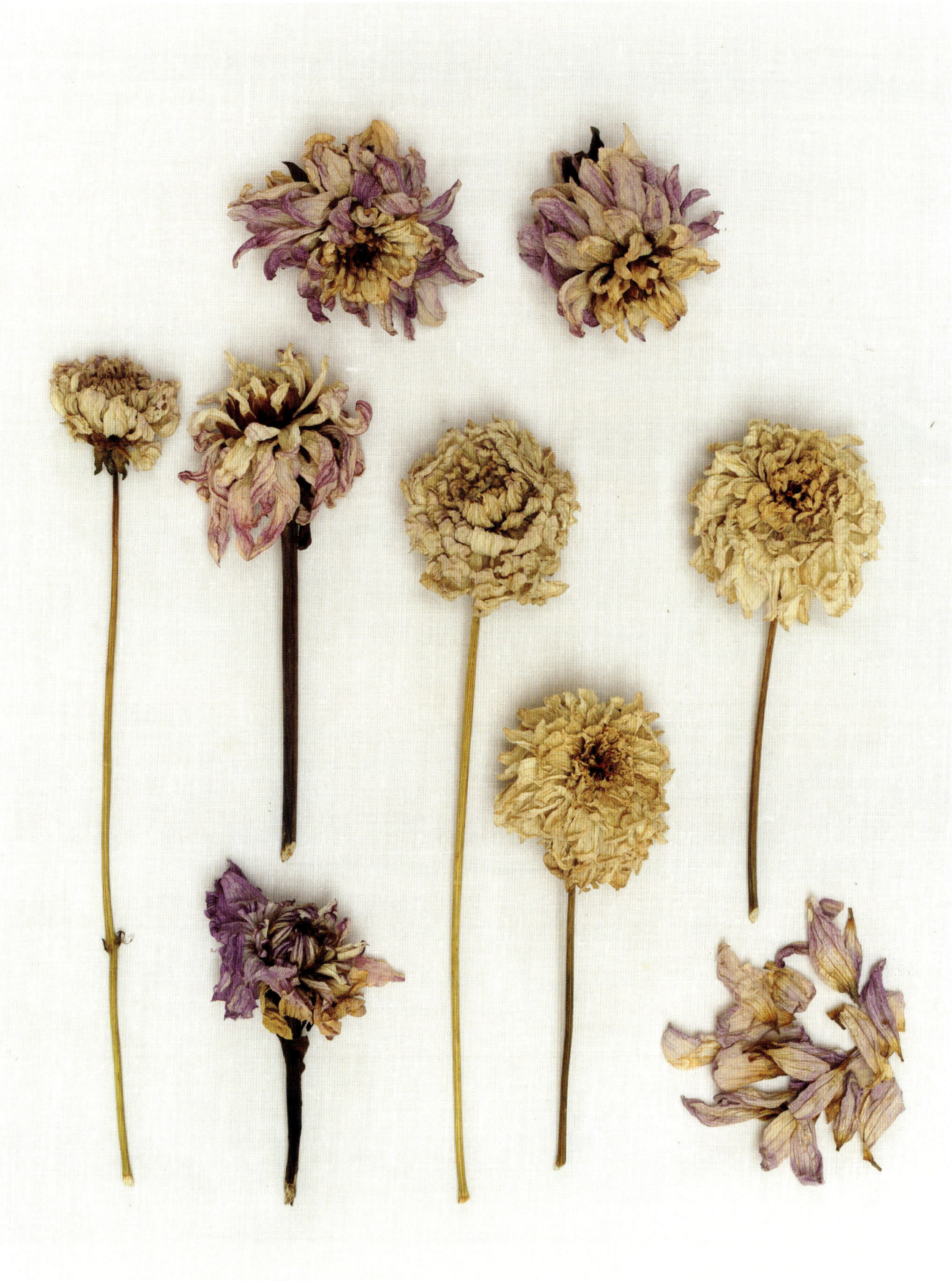

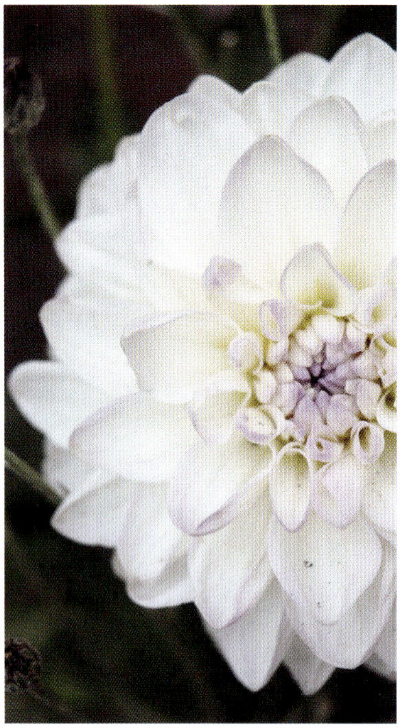

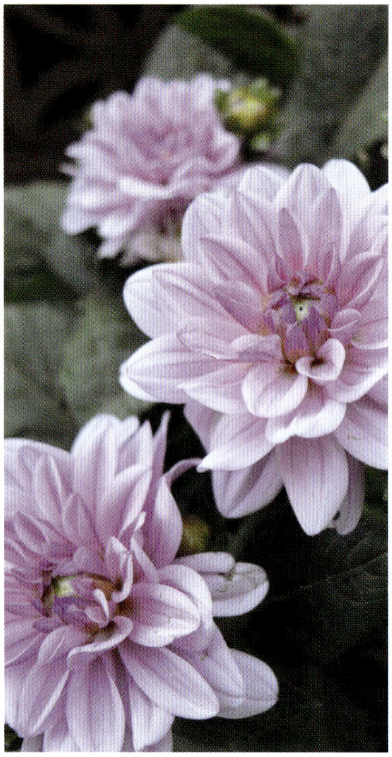

A GUIDE FOR GROWING . . .

- Dahlia tubers should be started in a pot indoors in spring in late March. Generally, bulbs should be planted at three times the depth of the height of the bulb. Place your tuber in a 2-litre pot that has a layer of horticultural grit at the base (approximately $^1/_5$ of the pot depth) to help with drainage, cover with peat-free multi-purpose compost, water, and place the pot in a warm indoor spot. Shoots will start to appear after around three weeks. It is best to cut back shoots so you have only five to ensure your dahlia is strong.
- Once the last frost has passed in May, you can transfer the dahlia outside. You should plant the tubers just under the surface of the soil and 75cm (30in) apart.
- While dahlias thrive better in the ground, they can be successfully grown in pots too. Be sure to check with the specific variety you are growing and ensure you have a pot with sufficient depth.
- You can also grow small varieties of dahlias from seed. Sow seeds indoors between February and April in moist compost and keep them well watered. Begin hardening off in early summer and then transport the seedlings and plant outdoors.
- Once planted out, dahlias require a lot of watering, especially during the peak of the summer months.
- Some dahlia varieties with big blooms can be top-heavy and will require a support such as a bamboo stick.
- Dahlias have a long flowering season, from late summer well into autumn.
- To encourage new growth, cut back flowerheads regularly. Unlike other flowers, the flowerhead will not continue to open once cut, so you should wait until the flowerhead is at its optimum glory before cutting.
- Over winter, dahlias should be stored in a dark, cool, frost-free place. Cover the tuber with insulating material such as a dry potting compost or wool tops. You can then bring them out again next March for repotting.

USING DAHLIAS AS AN EMBELLISHMENT

I prefer to grow varieties with small- to medium-sized dahlia flowers. The petals dry out well and are a much better size to stitch with. However, bigger dahlia flower varieties with large petals work excellently for dyeing. For a range of colours I would advise buying a collection of tubers that produce varied tones. My favourites are those in pink and white tones, but in terms of preserving their colour, the deep dark purple, red and pink tones work best.

Statice

Statice is also known as sea lavender, referring to its preference for growing in harsh environments with salty soils, native to coastal areas of the Mediterranean basin. Its papery flowers have earned it the nickname the 'everlasting flower', and it is especially popular in dried arrangements. In the Victorian era, the statice flower symbolized remembrance. Gifting the flower was a way to tell someone they were loved and missed.

BOTANICAL NAME: *Limonium sinuatum*

FAMILY: Plumbaginaceae (Leadwort family)

ETYMOLOGY: 'Limonium' comes from the Greek word *leimōn* meaning 'meadow', whereas the name statice is derived from the Greek word *statikos*, meaning 'causing to stand'. This mirrors the plant's ability to retain its shape and colour even after drying, suggesting standing still or stability.

ORIGIN: Originates from the Mediterranean region, including parts of Southern Europe, North Africa and Western Asia.

PLANT KNOWLEDGE: Statice has been used as a herbal remedy to soothe an upset stomach and aid digestion. It is thought to have psychological benefits too, being used to calm anxiety and balance the mind.

FOLKLORE: In the Victorian era in England statice was seen as a symbol of lasting memory, perhaps due to its reputation as an 'everlasting flower'. Its association with remembrance meant it was often used for celebrations of weddings and anniversaries.

WHY I GROW STATICE . . .

As I am a lover of lavender and rosemary, it is no surprise that statice – also known as sea lavender or marsh rosemary – is another favourite of mine. Statice petals work perfectly for the practice of *Stitching with Nature* as they are almost dried when they grow. This means that they retain their vibrant colour once harvested and dried out completely.

Another quality I find satisfying about statice petals is that they are almost always uniform in shape and size – as a perfectionist, the pairing of precise uniform stitches together with statice petals is very visually appealing to me.

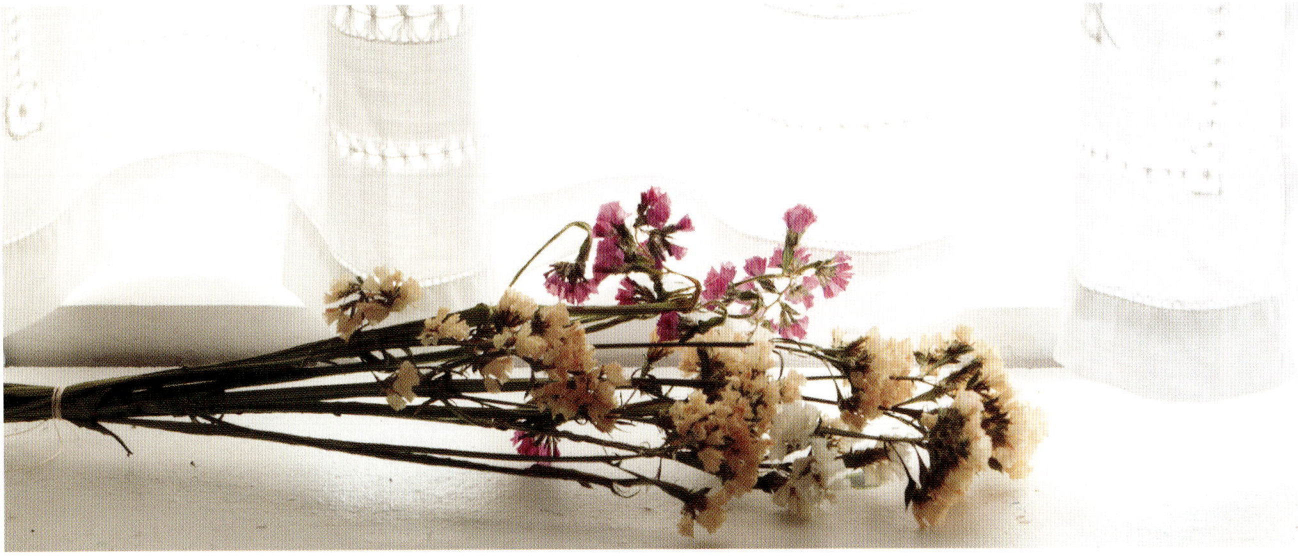

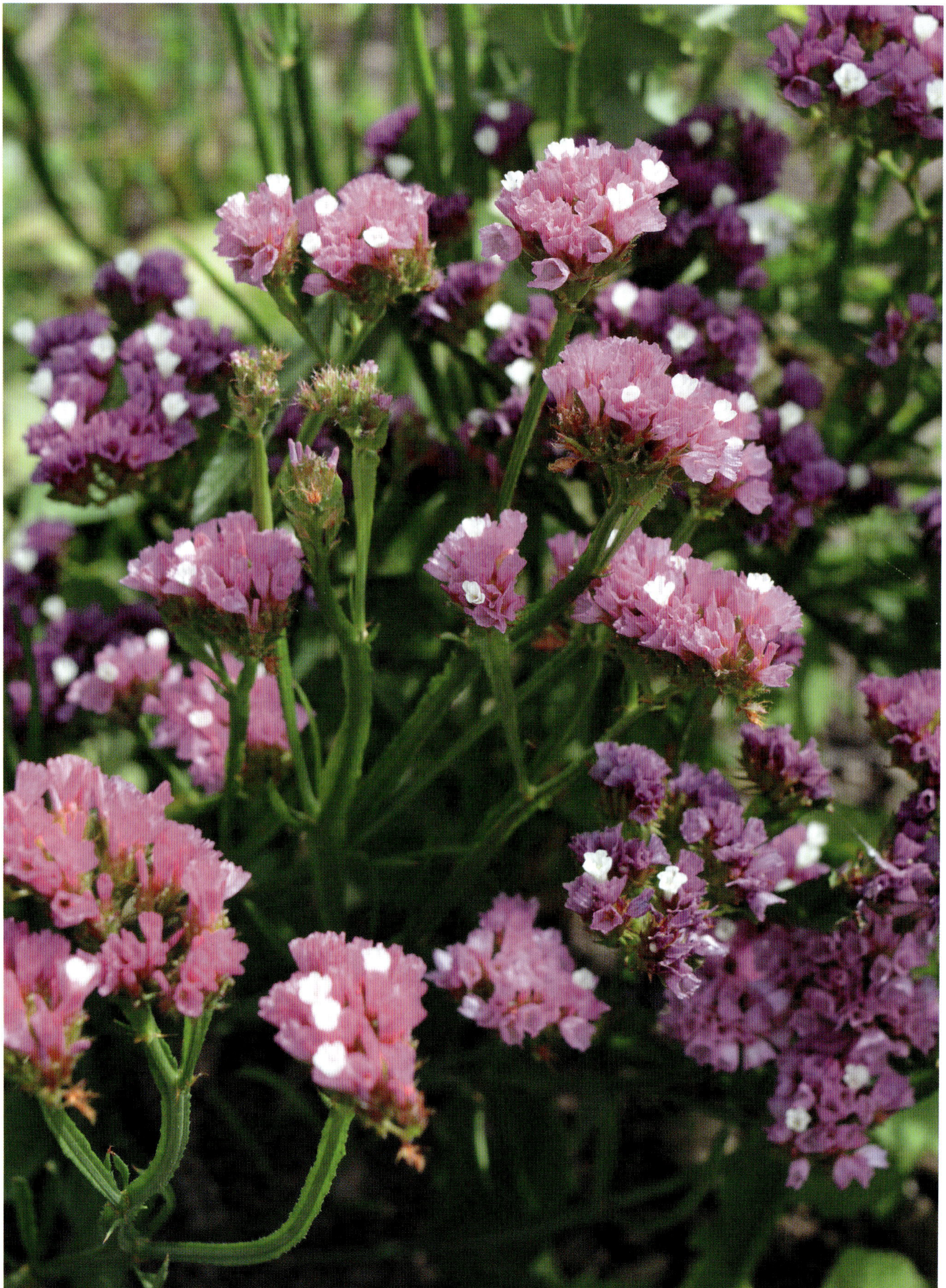

OPPOSITE Statice in bloom.

BELOW Harvested and dried statice petals ready to be stored.

A GUIDE FOR GROWING . . .

- Statice seeds should be sown under cover in March. Once the last frost has passed, they can then be gradually hardened off before planting out in a pot or in the ground.
- Statice plants will thrive best in full sun and well-drained soil.
- You should be mindful to avoid overwatering. Once established, water occasionally and through long dry spells.
- Harvest when all the flowers on a stem have opened.
- Statice is a productive plant and if regularly harvested during its flowering season it will continue to replenish and produce new blooms.
- Statice can be grown as both a perennial and an annual. In warmer Mediterranean climates it can be grown successfully as a short-lived perennial. However, in the UK it is often grown as an annual.
- At the end of the flowering season, pull up the statice plant and add it to your compost heap.

USING STATICE AS AN EMBELLISHMENT

Statice can be grown in a beautiful range of colours. Yellow and lilac are my personal favourites, though I enjoy cultivating several shades to create a more varied palette to choose from. These flowers retain their colour remarkably well once dried, often appearing almost identical to their fresh state. Unlike some plant materials that require time to cure, statice petals dry quickly, making them ready to stitch with almost immediately after harvesting. They are the perfect material for those eager to begin embellishing right away.

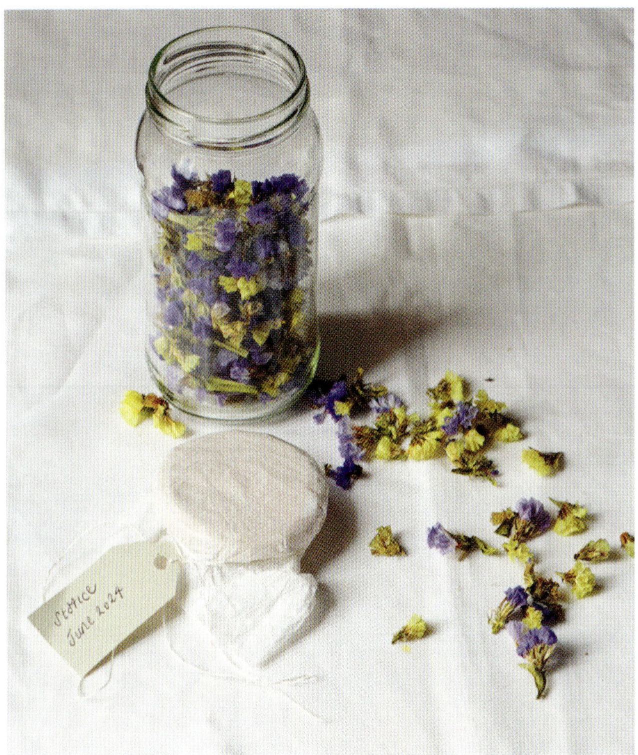

Other Flowers to Grow in Your Stitching Garden

- **Achillea:** Otherwise known as yarrow, achillea is a hardy perennial wild flower that produces flat-topped blooms that last throughout the summer months. Their colours can range from white, peachy oranges, soft yellows or vivid pinks. I especially like growing achillea to be used as an embellishment as they offer tiny clusters of flowers that can be left whole, offering you a full flowerhead embellishment to work with instead of single petals. Achillea flowers dry out quickly once harvested. You can find the white variety growing wild in abundance, so this is a flower you can easily forage for too.

- **Chamomile:** Chamomile (*Matricaria recutita*) is one of the oldest favourites among garden herbs. This hardy plant with restorative powers features delicate fern-like leaves and hairy, highly branched stems, creating a charming appearance reminiscent of daisy-like plants. It grows as a compact bush, and is a seasonal flower, blooming from June to July. Chamomile's historical use as a medicinal herb has led to its association with healing and recovery. It signifies the potential for physical and emotional healing. (Opposite, top left.)

- **Marigold:** Marigold flowers (*Tagetes* spp.) are aromatic, with deeply divided leaves and single or double flowerheads in shades of yellow, orange, red and brown. They flower from summer into early autumn. In the UK, marigolds are widely grown as a bedding plant, and their natural pest-repelling properties make them an excellent companion plant. Marigolds are a symbolic flower that have been used for centuries in decoration and sacred offerings, including in Mexico for Día de los Muertos and in India for Diwali and Holi.

- **Rosemary:** Rosemary (*Salvia rosmarinus*) is part of the Lamiaceae (mint) family, and is an evergreen shrub with aromatic leaves, native to the Mediterranean. Rosemary, for me, is a herb that goes hand in hand with lavender. The rich of combination of aroma and colour – lilac tones against earthy greens – is captivating. I started growing my own rosemary after being awakened to its remarkable potentials as a natural dye material.

- **Roses:** There are not many things I enjoy more than going around a garden smelling the roses, on the hunt to find the one with the sweetest scent. Roses come in various forms, from shrub roses, to climbers, to patio container roses. New roses in particular have been designed to have long flowering seasons. Often, roses can require a lot of space, or in some cases can be a more costly investment. However, parks and gardens are often rich with roses. Why not take a walk around your local park and gather the fresh fallen rose petals? (Opposite, top right and bottom left.)

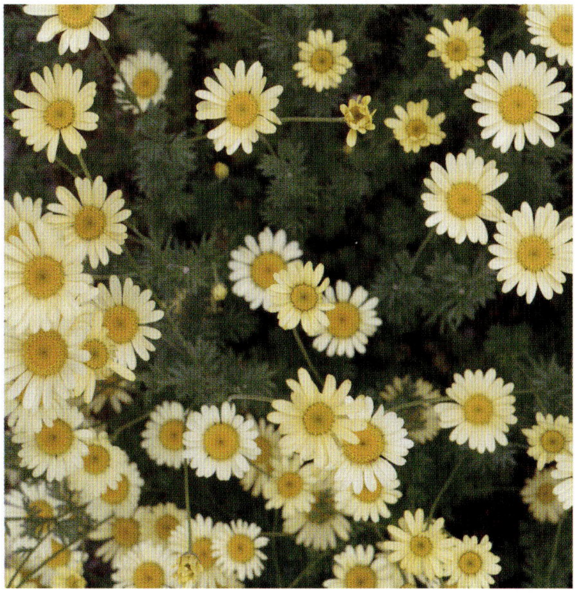

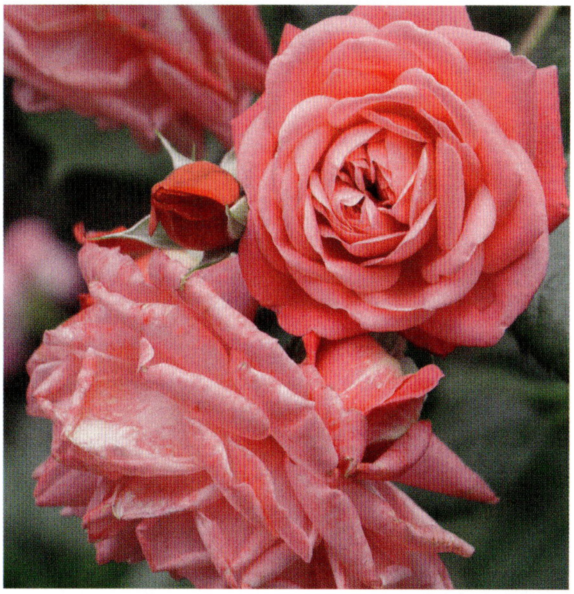

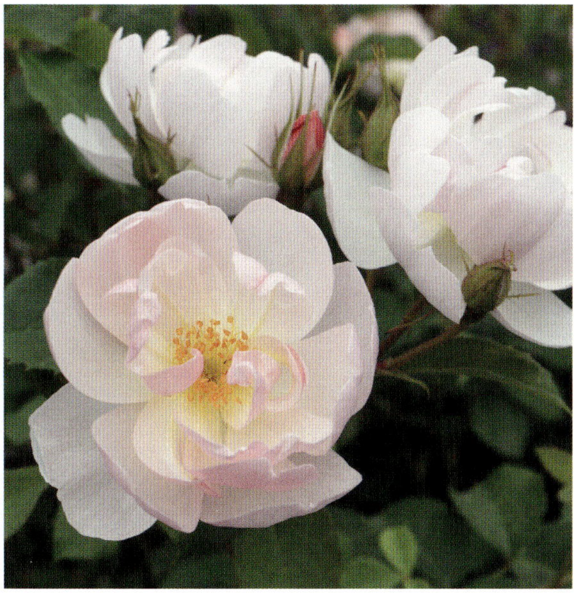

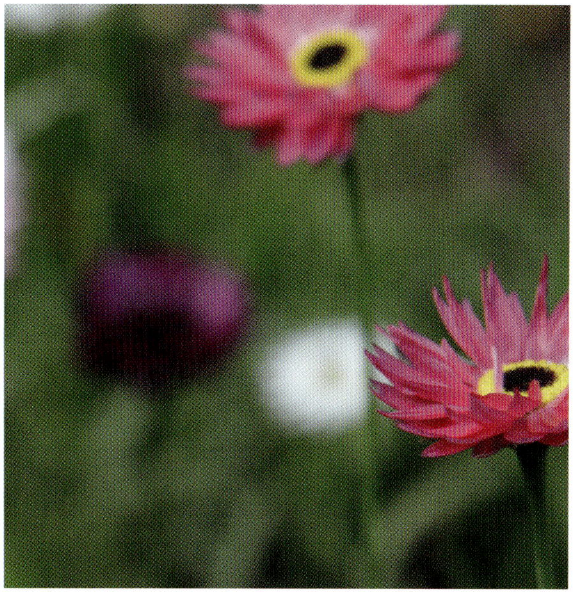

Strawflower: Native to Australia, strawflowers (*Xerochrysum bracteatum*) are often associated with immortality due to their dried quality offering longevity; thus they have become a flower symbolic of long-lasting love and relationships. Strawflowers are excellent for drying, retaining their colour and form extremely well, which makes them an excellent material for the processes featured in this book. Varieties can range from small, spiky-petalled flowers to larger circular blooms. (Above, bottom right.)

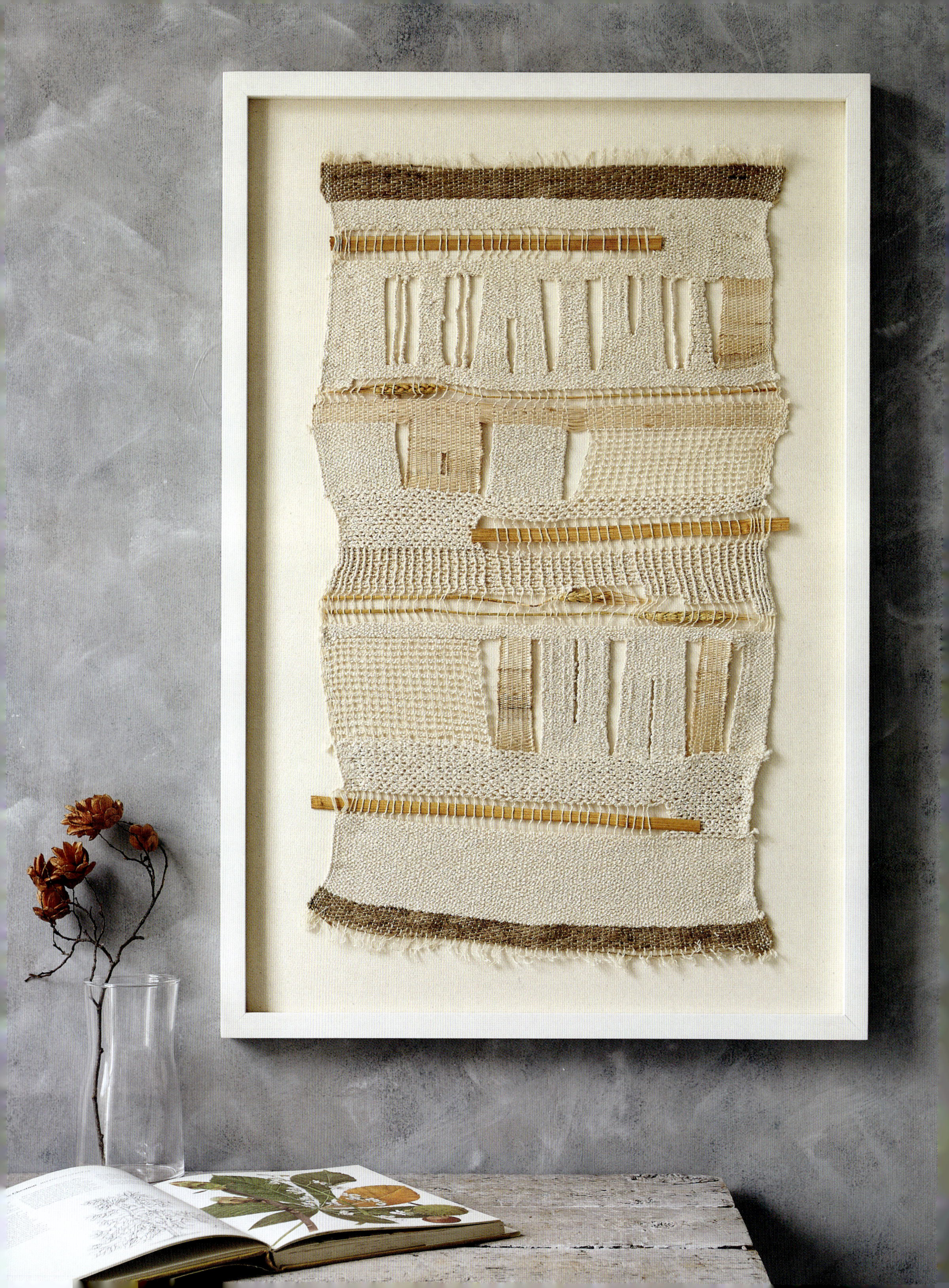

FEATURED ARTIST

Rachna Garodia

'It's like what Mary Oliver says: "It's all about paying attention." ... Sometimes the memory of a season, a memory of the colour can be as rich as the season itself; it might even be richer. Because with that memory you can add a few droplets of imagination and romanticism.'

OPPOSITE *Architecture* series (2018). Hand-woven using cotton, jute, banana fibre, wheat pods and bamboo.

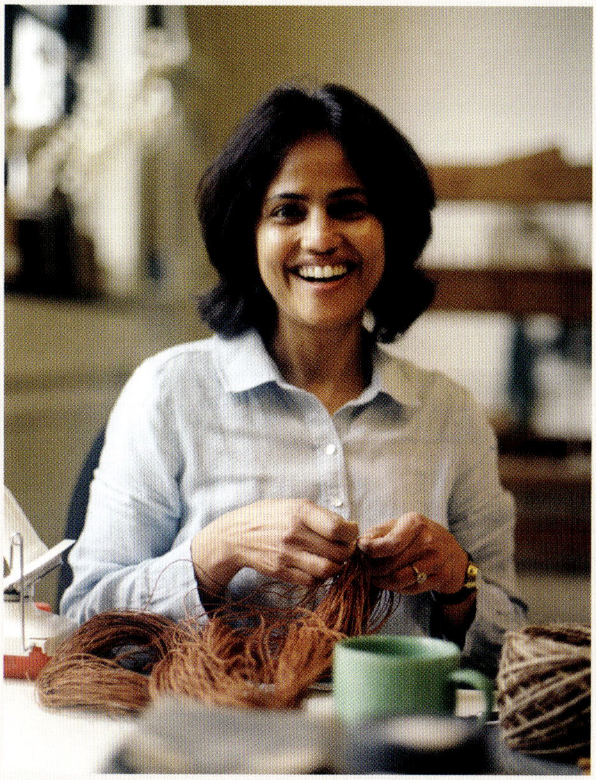

Textile artist and weaver Rachna Garodia's connection to nature is rooted in the everyday, through the ritual of daily walks in West London, through the ever-evolving seasons.

Rachna studied for her Masters at the National Institute of Design in Ahmedabad, India. She subsequently relocated to London with her family, and later trained in embroidery at the Royal School of Needlework. The intricacy of embroidery is very evident in her woven artworks today. Rachna discovered her working process of juxtaposing textiles and found materials – cotton, linen, silk and wool intertwined with bark, seedpods, branches and petals – during her studies at the National Institute of Design, and remains enamoured with it. 'My tapestries seek to bring the outside in,' says Rachna. 'When you look at my weave, the walk is there.'

KK: *What draws you to working with plants?*

RG: All plants inspire me, and I find inspiration in all of the elements of the plant; sometimes it's the roots, sometimes it's the stems, sometimes it's the buds, sometimes it's just the colours, or the texture, the dryness of a fallen leaf, for instance. Sometimes I feel you don't even need so much variety, you know: just one plant can offer so much detail.

KK: *Your pieces are closely tied to the seasons. Are you making in time with the seasonal patterns?*

RG: Nature's seasons are always on my mind, but I am not always designing in sync with the patterns. I work on commissions, so sometimes the theme of a piece and the colour palette is dictated by a client. I also work on multiple projects, two or three pieces at once, so I can be working with multiple seasons in mind simultaneously. There are times when I have to explain to clients that, when working with nature, my materials can be informed by the current season, so I might not be able to just pick up that exact leaf they would like and weave it into the design. Some things can't happen immediately. Sometimes the memory of a season, the memory of the colour, can be as rich as the season itself; it might even be richer. Because with that memory you can add a few droplets of imagination and romanticism..

KK: *Yes, and when you mix in a bit of your imagination, that's what makes your pieces unique to you. Are there challenges to working with such delicate plant materials on the loom?*

RG: There are times when I get very ambitious, and then realize it actually might not be possible. For example, I made a piece called *Mimosa* (2022). I love the bright yellow blossoms of the mimosa tree; they are so enticing to me, and I wanted to bring this into a weave. I spent years pressing the flowers, trying to retain that vivid yellow, but realized it was so ephemeral and quickly faded. So the final piece was a homage to the mimosa tree but woven with yellow threads and mimosa leaves..

KK: *Did growing up in India inform your relationship with nature?*

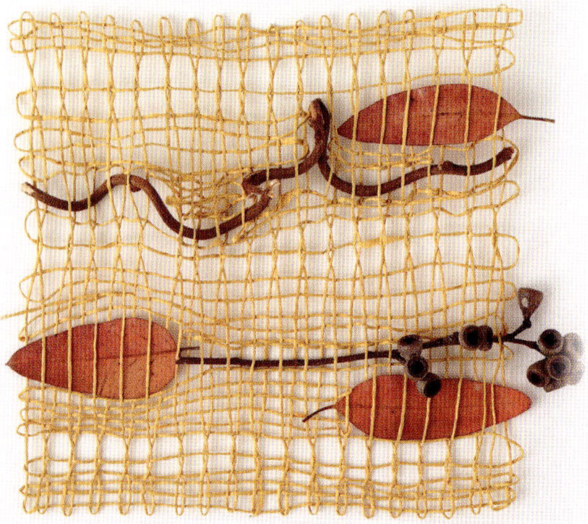

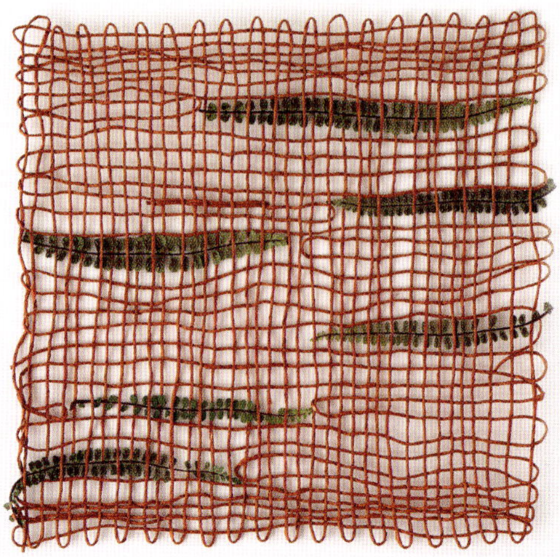

FAR LEFT *Nilgiri* (2023). Hand-woven with paper yarn and dried eucalyptus leaves and pods. 30 x 30cm (12 x 12in) in frame.

LEFT *Fern1* (2023). Hand-woven with paper yarn and dried ferns. 30 x 30cm (12 x 12in) in frame.

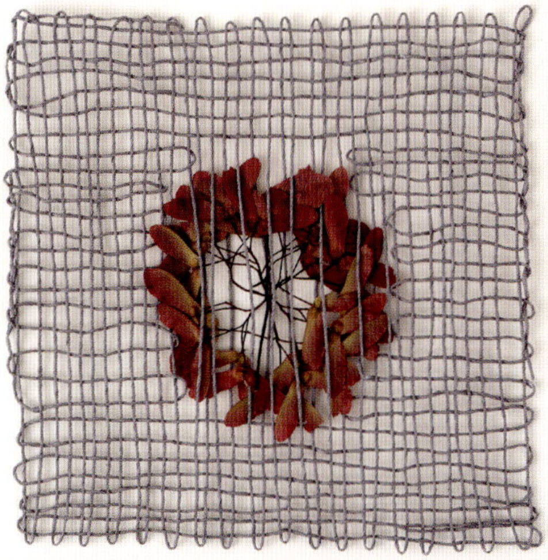

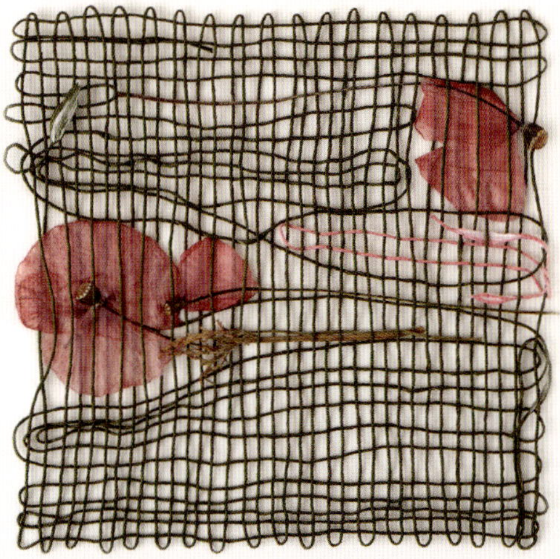

FAR LEFT *Maple* (2023). Hand-woven with paper yarn and maple samara, 30 x 30cm (12 x 12in) in frame.

LEFT *Poppy* (2023). Hand-woven with paper yarn and dried poppy flower, 30 x 30cm (12 x 12in) in frame.

RG: I've thought about this quite a lot recently. I grew up in a small town called Patna in Bihar, in the north of India. When I was little I used to love climbing trees, and I find it interesting how many trees I remember from our neighbourhood from the daily commutes between my home and school. Just the other day, my sister sent a photograph of a tree with white flowers and orange stems and it immediately transported me back to memories of a particular route we would take early in the morning where two trees had the same flowers. It's funny where things get logged in your mind.

KK: *Did you start working with plant materials while you were in India or was this more recent when you moved to the UK?*

RG: In India the climate can be very hot and dry. While studying for my Master's, I collected dried seeds and started combining them in my work. The seedpods were so lustrous and I started to explore stitching them onto a piece of fabric. I still have those samples now, from many years ago. It is the juxtaposition of yarns and textile with found organic materials that I became obsessed with.

KK: *It is quite amazing that many years later you can still find so much inspiration in this.*

RG: In some ways I feel like, oh no, I'm doing exactly what I was doing when I was 20 years old! But then I keep thinking, no, but the work has evolved. In India it is so noisy, the colours are so loud, everything is so bright. And in India when I was weaving, my designs had a very natural palette of browns and muted tones. Now, living in London for the past 19 years, how I weave is much more vibrant – like the mimosa, for example.

KK: *It sounds as though your making process is your safe place?*

RG: It's funny, I never thought of it like that, but yes: my weaving is almost like cocooning myself.

KK: *Would you say that mimosa is your favourite plant?*

RG: Oh no, no, no! I could not choose a favourite, it is like asking me to choose a favourite child. I love magnolias, I love dandelions – I could not pick.

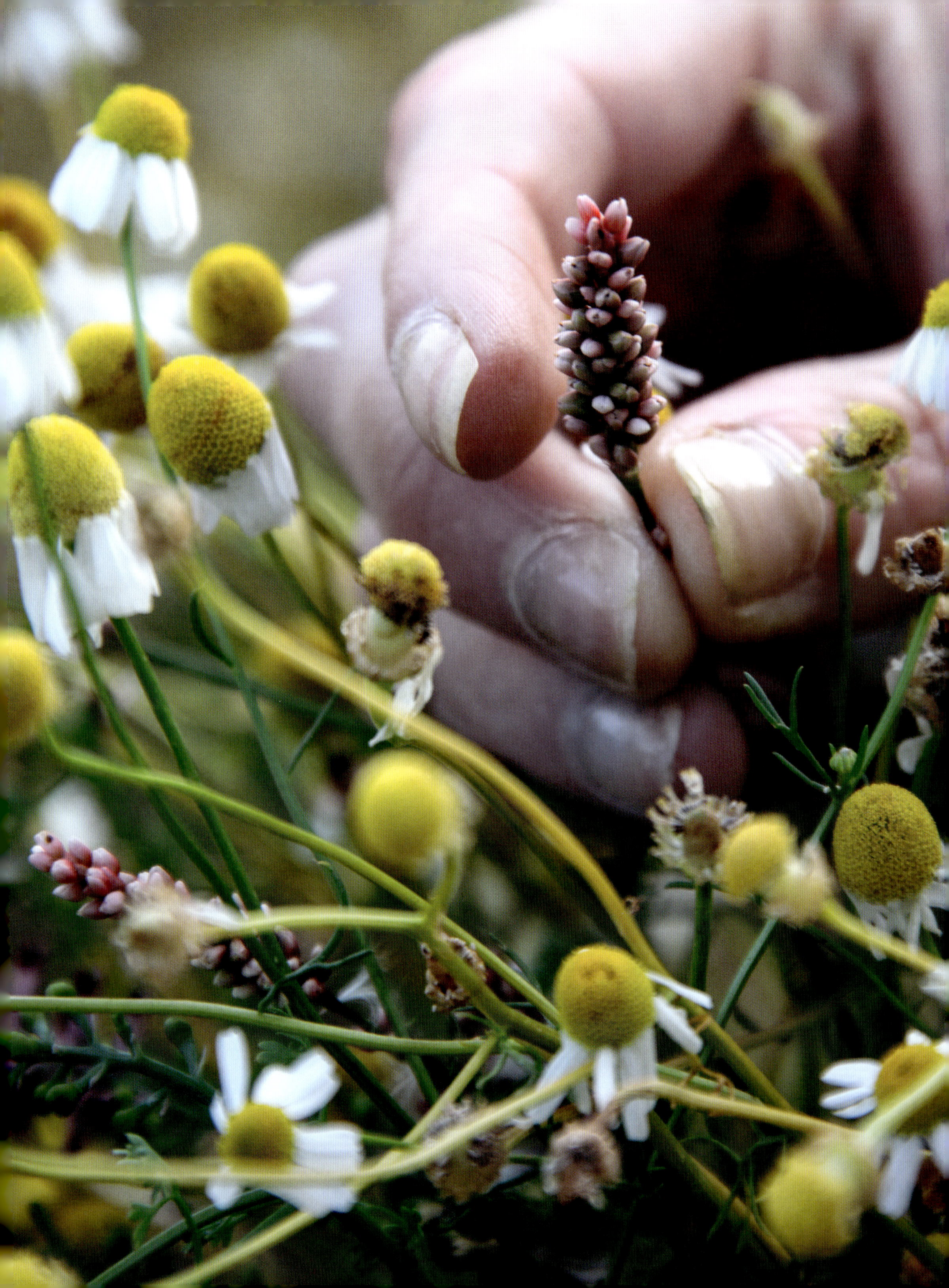

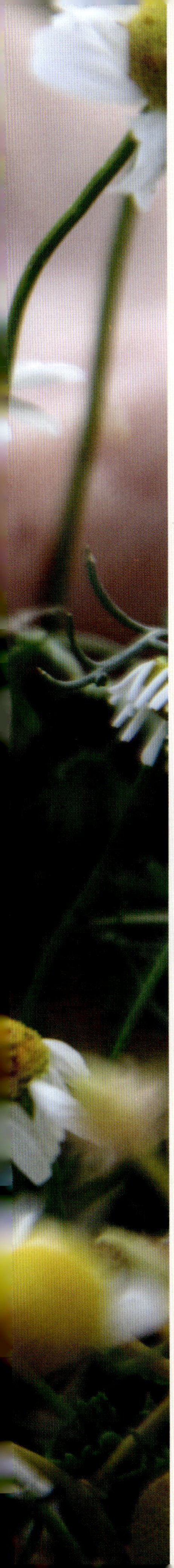

HARVESTING, DRYING AND STORING PLANT MATERIALS

'If you will take any flower you please, and look it over and turn it about and smell it and feel it and try to find out all its secrets, not of flower only, but of leaf, bud and stem as well, you will discover many wonderful things.'

GERTRUDE JEKYLL

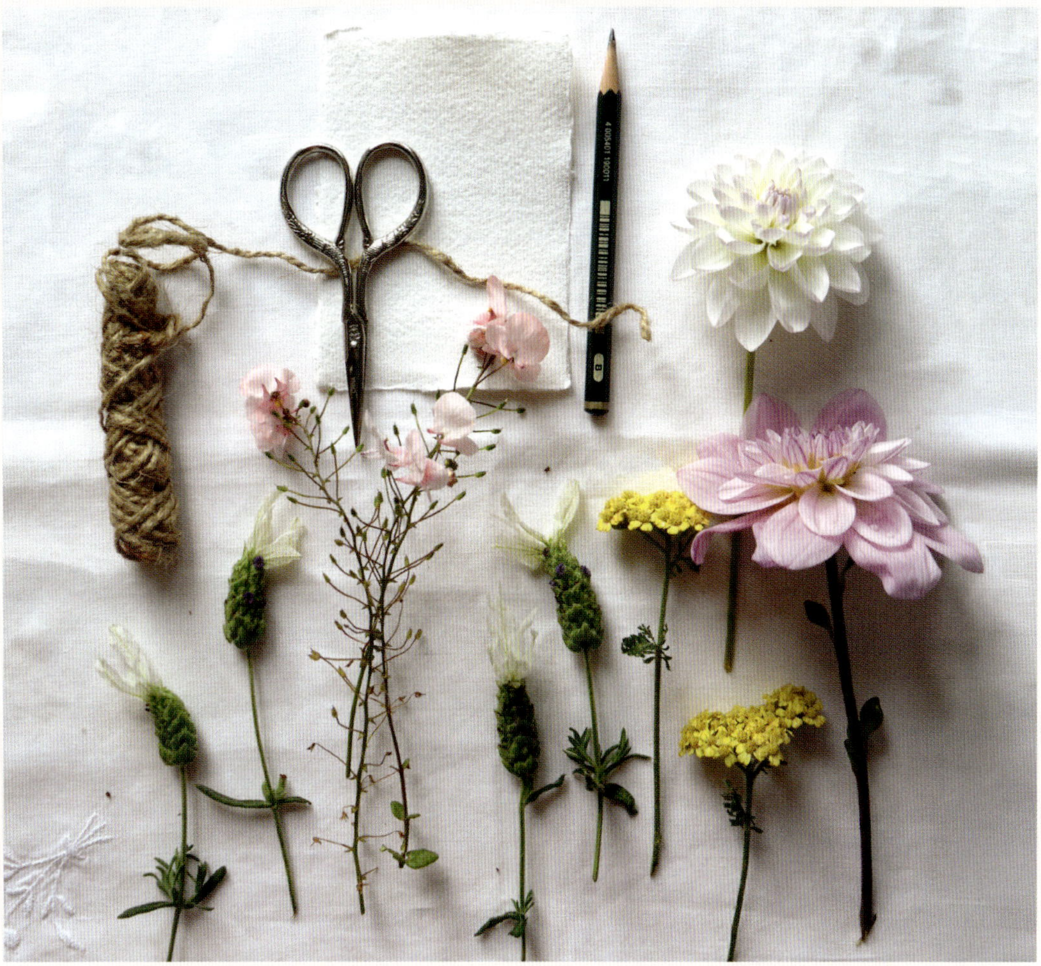

Harvesting, drying and storing are important processes in building your library of plant embellishments ready for stitching. These stages are just as important as growing the flowers themselves, and each deserves the time and care it requires. In keeping with the theme of the book, they are slow, ritualistic processes. Those that you can savour through late summer into autumn, as the evenings begin to draw in.

When stitching plant materials, I never work with fresh flowers. I always ensure they are fully dried out first. If you work with fresh materials they will continue to dry out on your cloth, creating moisture that could damage your textiles. Drying also allows you to select the flowers, seeds and petals that have retained their colour and form. Some petals fade or become too brittle; waiting until they are dry ensures you can choose your best embellishment materials.

Once dried, plant materials are usually stronger and easier to stitch with, you will find your needle passes through them more smoothly than when they are fresh.

In the pages that follow, I will share with you how to harvest your flowers and prepare them for safekeeping, ready for stitching.

Harvesting

Harvesting flowers is one of my favourite tasks in the garden. It's an intimate ritual and time for a quiet pause where I carefully cut each flower individually, taking time to appreciate what I have grown. I especially enjoy doing this in the evening, when the setting summer sun casts a golden light that makes the moment feel all the more magical. After cutting, I usually place the flowers in a vase by my bedside for a day or two before drying them. I love waking up to the sweet aroma of freshly cut flowers and the sight of their colours and shapes woven together – a fleeting arrangement that I savour before their next transformation into dried flora.

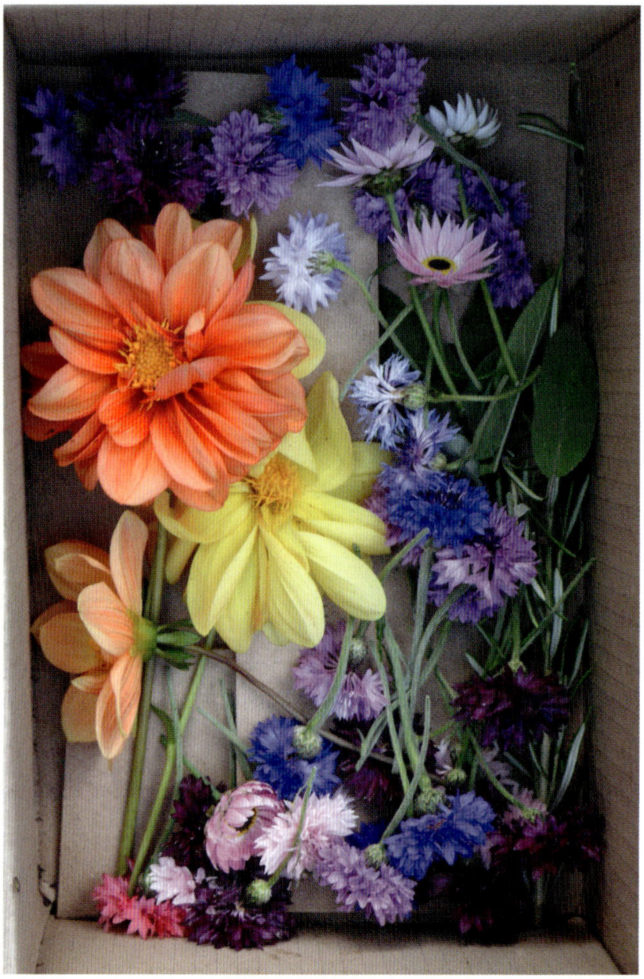

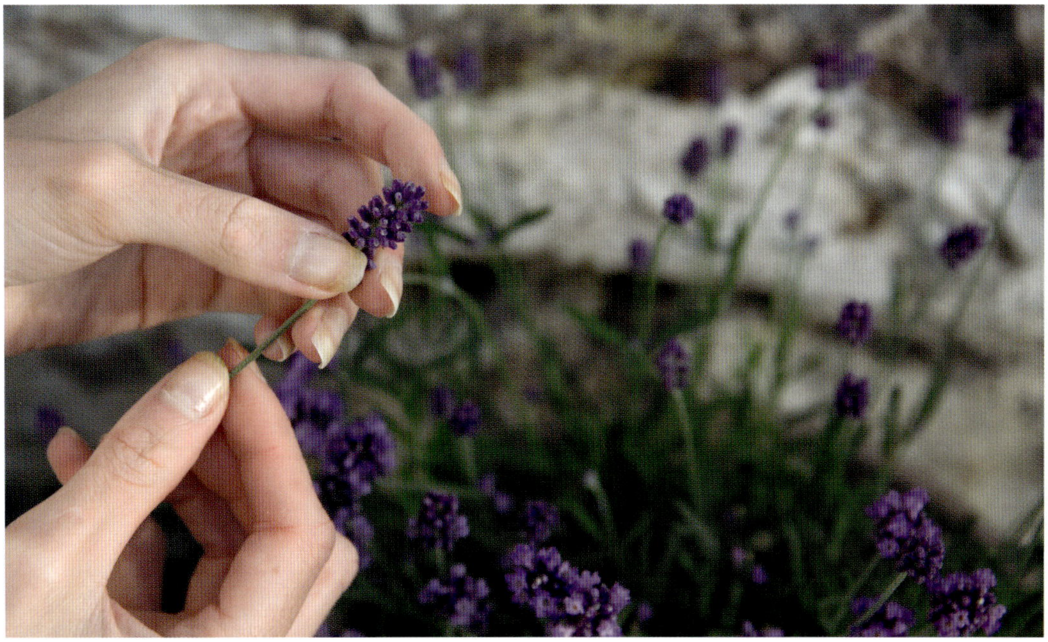

When to Harvest

- Pick a dry day to harvest, as you do not want flowers to be moist. Ideally, harvest after a few consecutive dry days for the best results.

- For pollinator-friendly flowers such as cornflowers and lavender, I like to stagger my cuttings, leaving some flowers behind for the bees and butterflies to enjoy.

- In summer, aim to harvest either early in the morning or later in the evening, when temperatures are cooler and the flowers are less stressed by the heat.

- Harvest regularly throughout the flowering season. This not only provides you with a steady supply of flowers but also encourages the plants to produce more.

- Be sure to deadhead any rotting or spent flowerheads to keep your plants healthy and productive.

- Cut flowers when they are at their peak: vibrant in colour, open and full of life. Avoid waiting too long: you do not want your cut flowers to be faded in colour, drooped or showing signs of drying.

- When cutting, always snip the stems at an angle. This helps prevent blockages in the xylem and allows the plant to take up water more effectively.

Drying

The next step once your flowers are harvested is drying. There are different ways that you can do this. Some people purchase a dehydrator, which works by speeding up the process and drawing moisture out of the plant. As with all techniques in this book, I embrace the slowness and natural rhythms of drying naturally, and not intervening with any machines. I like to observe the slow, subtle changes of colour, form and texture as the materials transition from fresh to dried.

For some of the flowers I grow that have multi-petalled, fuller flowerheads – such as marigolds or dahlias – there are two ways you could dry them. The first is to remove the petals from their flowerheads and lay them out individually on sheets of newspaper to dry. The second is to leave the flowerhead in its full form, as this way the petals retain an interesting three-dimensional shape. If you opt for this approach, be mindful that the petals will take much longer to dry out. For larger heads, such as dahlias, you can hang them upside down to dry.

Some petals, such as strawflowers and statice, dry almost immediately once cut. This is because their petals have a paper-like quality. For these varieties, I use a fine twine, tie a few stems together and hang them to dry above my studio desk. You could also hang your flowers to dry from picture hooks on your wall or, if you have one, a Clothesmaid is a perfect tool for hanging.

For seed materials, such as lavender, you should lie your sprigs of lavender flat on sheets of newspaper. Once dried, the easiest way to store your lavender seeds – and save you time so they are ready for stitching later – is to remove the individual seeds from their stem. Gently rub the lavender head between your fingertips to release the seeds. This allows you to store them more efficiently, reduces the space they take up and ensures they're ready for stitching whenever you need them.

I also collect old jam jars and use them to hold flowers while they dry. This method allows air to circulate around the blooms. Place just a few stems in each jar, spacing them out, and keep the jars on a shelf away from direct sunlight. This is a simple and space-efficient way to dry flowers indoors.

Drying time varies depending on the flower and the conditions of your space. Temperature, airflow and humidity all play a role. Keep your drying area well-ventilated and check the flowers every few days to monitor their progress.

I am often asked: how do you preserve your flowers? What do you put on them? I do not apply any form of coating to my flowers or interfere with the natural process. I expect them to be ephemeral materials and am mindful that I do not know how long they will last. I appreciate their temporality even when they are dried.

OPPOSITE Cornflowers drying on newsprint.

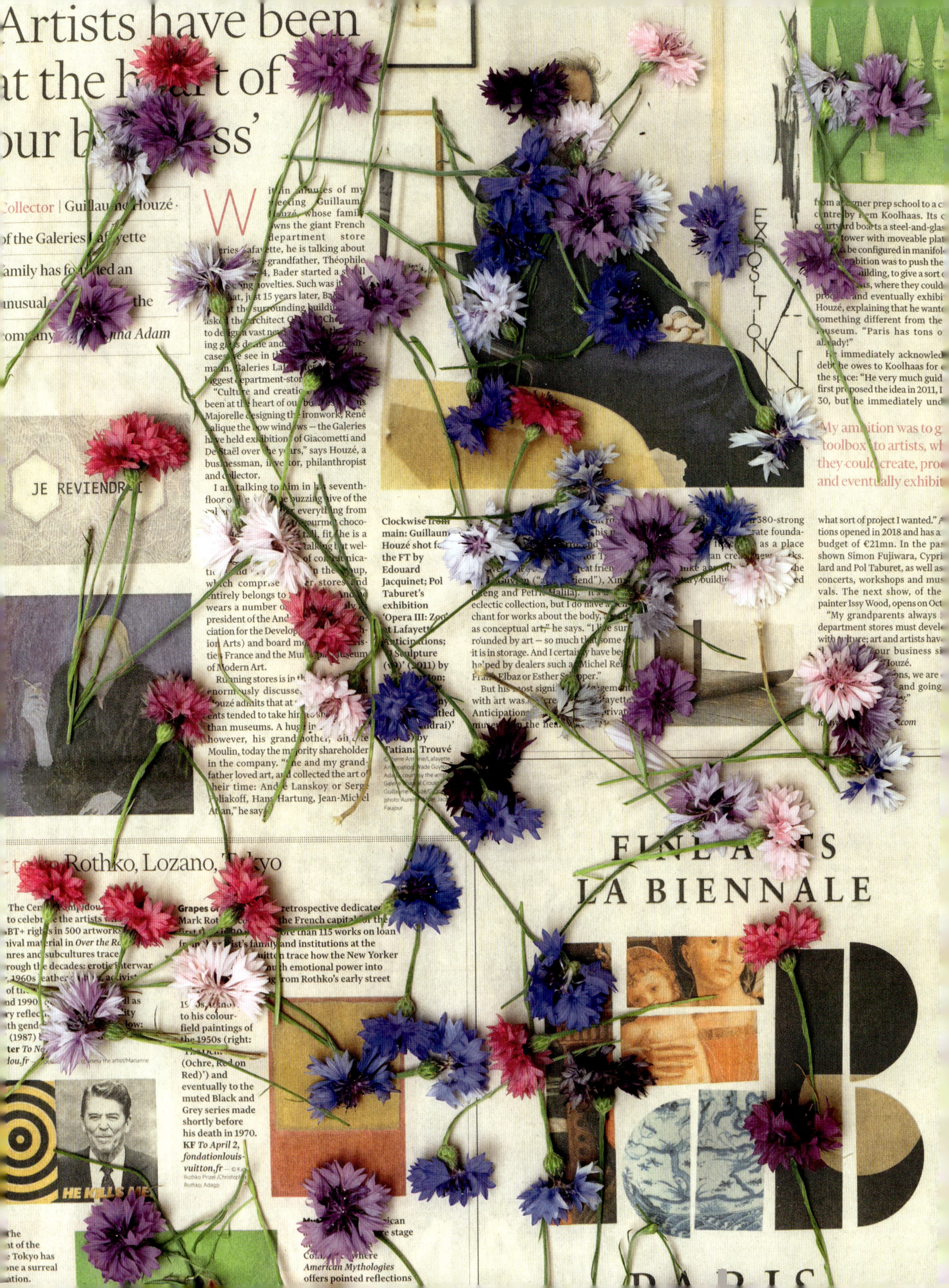
Artists have been
LA BIENNALE
Rothko, Lozano,

Storing

Once your materials are dried, you will need to store them carefully to keep them safe and protected until you are ready to work with them. Here are some tips on how to store your materials.

- Never seal them away in a container until they are completely dry.
- Store them out of natural light.
- I opt to separate my materials and not mix them up in case one particular plant shows signs of mould.
- Sealed containers that keep moisture out such as glass jam jars work well for storing your materials. Slowly gather these over the autumn and winter months. Look in charity shops for larger storage containers.
- Cardboard boxes such as shoe boxes also work well as storage containers.
- Label and date your materials with the year they were harvested and when you stored them.
- Check them every few weeks to catch any signs of mould.

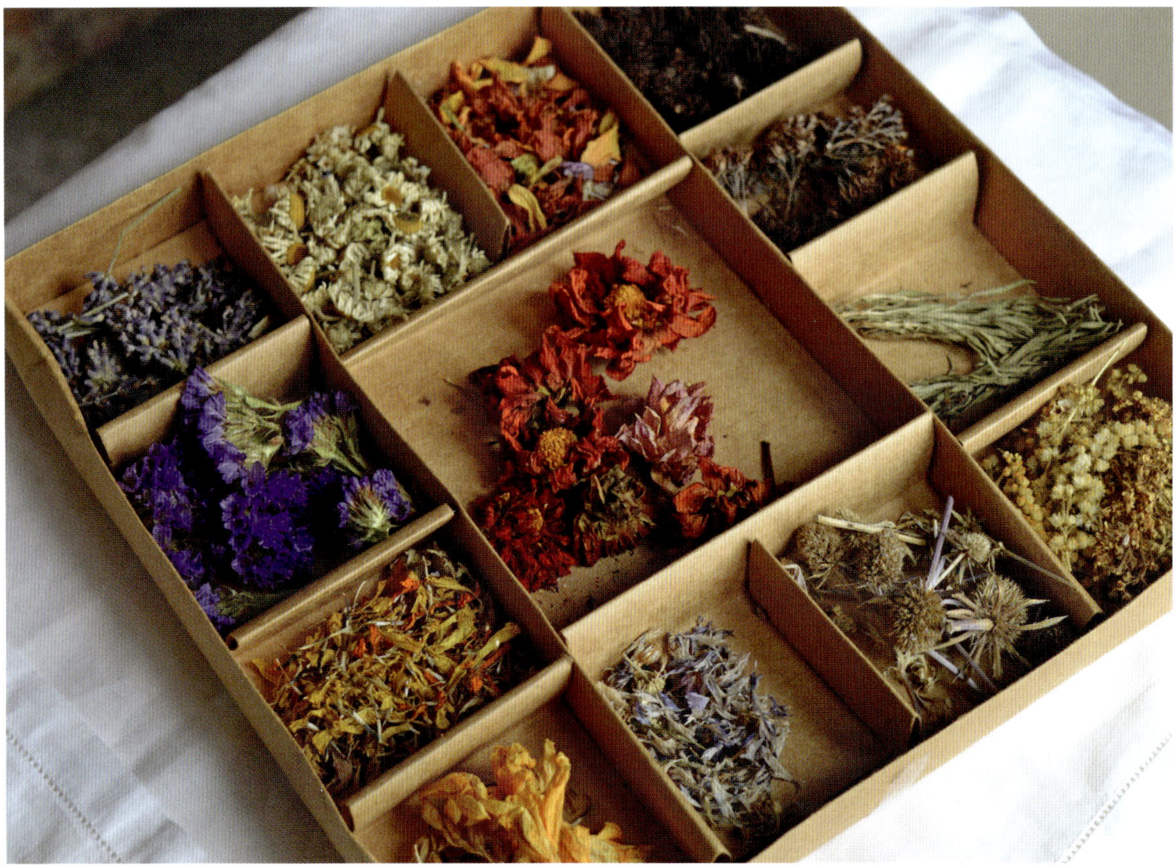

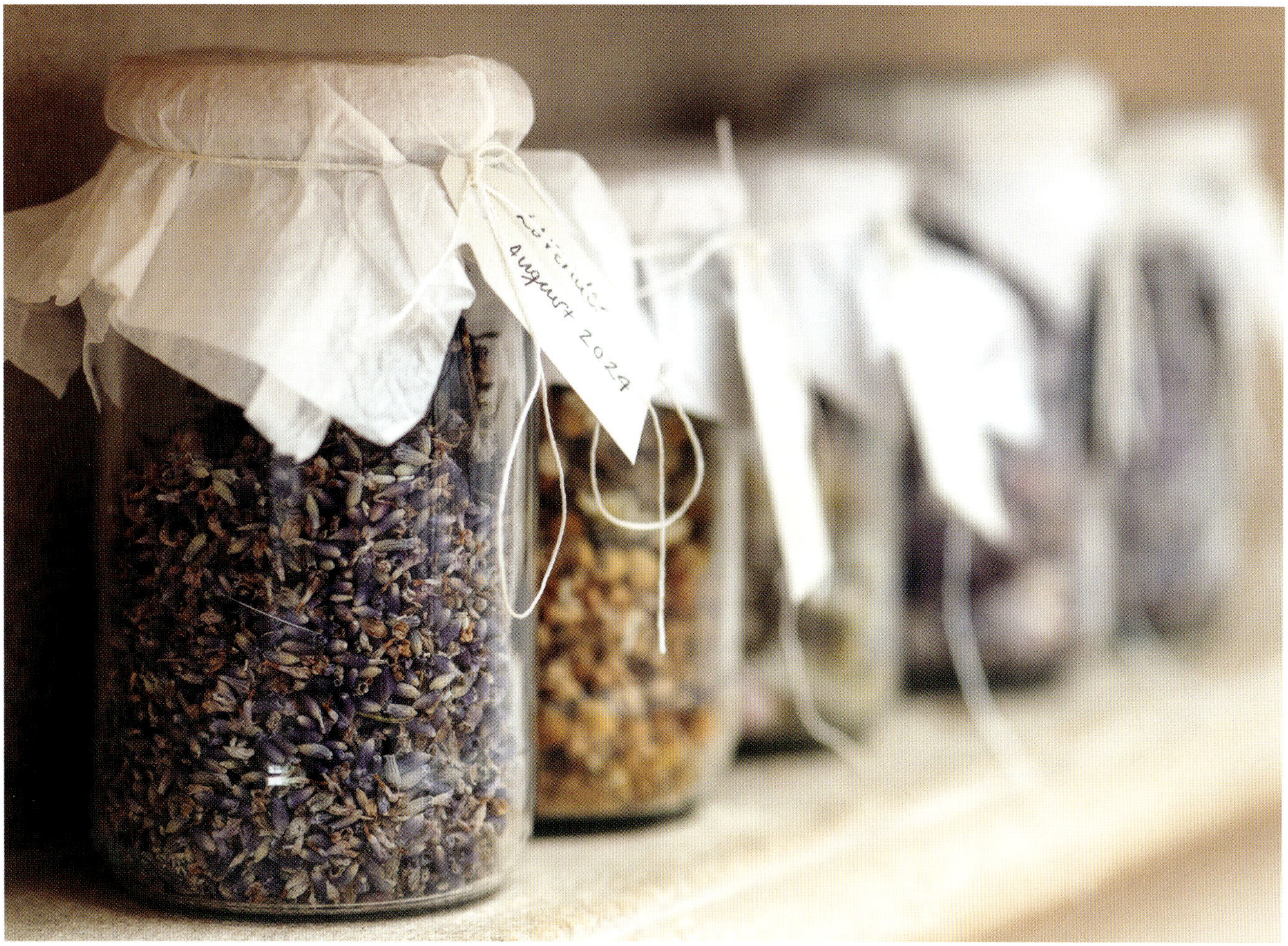

OPPOSITE Box of dried floral materials prepared for a *Stitching with Nature* workshop.

ABOVE Dried floral materials stored in glass jars.

SAVING SEED

Although annuals only flower for one growing year, once you have purchased a single packet of seeds and completed one growing cycle you will be able to collect and save seeds for next year.

Like humans, plants learn to adapt to their environment. By saving and resowing your own seeds year after year, you encourage bioregional adaptation. Over time, your plants become better suited to the specific conditions of your garden, resulting in stronger, more resilient plants.

September is the best month for collecting seeds. This task should be done on a dry day, when seedheads aren't moist. Select the healthiest plants to save seed from. You should collect seeds once the flower has fully matured, but before it begins to rot. Make sure seeds are thoroughly dry before storing, and keep them in brown envelopes. Check your seeds regularly to aid ventilation and catch any signs of mould.

Once you've embraced the rhythm of seed saving, consider connecting with your local seed swap. It's a wonderful way to exchange seeds, share knowledge and build relationships with other growers.

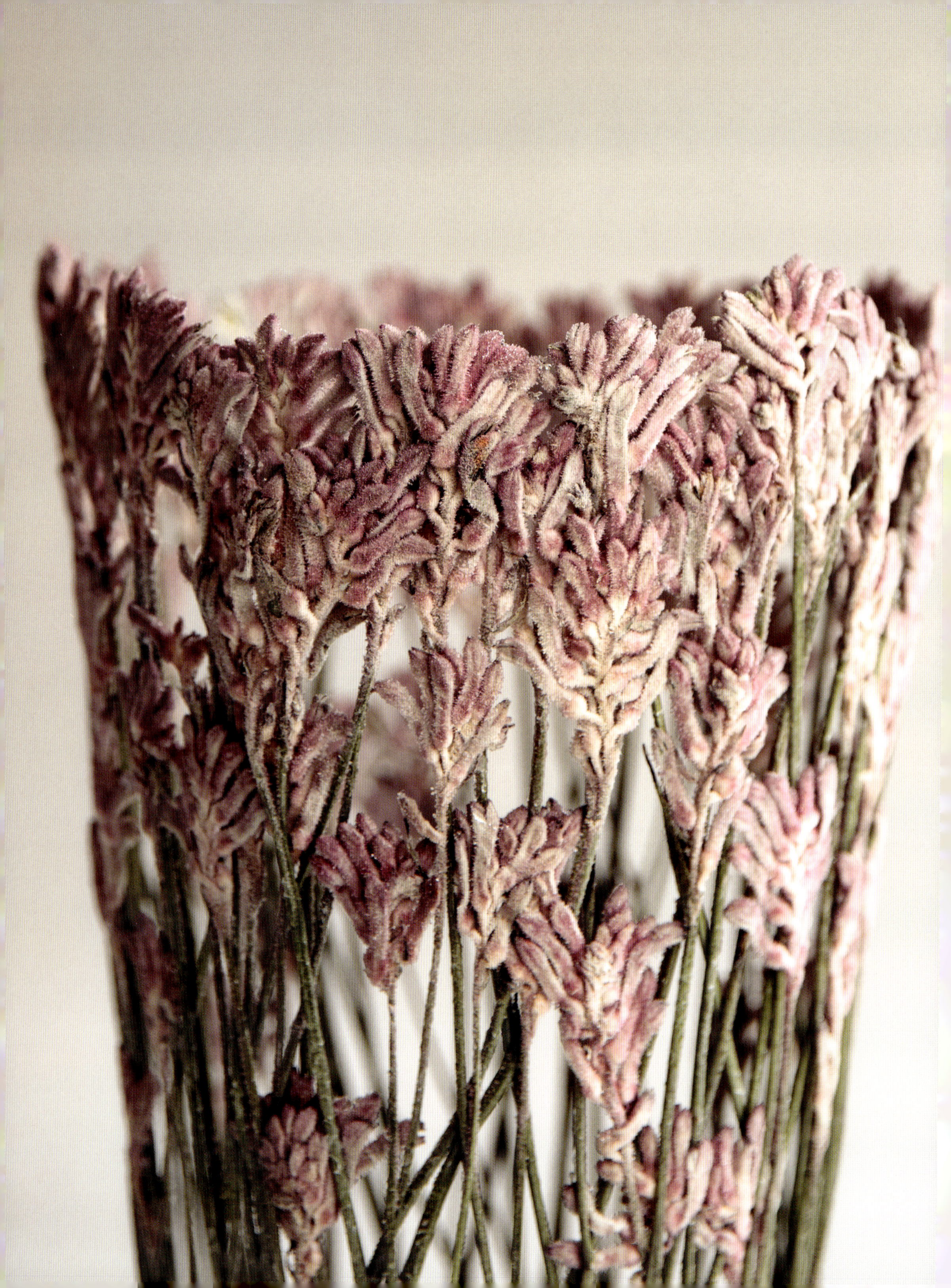

FEATURED ARTIST

Shannon Clegg

Tucked away in a studio in East London, Shannon Clegg works with flowers in a way that challenges traditional preservation. Through an imaginative technique, Shannon sculpts dried flowers into vertical structures that appear not just preserved, but alive – as if they are still in bloom and rooted in the earth. The flowers seem frozen in time, yet full of life.

OPPOSITE Detail of pink kangaroo paw sculpture.

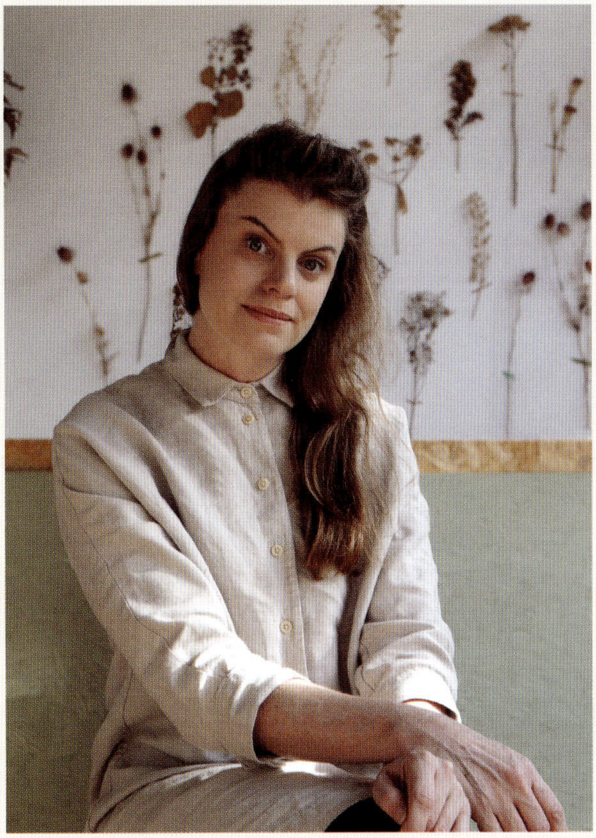

Blending botany with design, Shannon's method is meticulous. It is a process she began to develop organically using her knowledge and understanding of mould-making in ceramics as the groundwork. She spent the first six months experimenting with how to shape and retain real plant materials. The result is a rigorous process that involves creating custom moulds and pressing flowers over several weeks, preserving both their form and their colour.

Shannon's relationship with craft began early. 'Ever since I was about 12, I would find a way to make in my free time,' she recalls. Growing up in Cape Town, South Africa, her exposure to craft education was limited, with her school's focus exclusively on fine art – painting and sculpture. But at home she discovered sewing, developing skills to draft patterns and make clothing, which led to her training to pursue a career as a tailor.

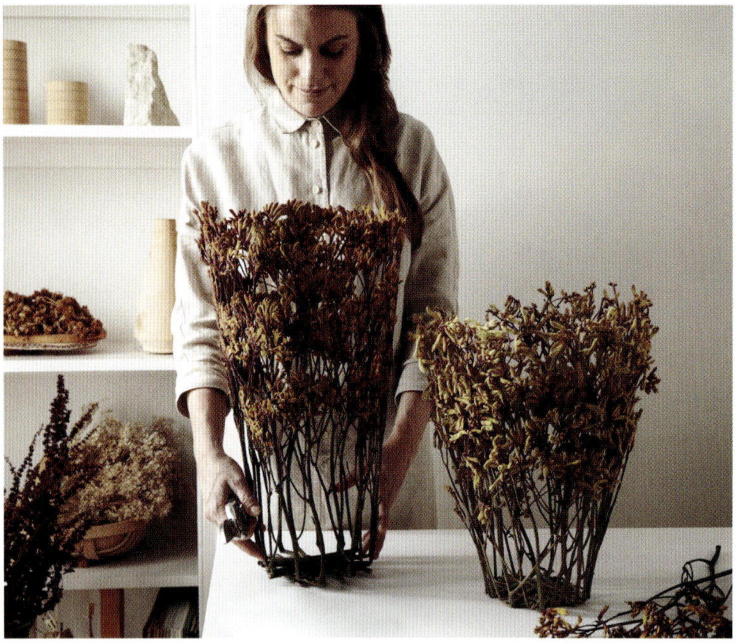

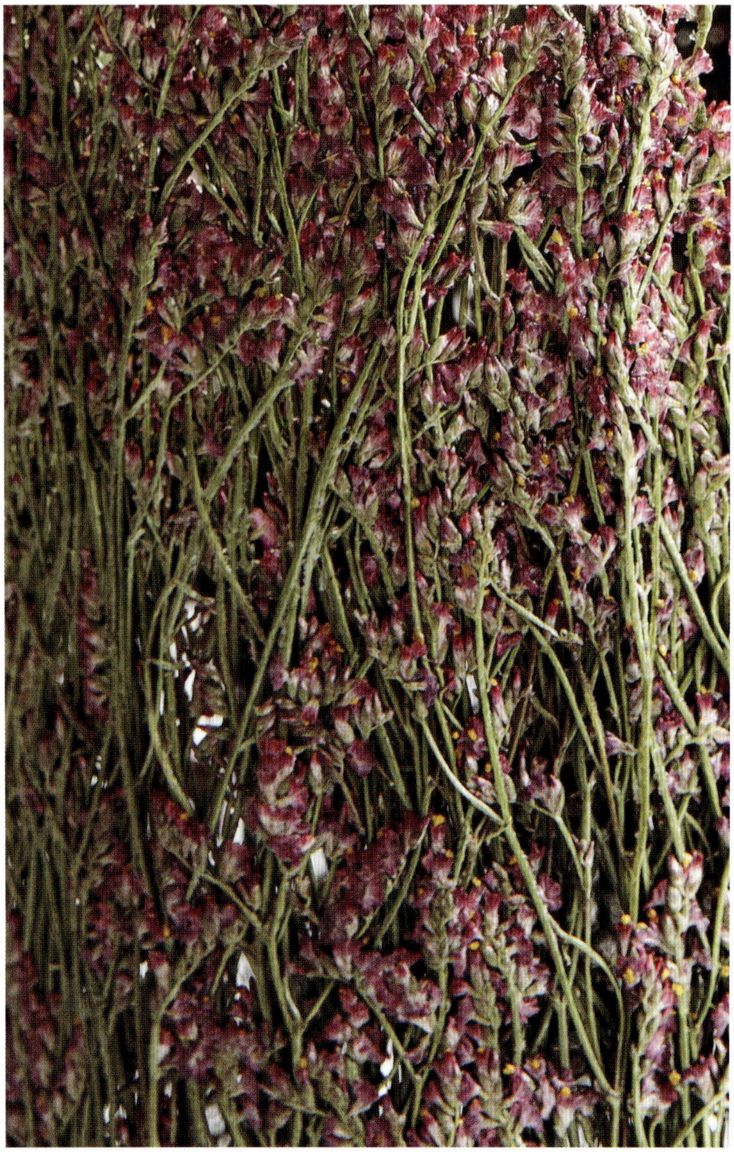

A short stint in the fashion industry in the late 1990s left her disillusioned, though it never dampened her instinct to make. At the time, there was little conversation around ethics or sustainability, and it wasn't a system she felt aligned with, nor one in which she could see a future. She packed her bags and moved to London in 2002, where an evening course in glass and ceramic casting opened up a new world of making, which felt more meaningful and better reflected her true values.

Shannon studied a BA in Contemporary Crafts at Falmouth University in Cornwall, followed by an MA in Product and Furniture Design at Kingston University in London, where she continued to hone her process.

Along the way, from the mountains of Cape Town, to the sea of Falmouth and the streets of the City of London, nature has remained a constant anchor in her practice. Reflecting on growing up in Cape Town, Clegg notes the region's extraordinary biodiversity. 'As a child, I think I took it for granted – it was all I knew. Behind our houses were expansive fields. After school, we'd just run through them until we had to be home by six. It felt limitless.'

Living in London made her appreciate that wildness more deeply. 'Now, I'm acutely aware of how precious those early experiences were,' Shannon says. 'Many children in the city here grow up with much more limited access to natural spaces.'

Her work today is connected to that human–nature relationship. It is also bound up in personal healing. During her brief period working in fashion, Shannon's father passed away. In the wake of that loss, making was more than just a means of creative expression; it became her therapy. 'I found a healing quality in the act of making, and similarly in being in nature. Those are the values I carry into my making practice now,' she says.

In Shannon's practice today she creates one-of-a-kind botanical sculptures that take the form of a vessel, and are a nod to a traditional vase. She works on private commissions and gallery pieces, and her sculptures have been exhibited and appreciated internationally from London, to Venice, to China.

But developing her flower preservation technique was far from easy. 'For the first six months, everything I made was a failure,' she admits. 'Everything was moulding or not holding its shape for long.' After much exploration, Shannon identified the most suitable flowers for the process. She now makes her pieces with strong, vibrant blooms such as statice (*Limonium sinuatum*) and kangaroo paw (*Anigozanthos* spp.). Her persistence paid off. Shannon spent hours researching in the Herbarium at the Royal Botanic Gardens, Kew, in London, learning from botanists and plant collectors how flora is documented and preserved across the globe. Today, she sources her blooms from New Covent Garden Market, often building close relationships with growers and sellers along the way.

Nature, she has found, is a powerful connector. She has experienced it in quiet moments with scientists in the archives – sharing stories of plants over cups of tea – and in the lively bustle of the flower market, where sellers joke and exchange news between stalls. Nature is something that we can all find a way of connecting with, both independently, and as a community.

As Shannon's connection to her materials deepens, so too does her longing to return to a place that is immersed in the natural world.

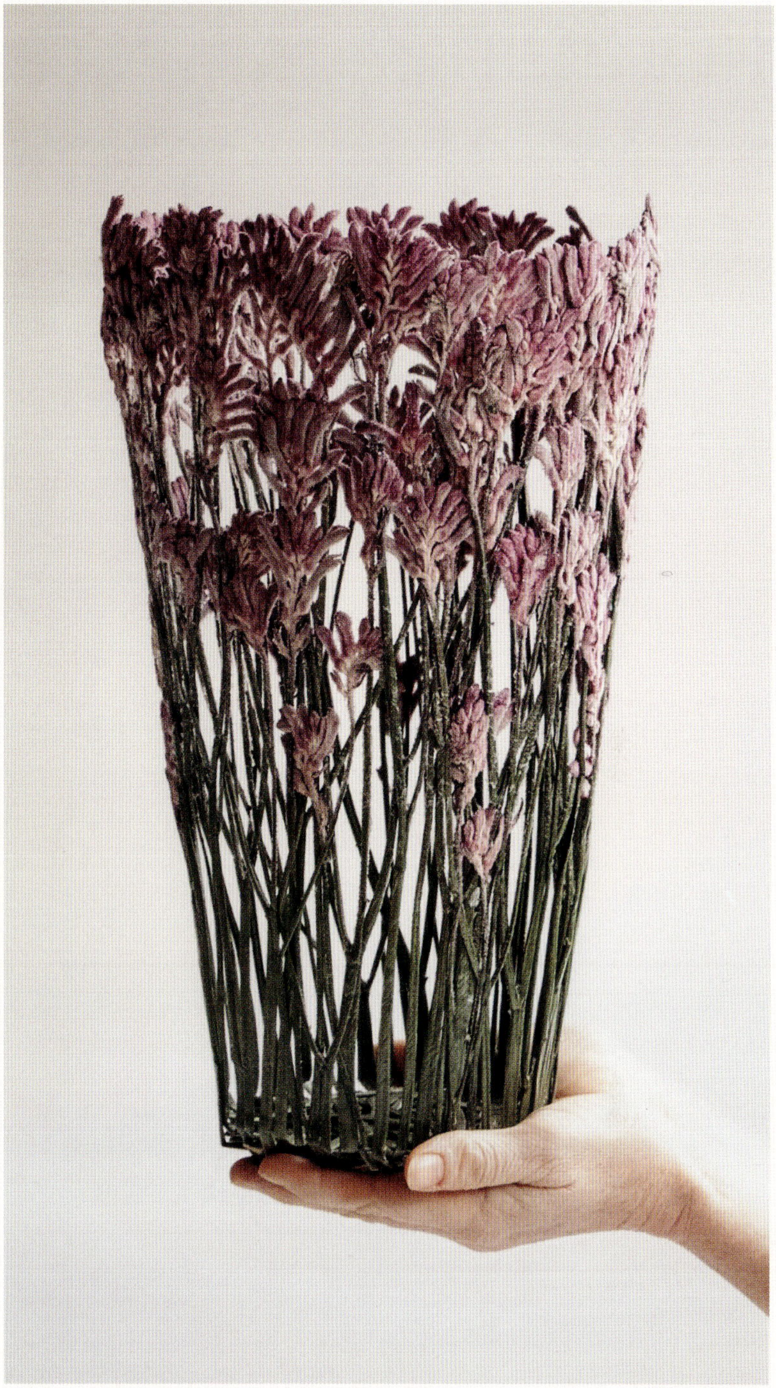

OPPOSITE ABOVE Shannon Clegg in her studio in East London.

OPPOSITE BELOW Detail of sea lavender sculpture.

ABOVE Pink kangaroo paw sculpture.

'I've reached a point where I need to move out of London ... I want to be surrounded by the wild again; to feel the changing seasons, the weather, the elements.'

Foraging

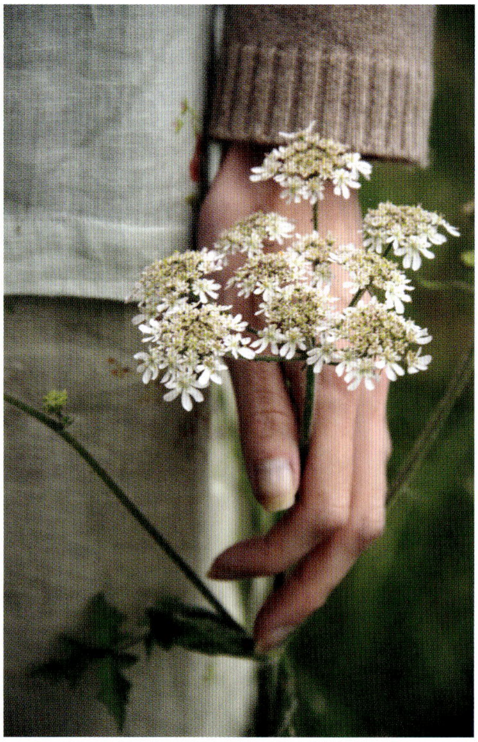

Don't be discouraged if you don't have a garden or space to grow. There are plenty of materials that you can find if you take a walk in a wild place in your local area. A place might be so familiar to you that you haven't taken the time to observe the plant life right in front of you. On our commutes we are often running to catch a train, responding to messages on the move, or finding the perfect playlist to soundtrack our walk, but if we are doing this we are distracting ourselves from noticing and being present with the landscape around us. Foraging is an invitation to stop and notice.

Taking a walk to forage or find new inspiration is my daily ritual. My most creative thoughts arise on foot; my deepest reflections, too. But more than anything, I feel most connected to the land when I walk *with* it, not just across it. To walk the same path day after day, season after season, is a sacred act. You begin to notice every small change: a bud here, a bloom there.

Even if the walk is not wild, just down your street, nature is always there if you look for it: wild flowers emerging through the pavement cracks, your neighbour's front garden, fallen leaves.

Even when living in a city like London I found great places to forage for wild flowers. While living in East London, for example, I would cycle along the canal in Hackney and go to Walthamstow Marshes in search of flowers.

Since moving to Malvern, foraging has become an increasingly important ritual for me. It is a process that has allowed me to feel grounded and to establish a sense of home in this new place to which I relocated alone. When you find yourself in a place where everything is new, you yearn for connection. It can take time to foster meaningful connections with new people, but forging a connection to nature can be almost immediate. I have moved between several different environments over the last few years, but knowing that I can always find connection with nature, wherever I end up, has been incredibly comforting.

Before you begin foraging, it is important to know what you are doing. You should enjoy the freedom foraging brings but you should not just pick aimlessly and disturb the landscape inconsiderately.

'Sometimes when you wander through the forest with an open heart in search of enchantment you find it.'

SHARON BLACKIE

OPPOSITE Foraging for pineappleweed (wild chamomile) in Malvern.

FORAGING SUSTAINABLY

- **Minimize your damage** – Ensure you don't disturb plants by trampling over them. Tread carefully, stick to paths where possible, or plan your route to the plant with minimal impact.

- **Forage sparingly** – Do not take all the plants and flowers from one place; pick little and from varied areas.

- **Forage mindfully** – In the first instance, I would pick only one stem or flowerhead, take this back to my studio, dry it and carefully observe it to see how the material dries, and make a small stitch sample with it. This way I can determine whether it is a material I can work with. This process avoids collecting wastefully.

- **Know your plant** – I would recommend using a plant identification app or referring to a local wild plant guidebook to ensure you know exactly what you are picking.

- **Know where you are** – Do not forage from sites of specific interest, conservation areas, private property, public gardens or parks. Ensure you stick to wild woodland areas, or pick plants that have grown wild in a hedgerow, along a path or an overgrown lane.

- **Be law-abiding** – There are specific wild plants that are illegal to forage. For example, the vivid violet of bluebells in April and May may look inviting, but the native British bluebell is a protected species and picking it could land you with a fine.

For further advice, The Woodland Trust have published an excellent Responsible Foraging Guidelines document. Visit **www.woodlandtrust.org.uk**

WHAT TO TAKE FORAGING . . .

- **Secateurs or small pair of scissors** – To cut your flowers.

- **Gardening gloves** – Ensure you wear gloves to protect your hands from delving into wild plants.

- **A small basket or bag** – To transport your foraged materials home.

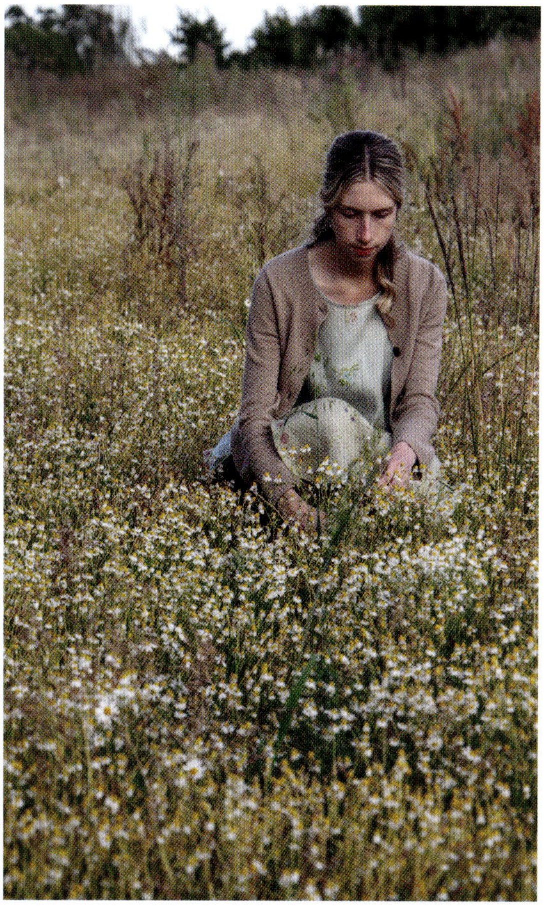

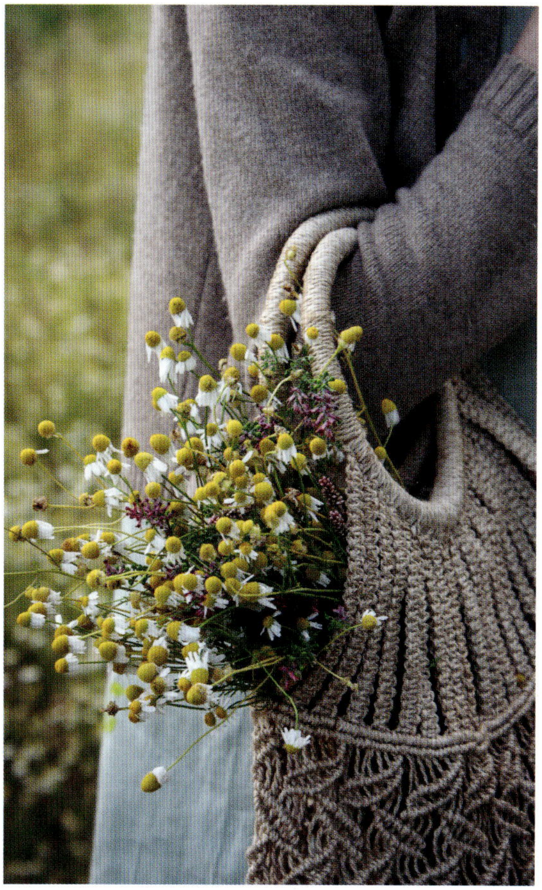

FORAGING THROUGH THE SEASONS IN THE UK

There are many plant materials you will be able to source on your wild walks, at all times of the year, which you could pick and use with these processes. While I forage far less in winter, nature still presents me with the occasional magical material – and its rarity makes it that much more precious.

Here are some ideas for flowers to gather which you could dry out and explore using their petals or seed heads as plant embellishments:

- **Spring:** Mallow, primrose and cow parsley.
- **Summer:** Red campions, common daisy, pineappleweed (wild chamomile), cornflowers, fallen rose petals, common knapweed, wild carrot, field scabious and corn marigold.
- **Autumn:** Golden rod, hawthorn, tansy, heather and yarrow.
- **Winter:** Old man's beard (*Clematis vitalba*), gorse and pine needles.

FORAGING FOR GRASSES

Grasses might be one of the most underrated plants. They grow together in drifts, which from afar can blend harmoniously to create a soft block of greeny-yellow hues. However, grasses, like all plants, have their own individuality and are rich with detail.

Lay with Me in the Long Grass was a piece I created during the spring of 2025. Each morning during the month of April, I would take my morning walk across the Link Common, walking through the long grass that skimmed my waistline. I set myself the task of selecting ten stems that caught my eye. Returning to my studio later that day after hours of writing, my evening ritual became stitching those ten strands of grass to a thin length of cotton organdie cloth. This piece began to take shape slowly over the month. As it evolved, I noticed that each strand of grass presented very different textural and tonal qualities. I laid each strand of grass delicately on the cloth, and used the couching technique (see page 82) to secure the grass embellishments.

So, when spring comes, take an early walk: enjoy the soothing rustle of grass against your body as you walk softly through it, pick a few stems and be inspired by their unique character.

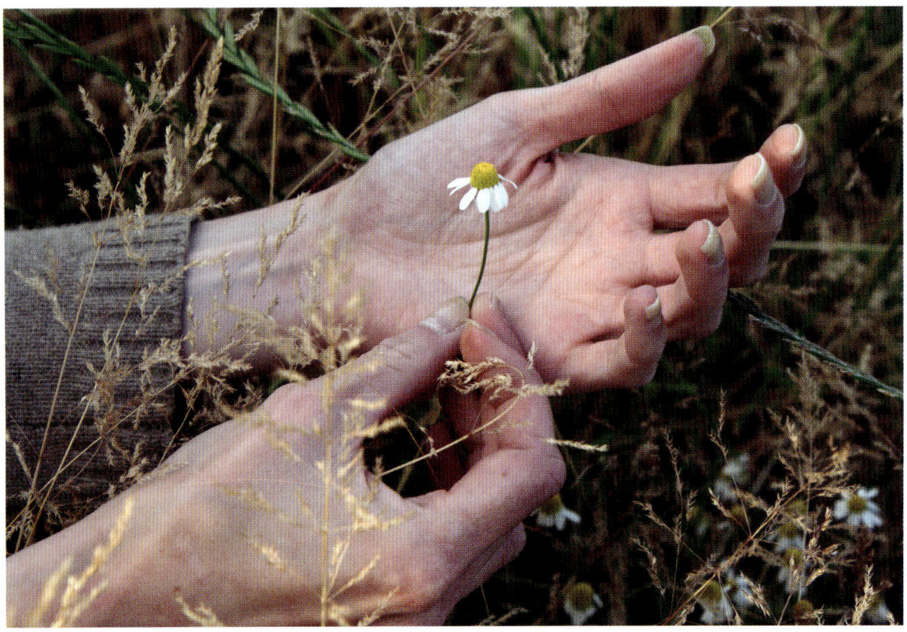

OPPOSITE *Lay with Me in the Long Grass* (2025). Cotton organdie, foraged grasses and silk thread, 56 x 200cm (22 x 79in).

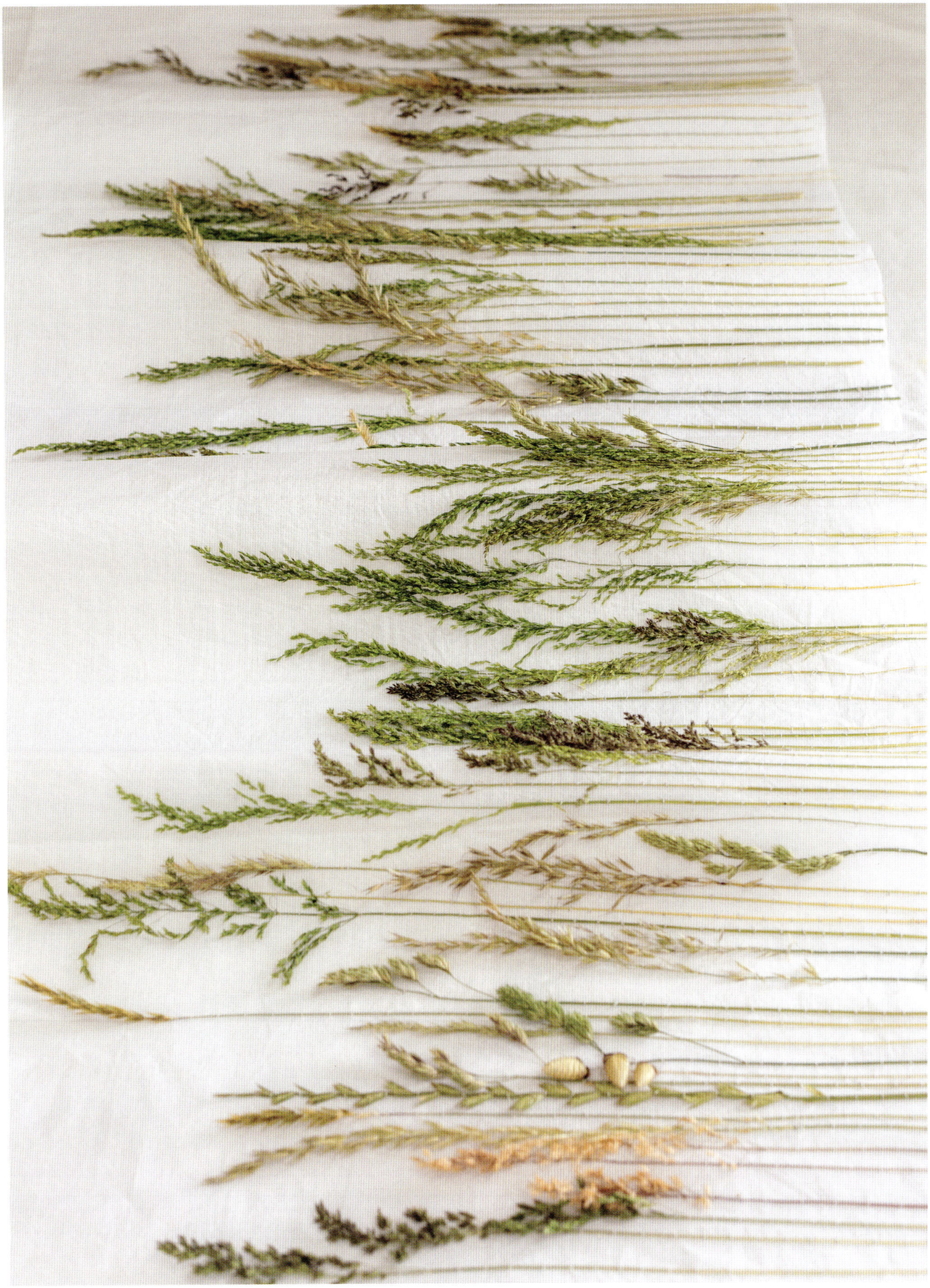

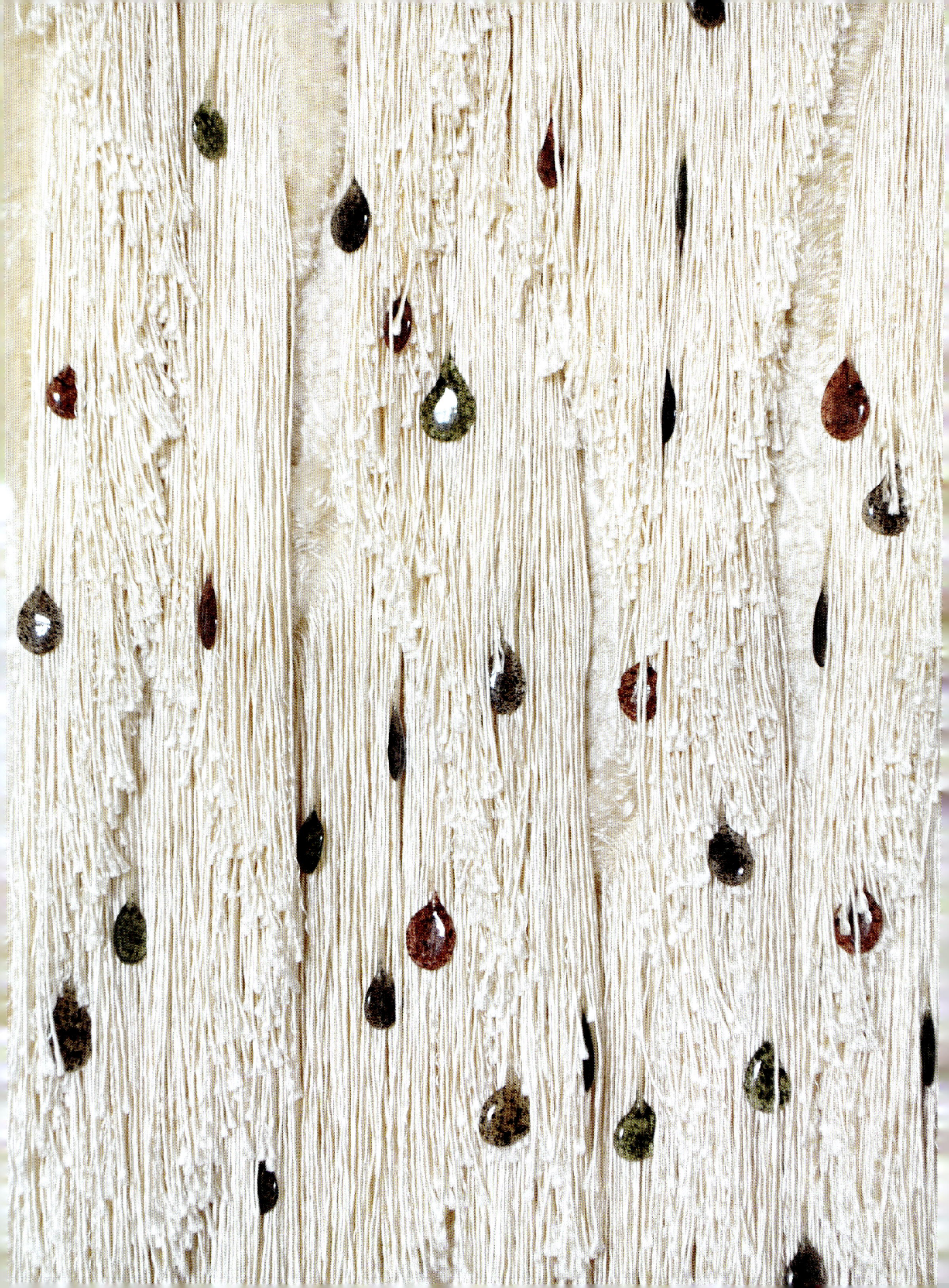

FEATURED ARTIST

Jasmine Linington

When I discovered Jasmine Linington's work some years ago, one thing stood out above all else: Jasmine has defined her practice to one material, by celebrating seaweed. Her commitment to uncovering the wonders of this singular element, through observing, listening and learning every aspect of this ocean treasure, is admirable.

OPPOSITE *Ripple Seaweed Bead Tassels.* Seaweed yarn, SeaCell fibre, seaweed coloured beads.

BELOW Jasmine with *Seaweed Ripple, No. 1* (2020). Kelp sequins, naturally dyed SeaCell fibre, 80.5 x 45.5 x 6cm (32 x 18 x 2½in).

A graduate of the Master of Fine Arts in Textiles programme at Edinburgh College of Art in 2019, Jasmine has remained rooted in the south-east coast of Scotland, where she has since established her studio.

After obtaining a specialist foraging license, Jasmine now harvests seaweed from her local beach. Alongside SeaCell fibre, she uses this material to explore a range of crafted techniques for reimagining seaweed in textiles, from natural dyes to intricate embellishments such as tassels and sequins made entirely from seaweed. The possibilities Jasmine presents for what we expect to find washed up on the shore, not in the cloth that adorns our bodies, is inspired.

Initially, Jasmine focused on the potential of seaweed in fashion, offering a natural alternative to the largely synthetic world of couture embellishments. Today, her practice has evolved beyond fashion, extending into bespoke commissions that are, undeniably, works of art.

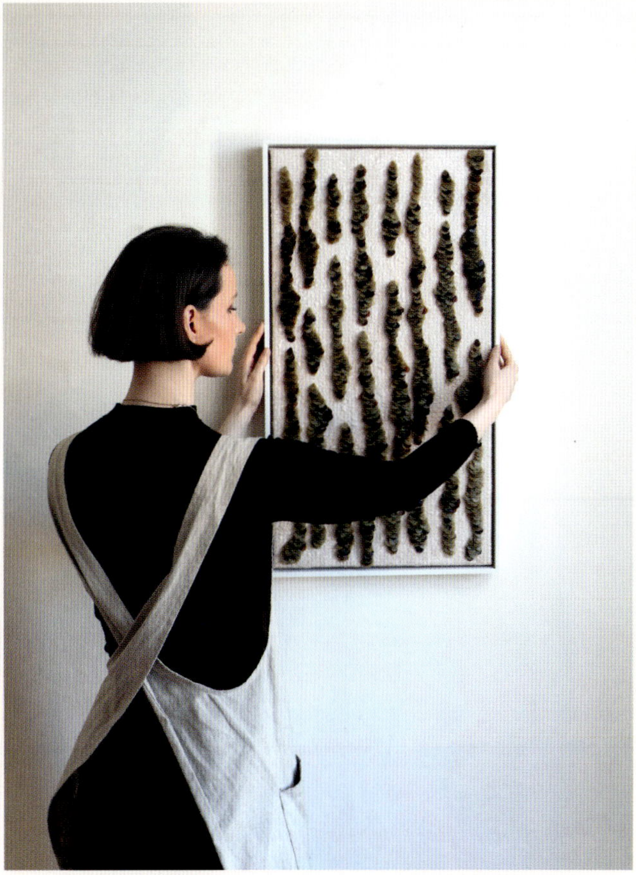

IN CONVERSATION WITH JASMINE LININGTON

KK: *The connection we have with nature as adults can often be traced back and informed by our experiences in childhood. Do you have any early memories of nature that are poignant to you?*

JL: Some of my happiest memories are of holidays on the beach in North Cornwall with my family. Running barefoot along the sand and wading through calm or choppy waves made me feel completely free. I was mesmerized by the changing patterns where water met sand. The beach was a sanctuary away from homework and routine, and those early experiences with nature filled me with calm and sparked my love of the natural world.

KK: *What role does nature play within your work today?*

JL: The beach serves as my muse. Seaweed's textures, shapes and wide palette of colours captivate me; I vividly recall realizing how varied and bright its hues can be. Over the years, I've explored its versatility by transforming kelp into sequins, crafting beads from its colours and extracting pigments for subtle natural dyes. The ever-changing ripples in the sand also inform my work – their fluid patterns inspire motifs in my textile pieces. Seaweed and microalgae grow rapidly, making them sustainable materials, and working with them allows nature to shape both the aesthetics and ethics of my practice.

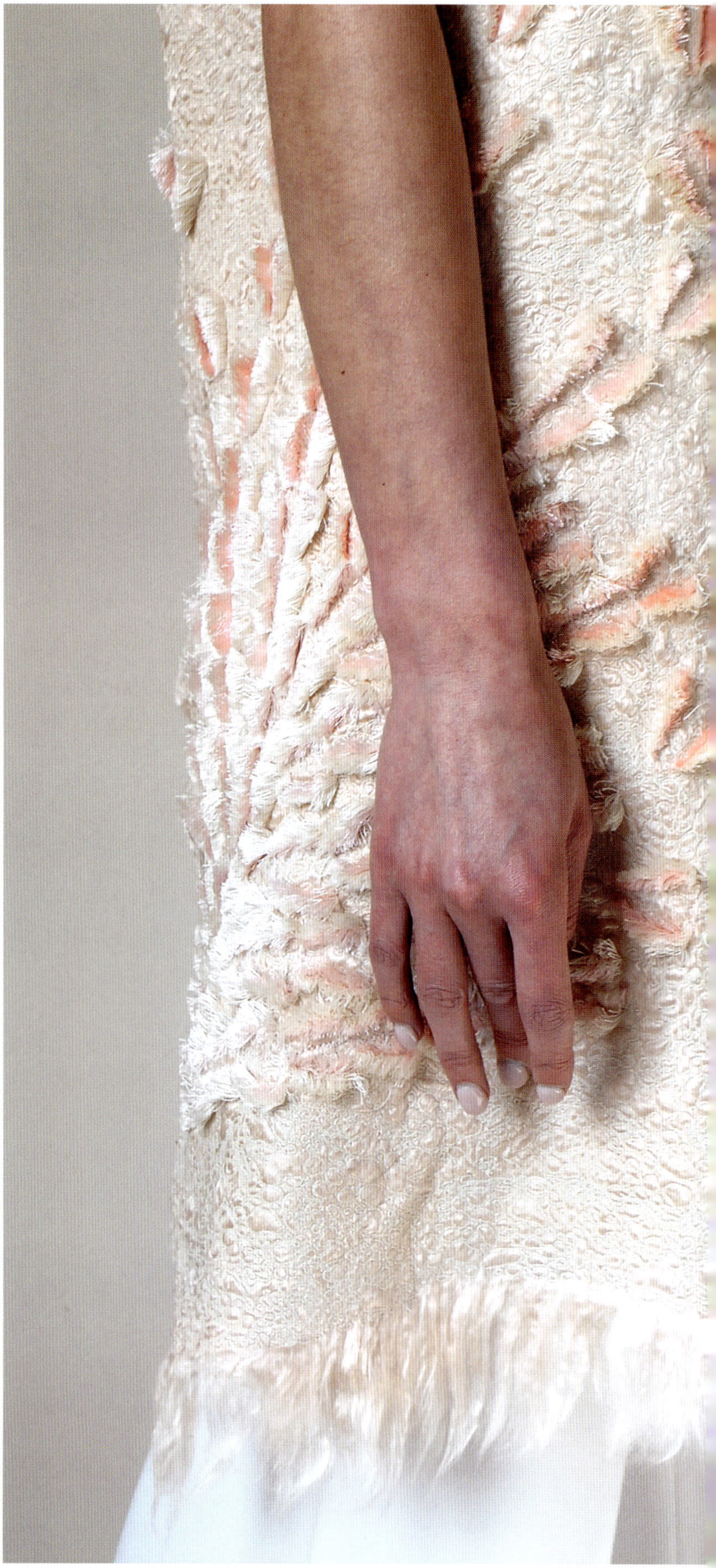

RIGHT *North Berwick Lido*. Naturally dyed SeaCell fibre.

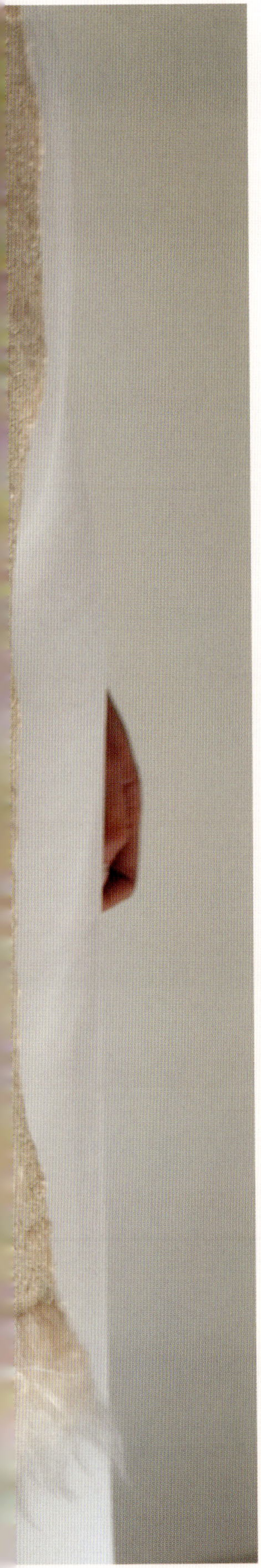

KK: *In my experience, the materials I work with have become teachers in their own right. Through them, I've unearthed a deep source of plant knowledge. These materials hold a kind of philosophical weight that is incredibly powerful, I believe. I wonder: what has seaweed taught you?*

JL: Working with seaweed has taught me patience and adaptability. At the start of my journey, I knew very little about handling seaweed, so I approached it with curiosity and an open mind. Through trial and error, I discovered that each species has its own purpose; these lessons have shaped my practice and guided how I work with the material. I had no idea where this journey would take me, and that uncertainty has been a lovely part of the experience. I love that seaweed has taught me to respect the material – to collaborate with it rather than force it. Finding ways to use it effectively and durably, giving it longevity, is central to my work. On a personal level, gathering, preserving and transforming seaweed has taught me to slow down and appreciate the subtle beauty in materials we often overlook.

KK: *Focusing your practice on one plant material shows impressive dedication. What is it about seaweed that makes this an interesting material for you to keep working with?*

JL: I keep coming back to seaweed because its diversity feels endless. Some species have delicate, lace-like fronds; others grow into thick, leathery ribbons; some are dotted with bubbles, and each has its own texture and colour palette. I'm mesmerized by how its look shifts when it's wet, dry or preserved, and how it plays with light. Beyond its aesthetic qualities, I'm drawn to seaweed's ecological significance – it's a keystone species in coastal environments, providing food, shelter and oxygen, as well as absorbing carbon. Using seaweed allows me to explore themes of sustainability, regeneration and the intersection between human and non-human worlds in a tangible way.

KK: *You gather your seaweed along the Edinburgh coastline. What does foraging as a process mean to you?*

JL: Foraging has become both a ritual and a form of mindfulness for me. It requires careful observation of tides, weather and seasons. It fosters a deep sense of attunement with my environment. When I gather seaweed, I follow sustainable practices – taking only what's abundant and leaving enough to regenerate. This ritualistic approach makes the act of foraging meditative; it's a time to slow down, listen and connect with the landscape. It also deepens my understanding of place: knowing where certain species grow and how they change over time creates a relationship with the shoreline that influences my art and my sense of belonging.

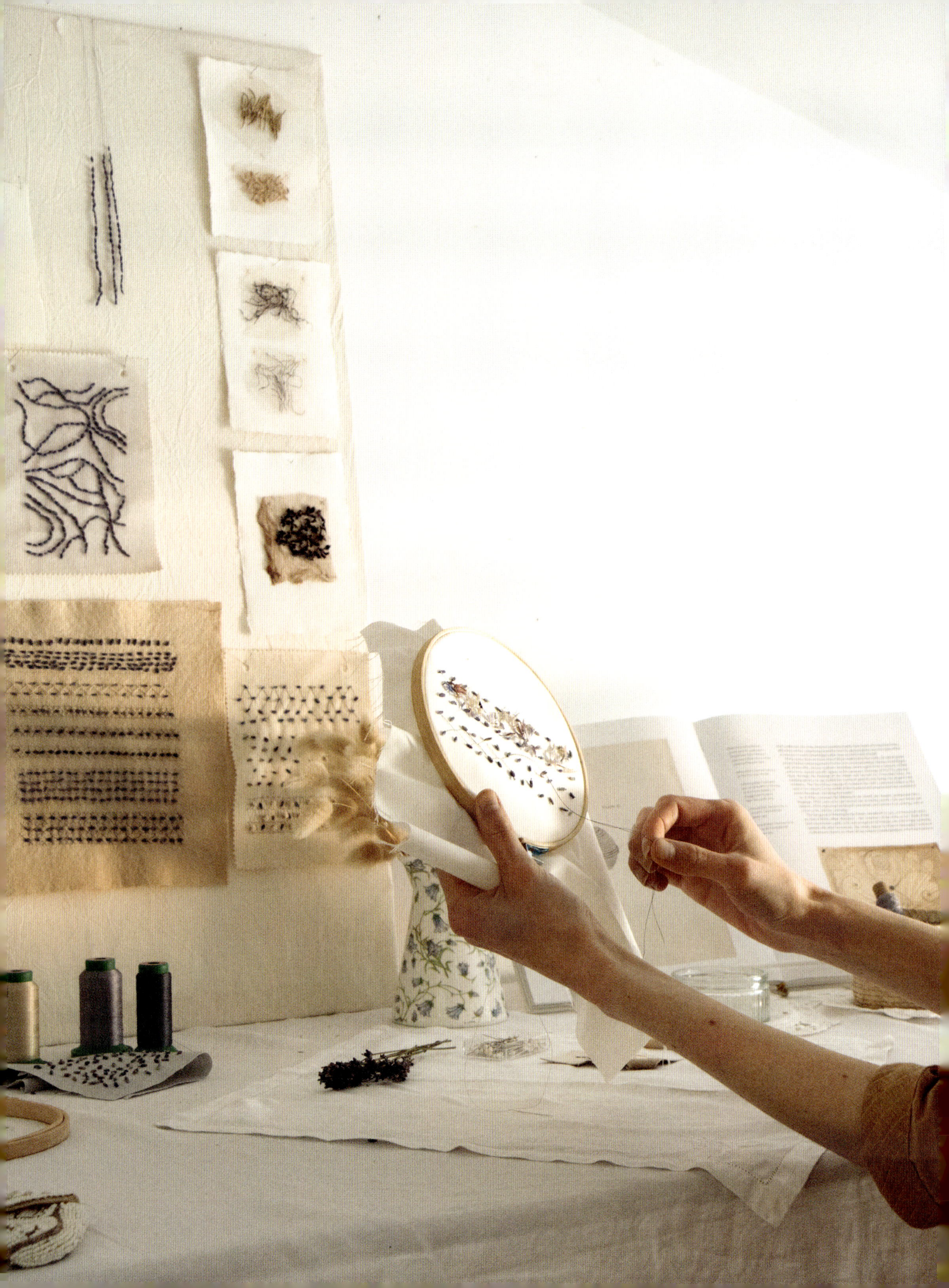

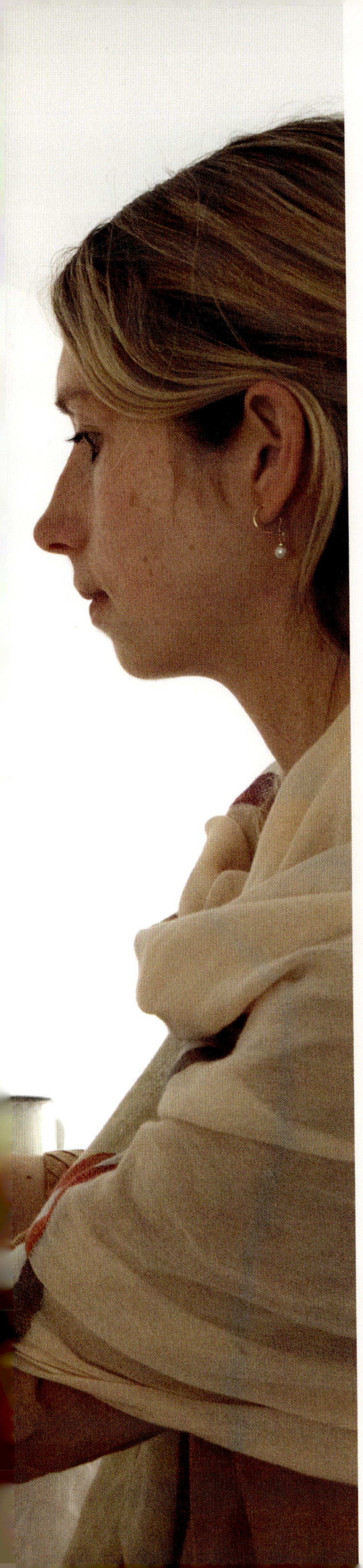

STITCHING WITH PLANT MATERIALS

'I always had the fear of being separated and abandoned. The sewing is my attempt to keep things together and make things whole.'

LOUISE BOURGEOIS

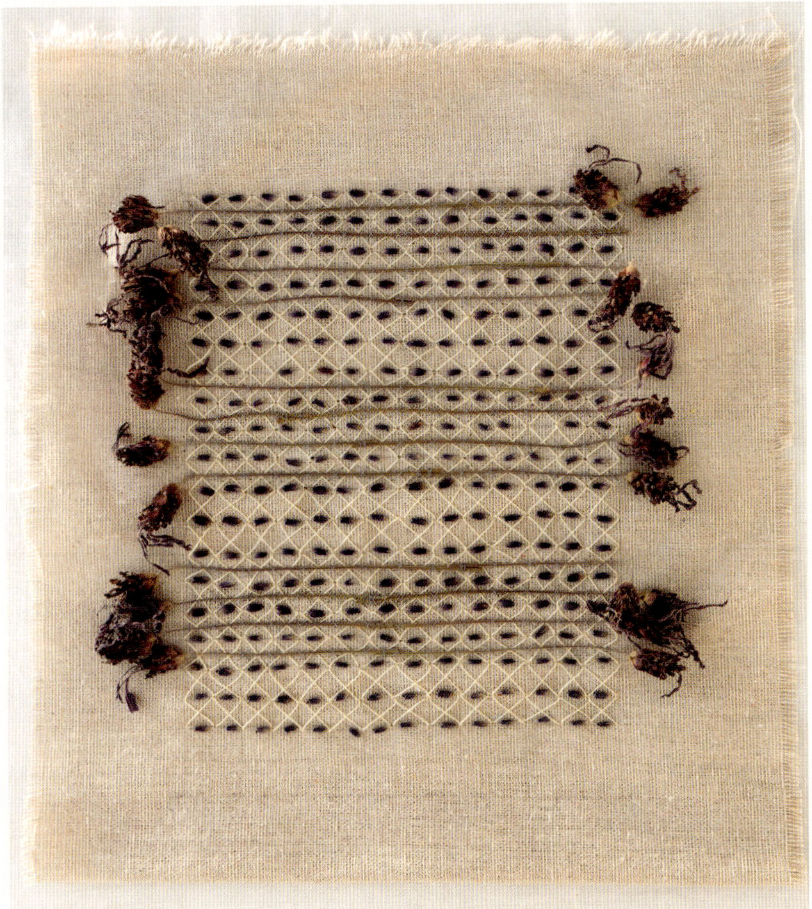

Wherever I go, my embroidery toolkit comes with me. On a long bus journey, a train ride, a holiday, I know that I will find time to stitch. For a hand-embroiderer, a good set of sewing tools is essential. In time you will find the perfect size of needle, your favoured set of snips, and your preferred hoop to work with.

Learning to stitch with plants can be delicate work; you must have a gentle hand, as the materials you are stitching with are often fragile, even once dried. This is why it is slow work: you must not rush the process, instead taking your time so that your materials do not break. With practice, you will find a slow yet rhythmic flow between your stitching hand and nature.

In terms of fabric, I would recommend working with a linen or cotton fabric that is not sheer. This means that you can focus on what you are doing on the right side of the cloth instead of simultaneously having to consider the design that shows on the back. Once you are confident with the techniques and move onto the creative exploration section, you can begin to explore more sheer, slippery fabrics if you wish.

Depending on the fibre, the thread you use can vary in thicknesses but also in texture. This is important to note as the plant materials are delicate and when stitching you want your needle and thread to slip through the petal seamlessly. This is where using textural thread or yarn can be difficult. My preferred thread is silk, as it has a fine and even quality. I love linen, but linen thread is not as fine and has a textural quality, so is not always appropriate for use with delicate plant materials.

BELOW Dried flora embroidery sampler, exploring various hand stitches using statice, rosemary and California sea lavender (*Limonium californicum*).

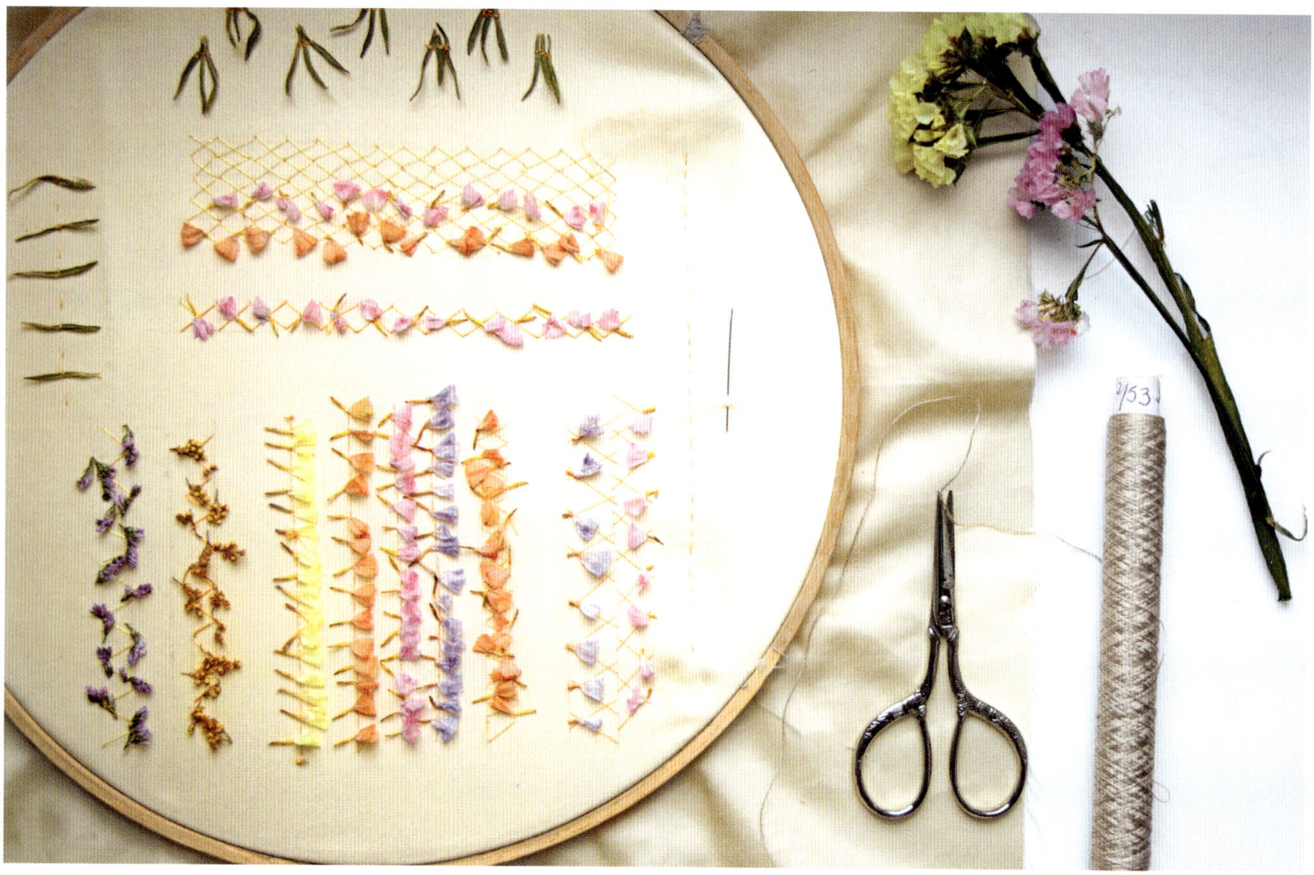

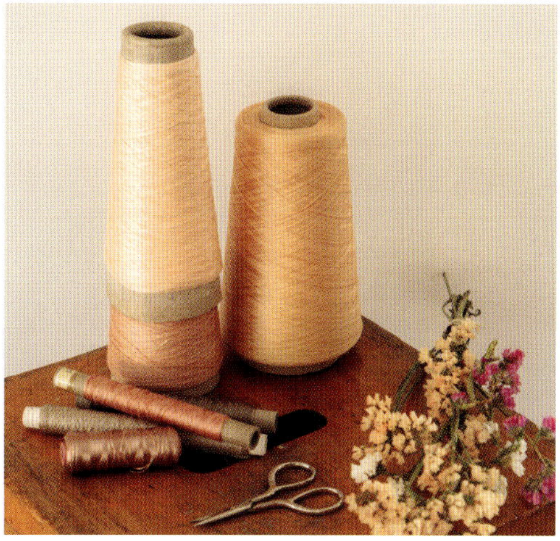

Embroidery Tips and Things to Consider

- **Selecting your needle** – There are many different needles available, each one more suitable for different styles of embroidery. I work with a size 10 bead embroidery needle. For this embroidery style you want to pick a sharp tip. As I recommend using a fine thread such as silk, you will need only a small eye. I find selecting a beading needle of a shorter length works best.

- **Length of your thread** – You might think that cutting a long length of thread will save you time, but with an intricate process, a long length of thread can often make things more difficult. You also risk catching your length of thread on the plant materials you have already stitched down, which could ruin your design or involve going back to fix things. A useful guideline is that if your thread is longer than the length of your arm it is too long.

- **How to make a knot** – Do not worry about your knots being visible on the back of the cloth: if you are also working with a fine beading needle and fine thread as advised, your knot will only need to be very small and will not be visible. I simply tie two knots, one on top of the other, at the end of my length of thread, cut off the excess and then thread my needle.

- **How to thread your needle** – First cut your thread at an angle to make it easier to thread. Then hold your needle at eye level with the needle eye facing you. This should allow you to see clearly and get the angle of your thread aligned for threading.

Sewing Tools

These are the sewing tools I find essential for my textile practice.

- **Carry case** – I keep my tools neatly in a handmade French beaded purse that I purchased at a flea market many years ago. With age, it is slowly starting to lose its beads, but I am so connected to it I could not imagine storing my tools in anything else.

- **Embroidery hoops** – I have a range of hoops. My choice of hoop is often determined by the scale of the piece I am working on and where I would like to position myself. When working at my desk, I use a table-clamped wooden hoop, 20cm (8in) wide. While many people prefer a table hoop, I enjoy the simplicity and freedom of a small simple hoop most. I love the ability to pick up my work and take it with me wherever I go. My friend Penelope gifted me a tiny spring metal hoop from a haberdashery in New Zealand. I find this excellent for testing out small samples of new materials or when working with trickier fabrics such as silk, which can be too fine to keep taut when working in a wooden hoop.

- **Fabric marker** – If you want your designs and stitches to be precise and even you can mark your patterns or guidelines directly onto your cloth. I use a fabric pencil for this, which I keep sharp at all times. The marks can be easily erased away.

- **Fabric scissors** – A high-quality pair of fabric scissors is an essential investment. Once you have bought a pair, always keep them under your watchful eye and never use them on paper or non-textile materials. Merchant & Mills supply an excellent range.

- **Needles** – You will need a set of fine needles. They can be tricky to work with, but select the finest that you feel comfortable with. I use beading needles.

- **Seed dish** – I find a small glass ramekin is perfect; it stops the seeds from blowing away and the glass makes them easy to see.

- **Snips** – You will need a sharp set of fine snips. You may need to replace these over time as you will be cutting stems, leaves and so on, which can cause the snips gradually to become blunt.

- **Tweezers** – Tweezers are a handy tool that allow you to pick up and position your dried materials on your cloth.

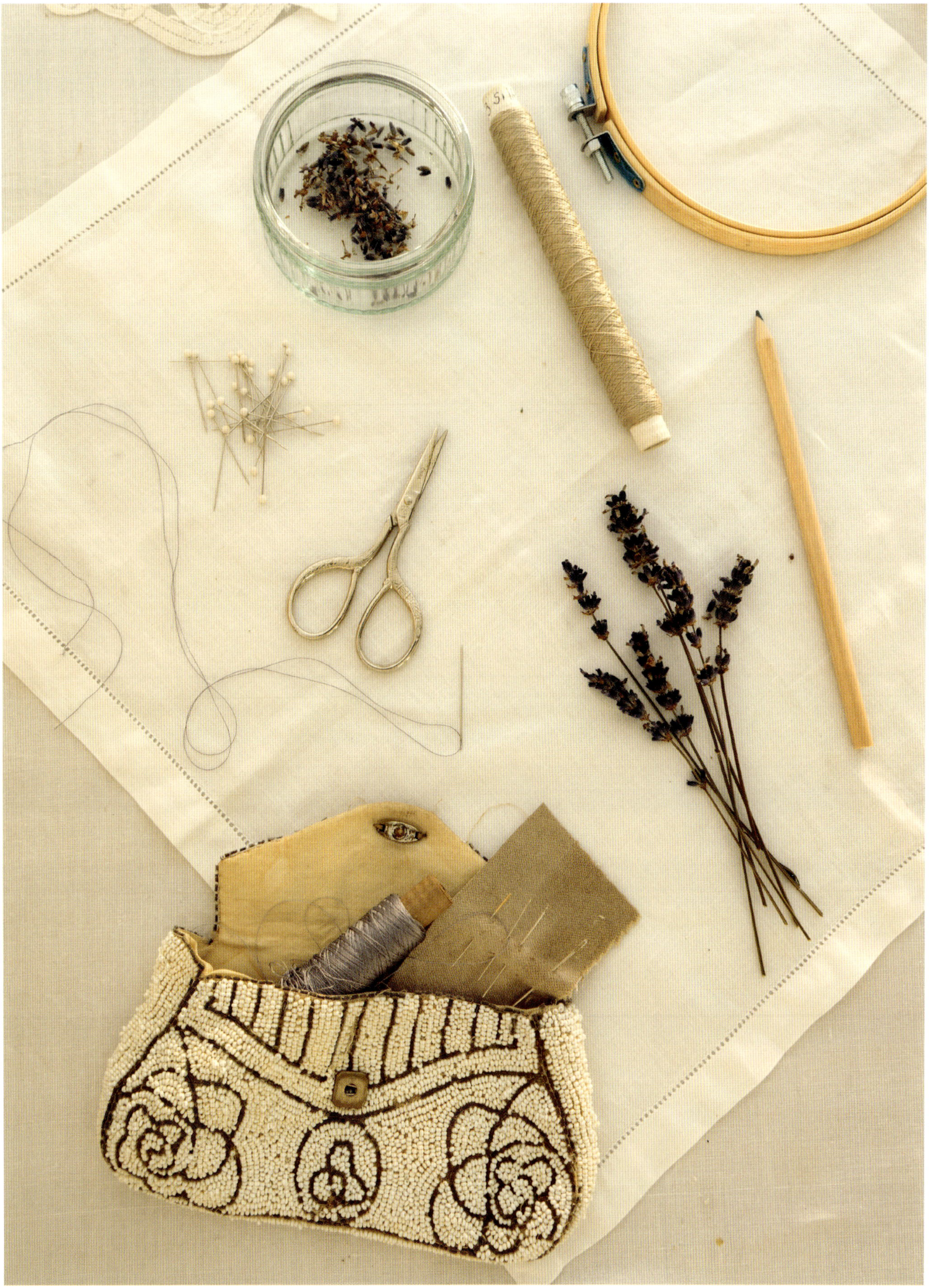

Working with Plant Embellishments

Before we begin the embroidery techniques, you might be wondering how these plant materials can be threaded through a needle just like traditional embellishments. Below I reveal where the strongest point in your plant material is to thread through your needle. Of course, this is just a guide. The process is often a case of trial and error, as some crops or varieties might be stronger or more delicate than others. You may need to carry out some testing and personal exploration to find out.

1 **Achillea** – Once dried, achillea offers tiny, full-headed flowers that are surprisingly strong. To stitch with them, pass your needle through the outer shell that is holding the flowerhead together. Take your needle through in a horizontal direction; this avoids catching the delicate petals and keeps the flowerhead intact.

2 **Chamomile** – The best place to stitch with chamomile is through the stem. Therefore, keep a small amount of the stem attached to the flowerhead. Avoid stitching through the central yellow floret as this will most likely cause it to break apart.

3 **Cornflowers** – Their petals might appear to be too small and delicate to work with, but you may be surprised at their strength. The flat petals work best, as others might shrivel up and become too small. Petals on the outer edge, furthest away from the pistil (the centre of the flower), work best as they are slightly larger than the petals at the centre. When threading, pass your needle through the centre of the petal. This provides the most surface area around the entry point, helping the petal to stay intact.

4 **Dahlias and roses** – Dahlias and roses will produce large, full-bodied petals that can be used in their natural three-dimensional form or carefully cut into smaller fragments, depending on your design. Select the most robust petals to work with; some will be too brittle and will immediately tear with the needle.

5 **Lavender** – Lavender seeds were almost designed to be used just like beads. When you remove a seed of lavender from its stalk and observe it closely, you will notice a tiny hole at the top of the seed. This natural opening is just the right size for a needle to pass through, so you can thread the seed on it as if it were a bead.

6 **Marigold** – In one individual marigold flowerhead you will get more than a dozen single petals that are perfect to stitch with. To unlock the petals, crack the flowerhead open on the side of its shell to release the individual petals. At the base is the strongest point to stitch with. Alternatively, the long stem of the marigold petals means they work well with the couching technique (see page 82).

7 **Statice** – To release the individual statice petals, hold the petals between the fingers of one hand and gently pull on the stem with your other hand – this will separate the petals. The strongest part of

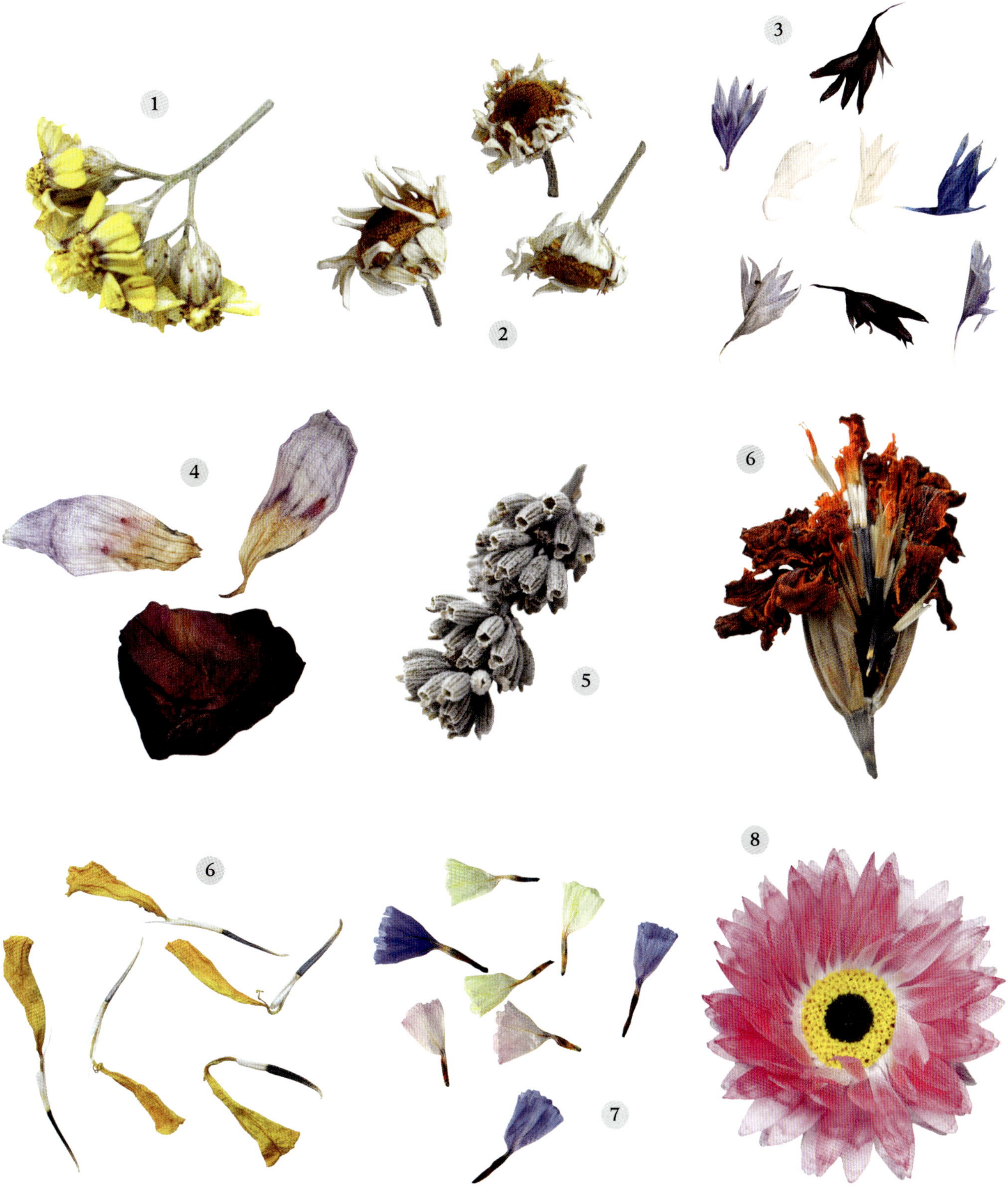

the petal, and the best place to thread your needle, is where the petal meets the pistil. The pistil itself is too thin for your needle, but the base of the petal is strong enough to pass a needle through without tearing.

8 Strawflowers – You can work with strawflowers in two ways: either gently separate the petals from the flowerhead and stitch with them individually, or use the full flowerhead for a more three-dimensional material to work with.

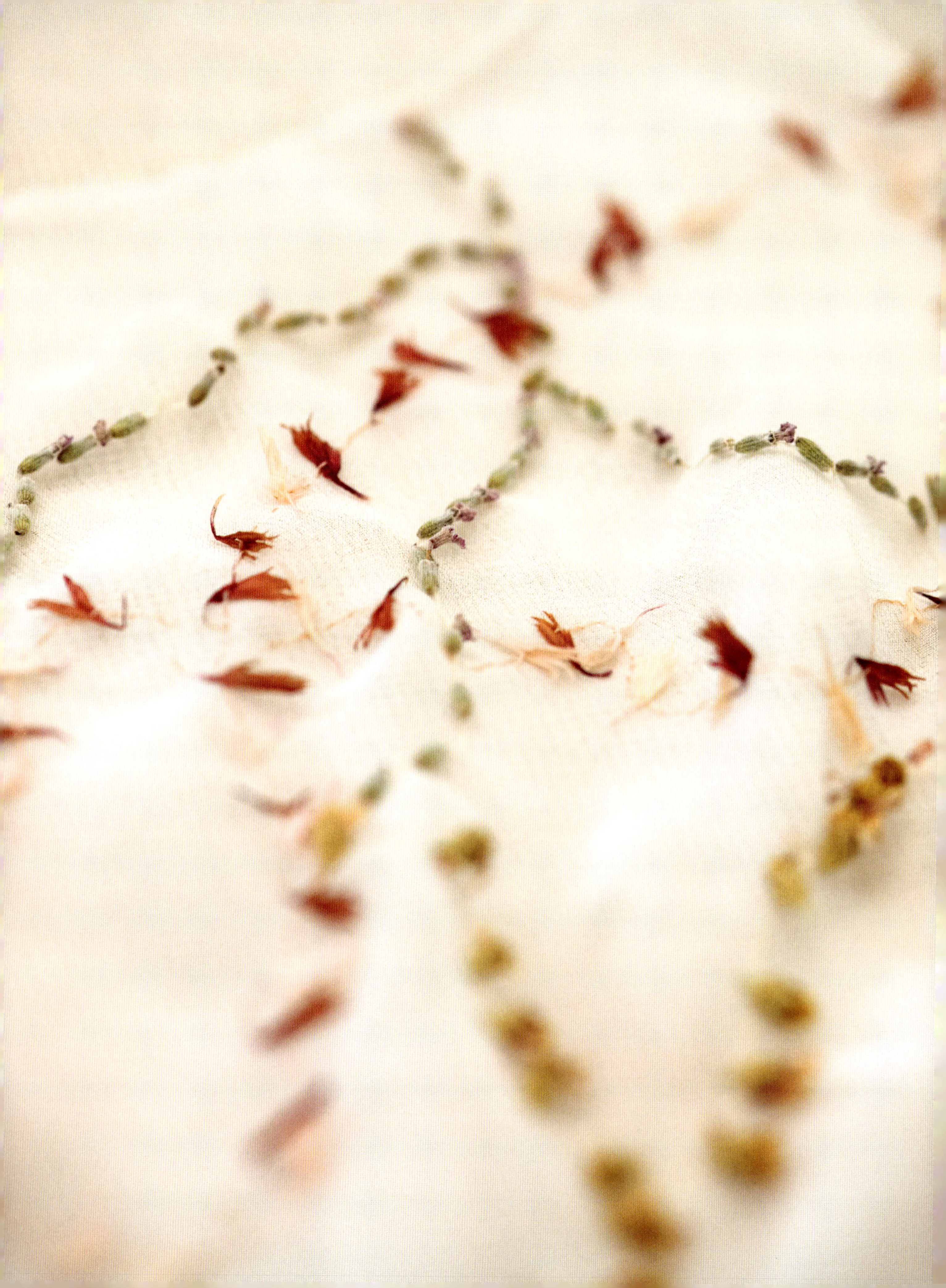

Stitching Techniques

'You push your threaded needle in one side of the cloth and pull it out on the other, on and on in rhythmic sewing, until you have made something that matters: a thing of beauty and meaning, an embroidery that holds your spirit fast within its threads.'

CLARE HUNTER

The techniques I have chosen to share with you are those that I have practised and perfected together with my plant embellishments. They are traditional embroidery stitches, familiar and nostalgic, perhaps reminiscent of learning to hand-stitch at school, like the humble cross stitch. While the stitches themselves remain true to their traditions, it is through incorporating flowers and seeds that you can achieve unexpected and unique results.

The techniques in this chapter progress in difficulty, beginning with a simple seed stitch and gradually advancing towards the more intricate interlace techniques at the end, stitches that require the most patient and delicate hand. Gently progress at a pace that is comfortable for you, taking each stitch slowly, enjoying the quiet repetition of each process.

For some stitches, such as double darning, I provide variations to try, like circular double darning. In this way, you can build upon the foundational technique and explore more organic, free-flowing compositions.

In each technique I have suggested a particular flower, petal or seed to use. But do not let this limit you, this is merely a material starting point. In double herringbone, for example, I combine lavender and achillea; I encourage you to experiment too, weaving together intriguing combinations of threads and flowers.

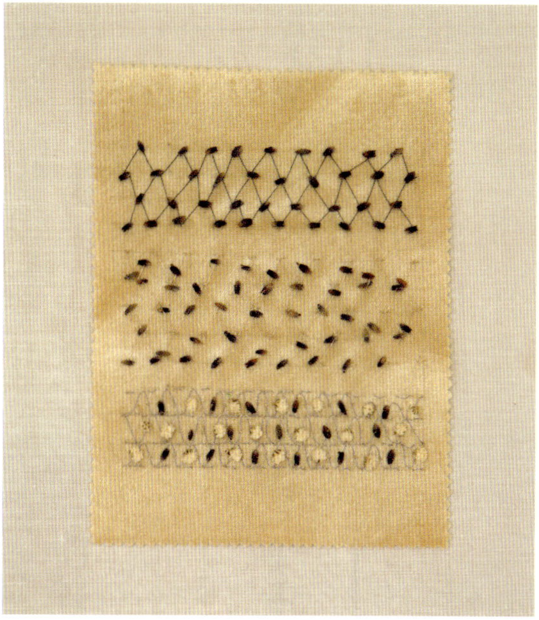

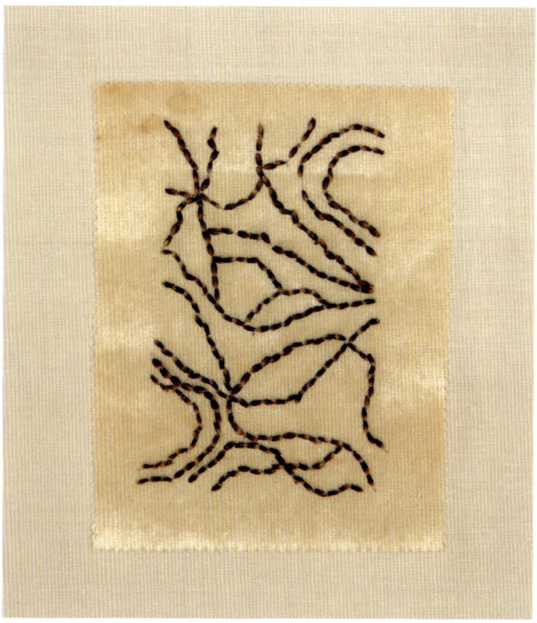

Seed Stitch

USING CORNFLOWERS

The seed stitch is a simple yet soothing technique to practise. It is the perfect way to ease into working with plant materials. I love how its simplicity allows you to get lost in the rhythm and randomness of each stitch, creating a meditative, organic flow.

STITCH STEPS . . .

1. Thread your needle and take it up through the back of your cloth.
2. Take your needle through your petal and back down through your cloth as close as possible to where you began so no thread is visible on the surface of the cloth.
3. Select the next point for where you would like your next petal to be and take your needle up through the back of the cloth.
4. Repeat step two, stitching down your second petal.
5. Continue making seed stitches with your petals in randomized directions until you have covered your cloth.

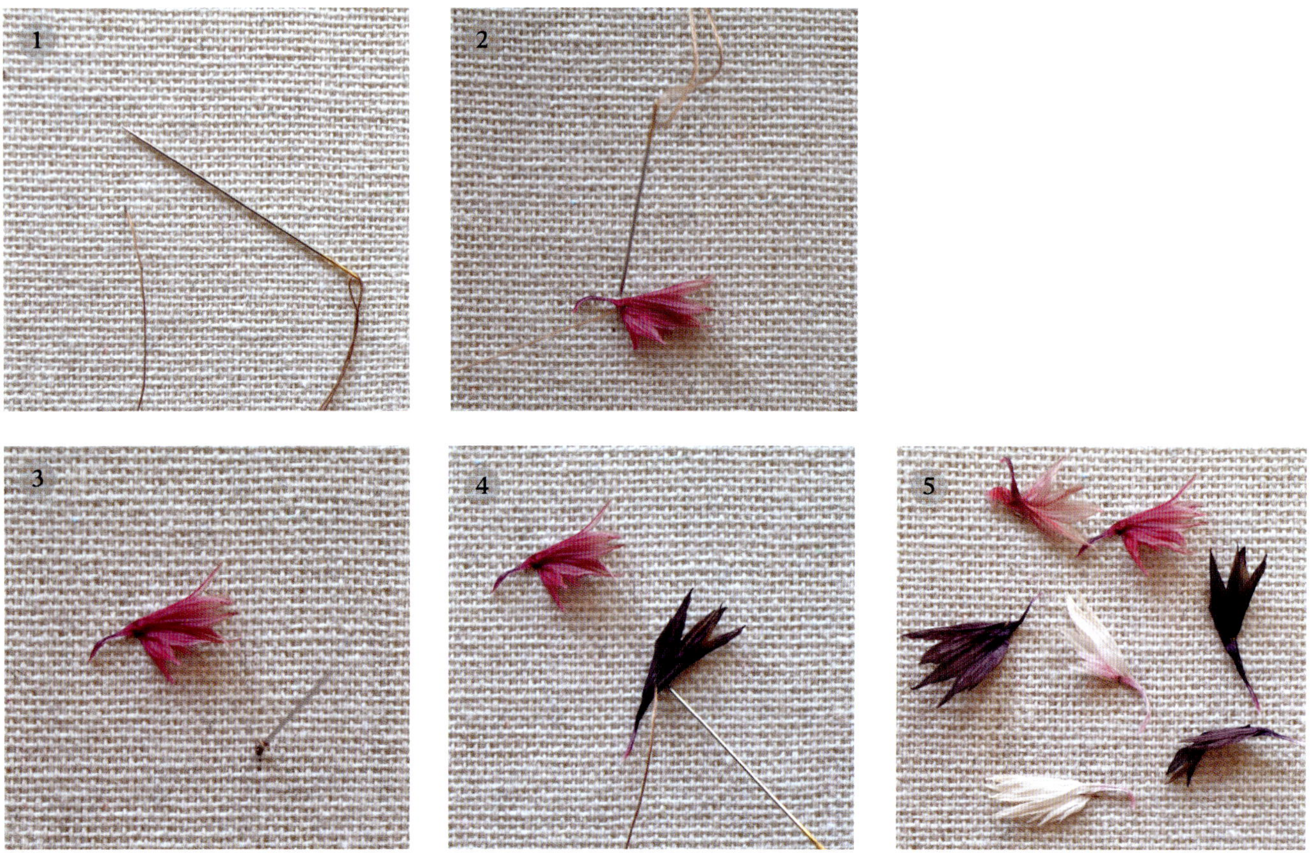

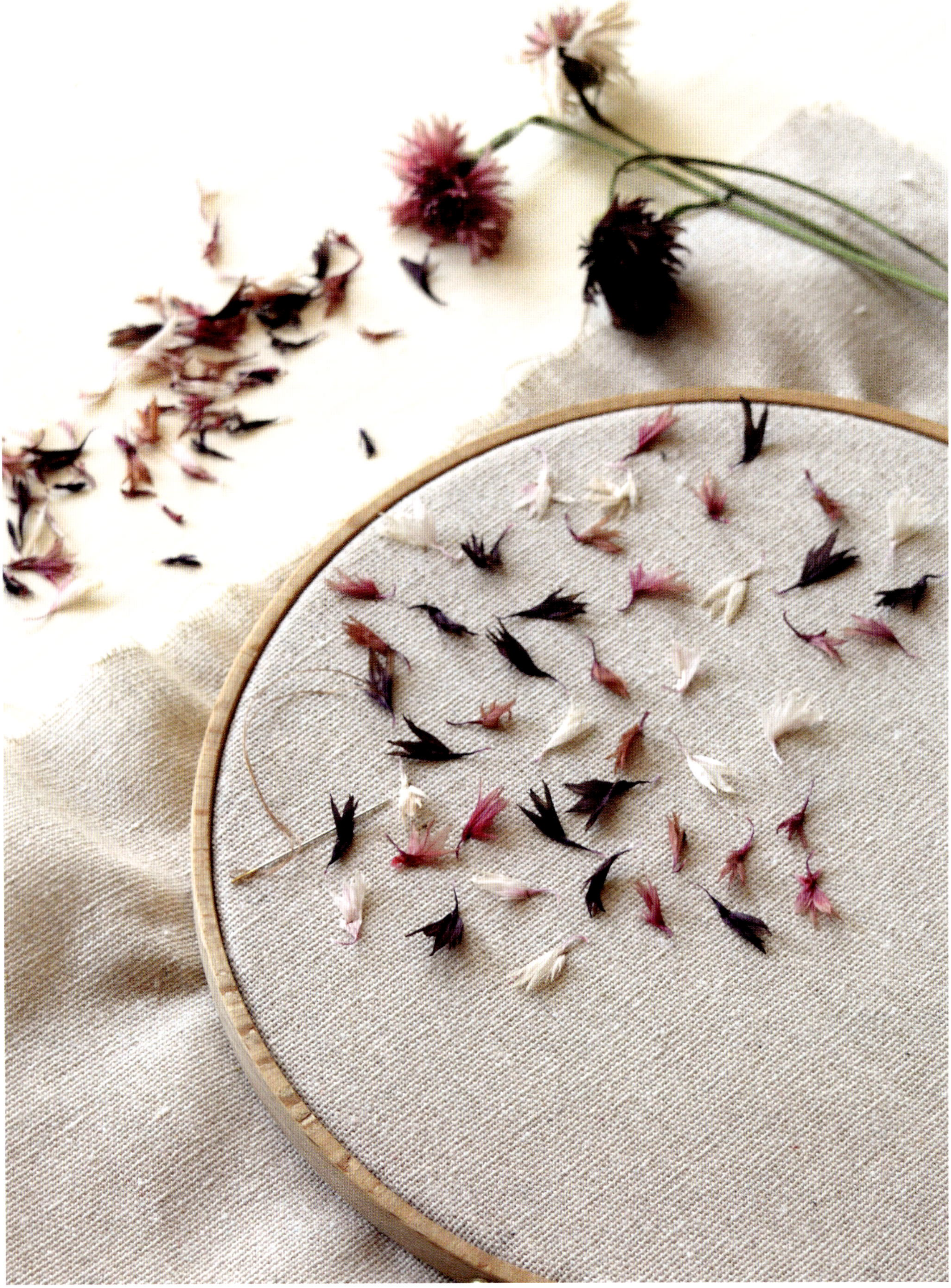

Couching

USING FLORA THAT ARE STILL ATTACHED TO THEIR STEMS

The couching technique works well for tiny flowerheads where you might prefer not to cut them away from their stem but rather include the stem as part of the design. This method allows you to secure the flower to the cloth without piercing through the flower or the stem itself, causing the least disruption to its structure.

STITCH STEPS . . .

1. Thread your needle and take it up through the back of your cloth, then place your plant material on top of the cloth with the stem as close to your thread hole as possible.

2. Take your needle over the stem and back down through the cloth, back through the same stitch hole if possible, or for thicker stems as close as possible.

3. Depending on the length of the stem, you can place another couching stitch over another point on the stem 1–2cm ($\frac{1}{2}$in) apart, to ensure it is extra secure.

4. Lay your next flower on the surface of the cloth in your desired place and repeat steps 1–3.

5. Continue the process until you have completed your desired design.

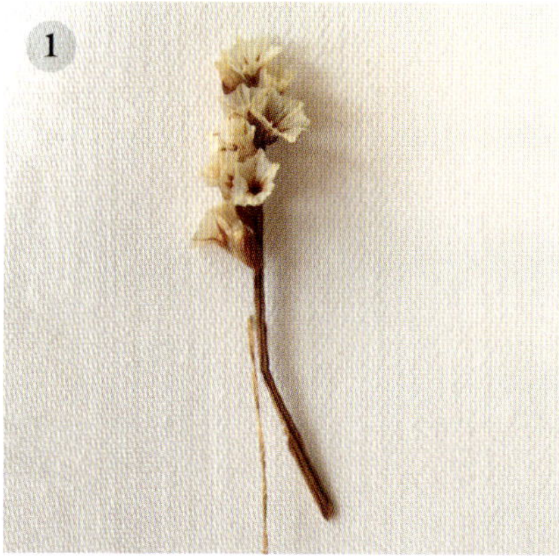

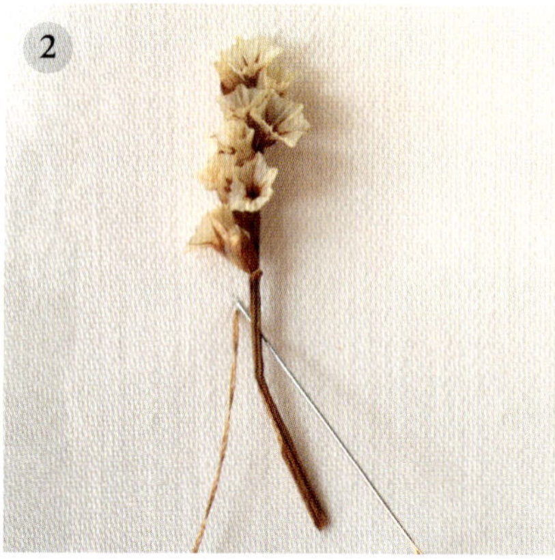

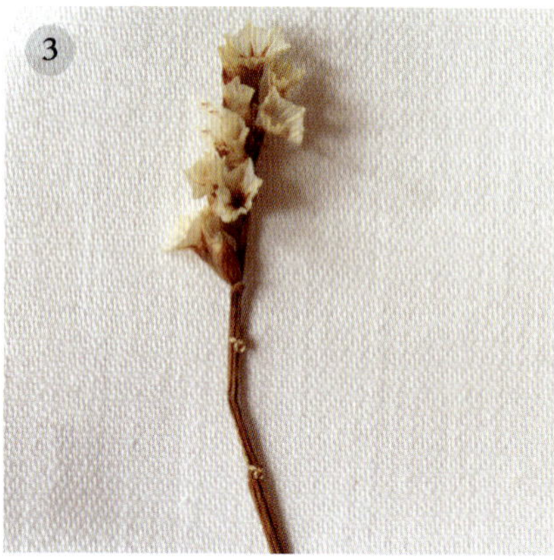

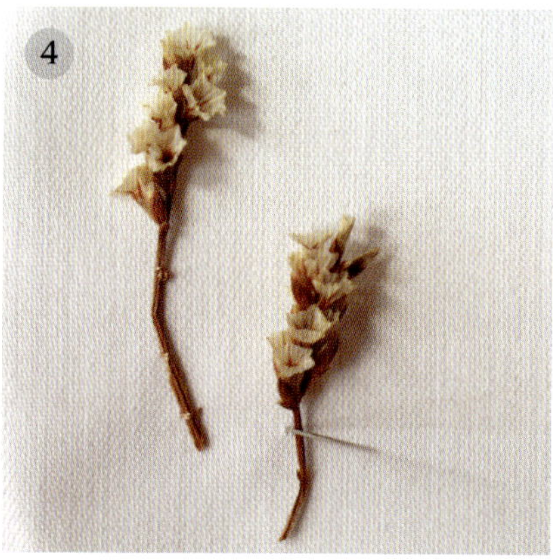

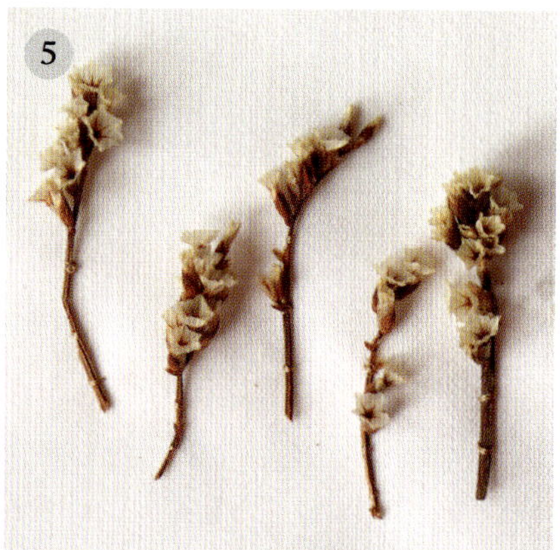

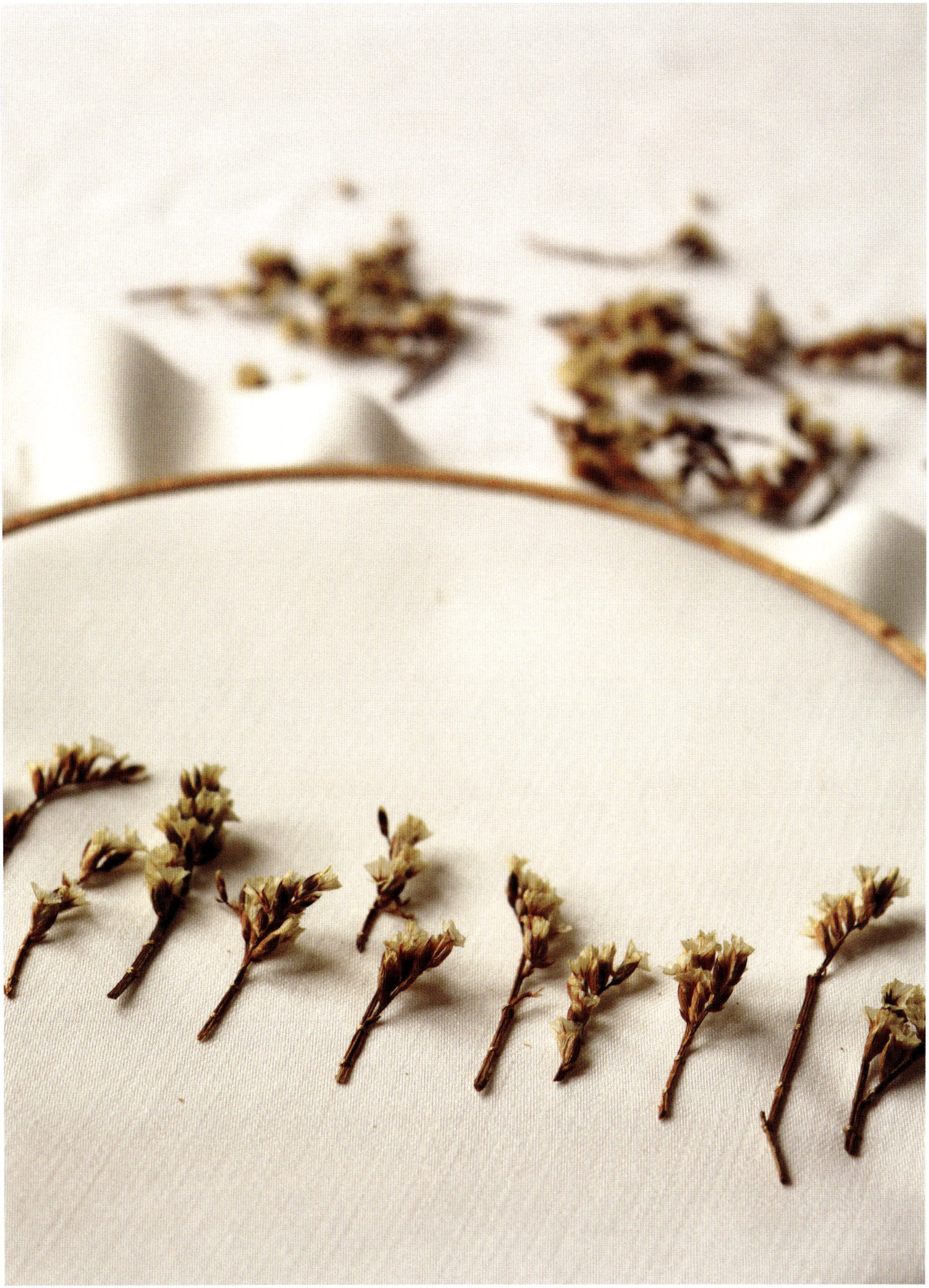

Couching with a Single Thread

USING SEEDS OF LAVENDER

In this technique, lavender seed beads are worked onto a single thread. The thread is then couched down to secure it to the fabric. The thread will be invisible and thus the seeds look as if they are floating on the surface of the cloth. This is a quick technique to work with compared with some others we explore in this book.

STITCH STEPS . . .

1 Thread your needle and take it up through the back of your cloth wherever you wish to start.

2 Take your needle vertically through the seed, and repeat this until you have attached several seeds to the thread. You should work in short lengths of around four to six lavender seeds so you can maintain control and avoid damaging or breaking the seeds.

3 Once your seeds are attached, lie the thread down on your cloth in the position you would like, and take your needle down through the point of your final bead. You might wish to mark your lines on the cloth so you have a guide to follow, or take a more intuitive approach.

4 Go back up through the cloth between every second lavender bead and make a small stitch over the thread to secure the couched line in place.

5 Continue couching every two or three beads along the line back to the start. It is important to ensure your couch stitches are small and discreet so they are not visible.

6 You could then extend this couched line by beginning again at your final lavender bead, or start a new line entirely.

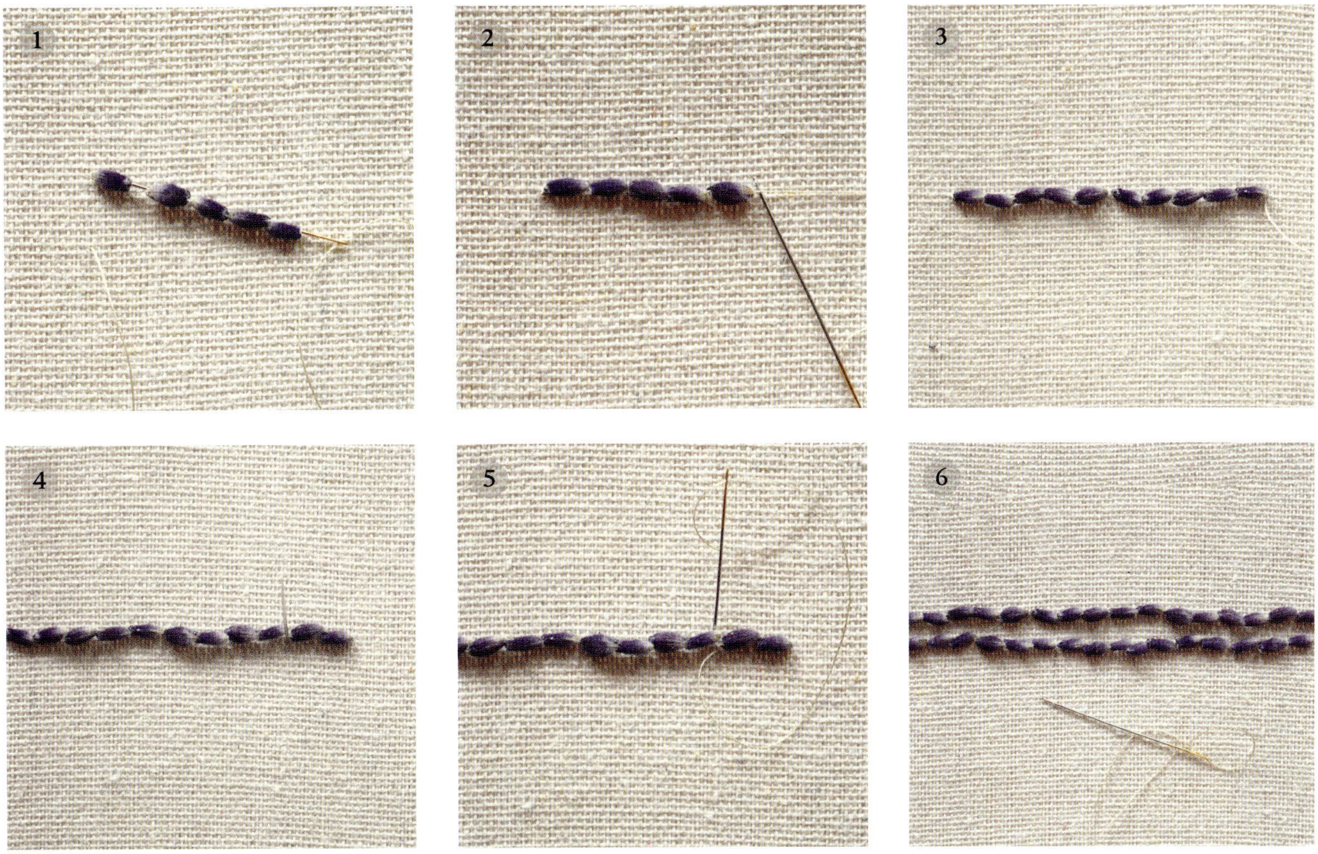
1
2
3
4
5
6

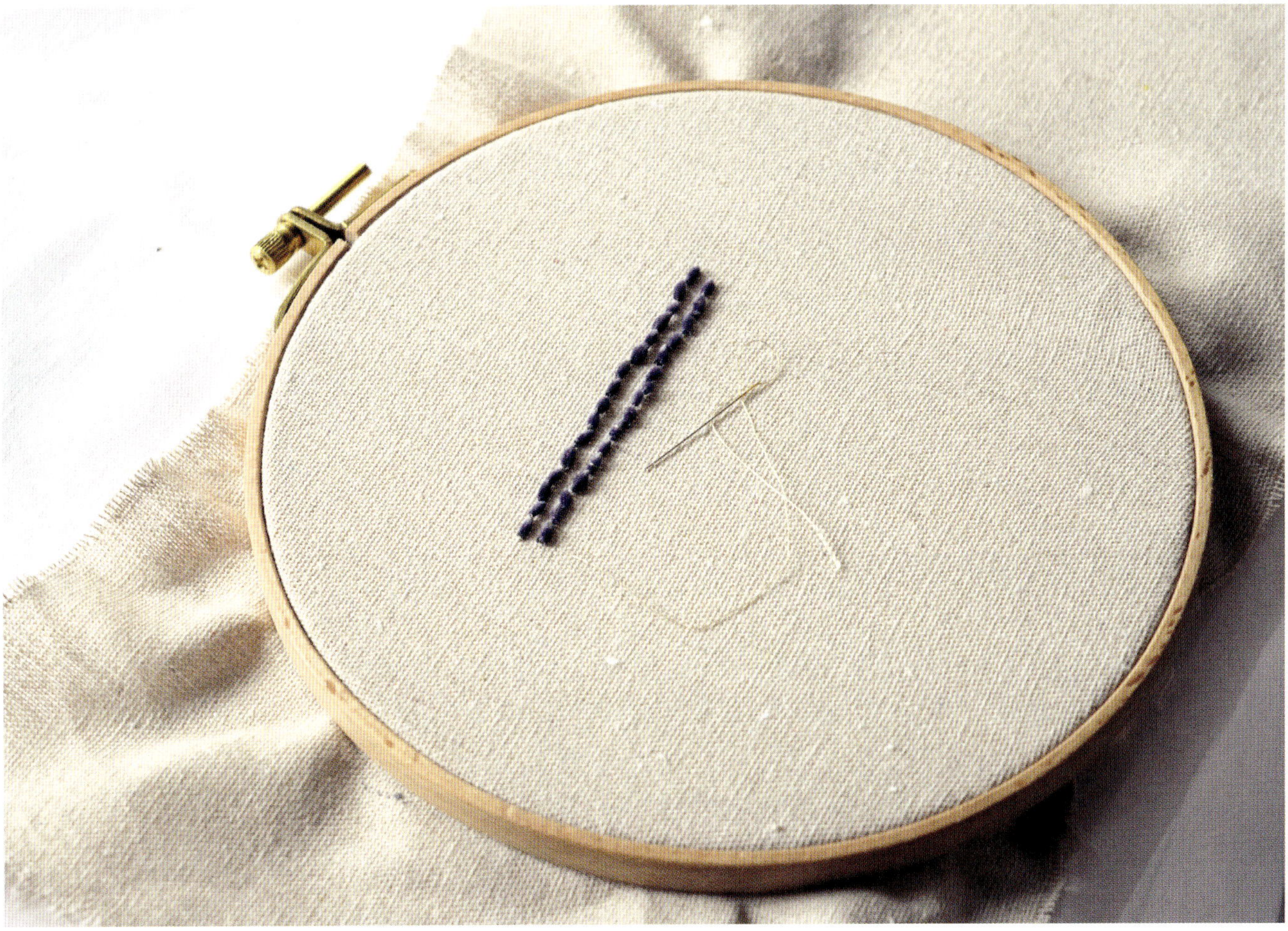

1

2
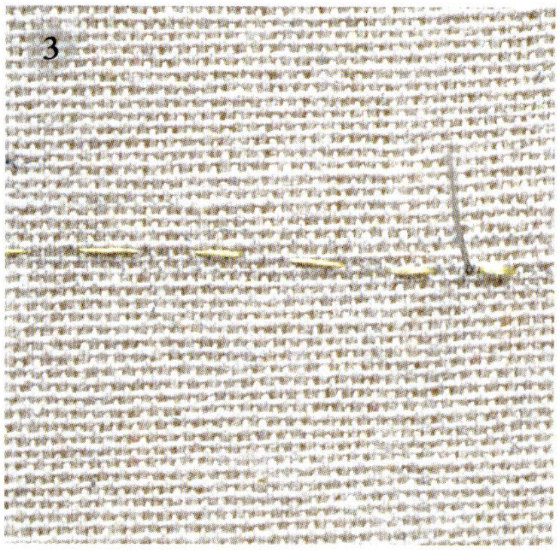
3
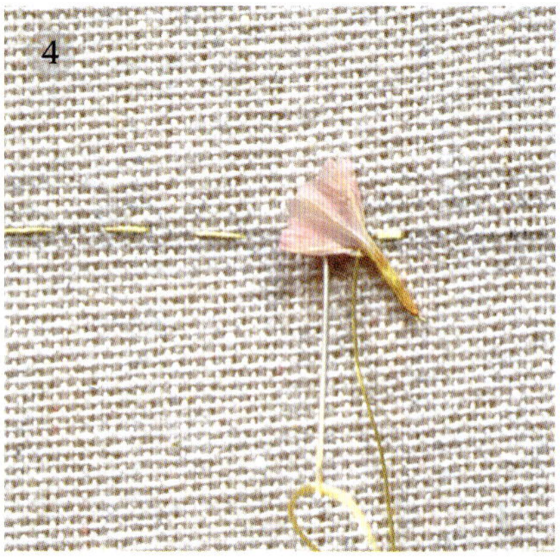
4
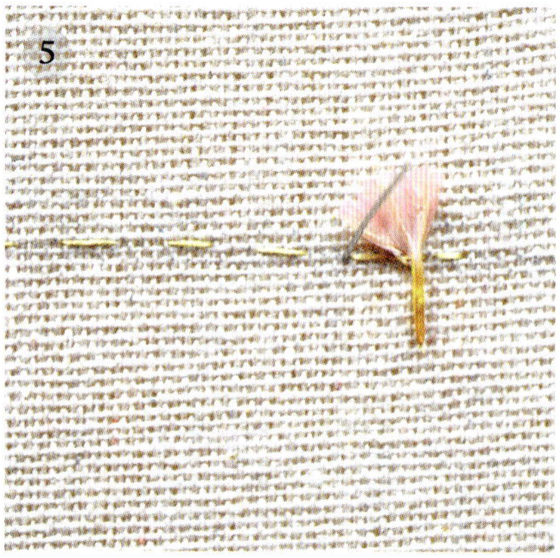
5
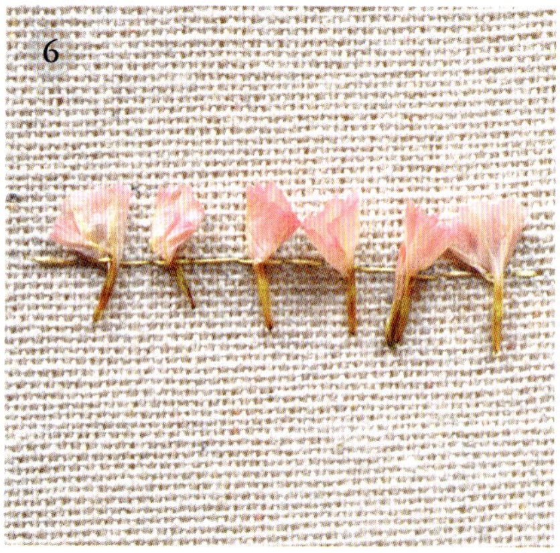
6
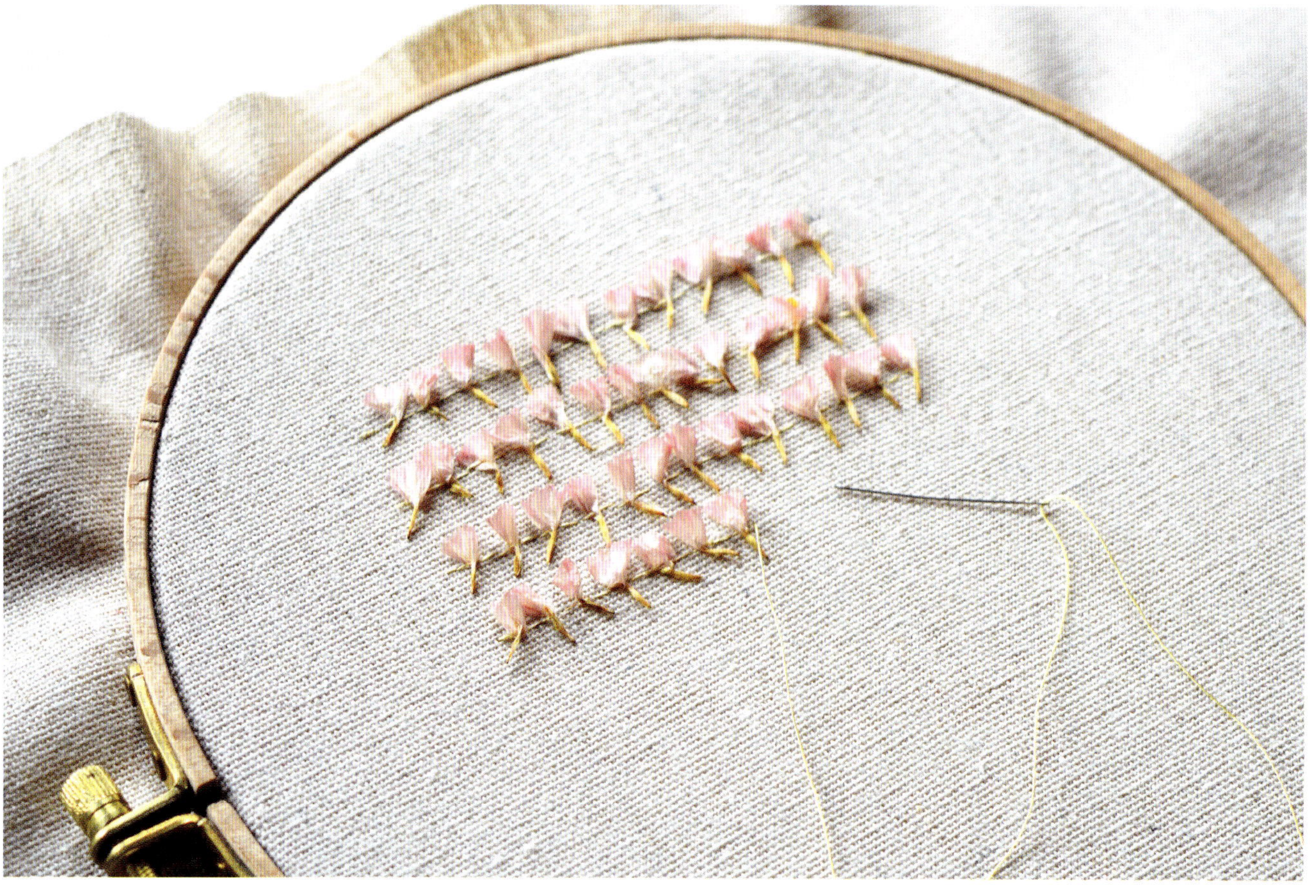

Double Darning

USING STATICE PETALS

Double darning is a type of filling stitch where lines of stitches are typically worked in parallel lines close together. Here we will use it as a method of creating a continuous stitch line flowing with flowers. I find the result of perfectly aligned parallel rows of petals beautifully satisfying.

STITCH STEPS . . .

1 Draw a straight line across your cloth with your fabric pencil. Thread your needle and take it up through the back of your cloth, then make a straight stitch approximately 1cm (3/8in) in length (smaller stitches mean that your petals will be closer together).

2 Leave a 1cm (3/8in) gap and make another straight stitch. Continue stitching a line of straight stitches, ensuring that each stitch is even with an equal 1cm (3/8in) gap in between each stitch.

3 Once you reach the end of the row, you will go back and fill in the spaces between each stitch. Take your needle through the back of the cloth at the first point where you made your last straight stitch.

4 Thread your petal and pull it down the thread so it is flush on the surface of the cloth. Then take your needle back down through the final point of your penultimate straight stitch (so that you close the gap).

5 Move on to the next gap and repeat step 4.

6 Continue working your way back down the row, securing a petal in each gap. You will create a continuous row of joined stitches and petals, where the thread runs seamlessly.

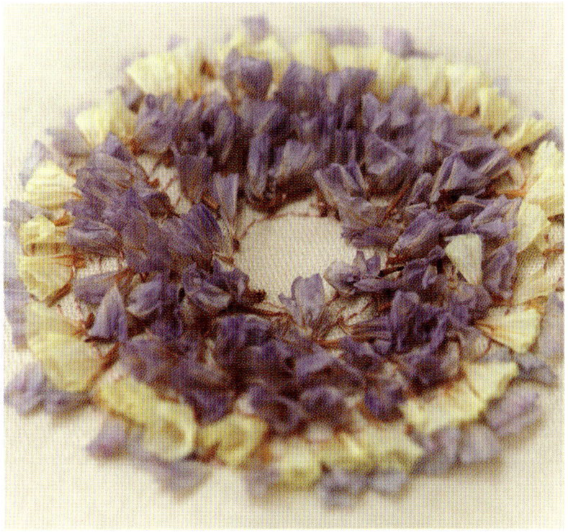

CIRCULAR DOUBLE DARNING

This technique does not only have to be worked in straight lines.

STITCH STEPS . . .

1 Use a compass to mark out your cloth with concentric circles, approximately 2cm (3/4in) apart.

2 Work from the outer circle in. First make your row of straight stitches on all of your circles.

3 You can then go back to the outer circle and fill the spaces with your double darning stitch, threading each petal as you go.

Cross Stitch

USING DAHLIAS

The cross stitch is a classic and quintessential hand-embroidery technique, which many of us might remember from our early days of learning how to stitch at school. It is made up of two straight stitches that cross over each other on the diagonal.

STITCH STEPS . . .

1 Mark out parallel lines on your cloth. The width in between your lines should depend on the type of petal you are embellishing with, so allow more space for bigger petals. The dahlia petal is large; thus your lines should be approximately 3cm (1¼in) apart. Bring the needle up at the bottom left of the square and work the second straight stitch from the bottom left of the square, over the top of your first straight stitch across to the top right.

2 Take your needle up to the top of the cloth through the bottom right hole of your cross. You can begin the second cross stitch from this point.

3 Take your needle diagonally across your first stitch and through the cloth on your top line. It is important to ensure that your stitches are even in length to form an accurate cross.

4 Continue working a series of joined cross stitches until you reach the end of the row.

5 Now, take your needle up through the middle of your final cross stitch, take your first petal and thread it through the central point of your cross stitch.

6 Now, move onto your next cross and secure a petal at the central point of the stitch, like you have just done in step 5.

7 Continue back along the length of your row of adding a petal at the centre of each cross stitch. Ensure your petals consistently face in the same direction.

8 Once you have completed a row, you can continue the process by building joined rows. This creates a lovely block of cross stitches that covers the entire surface of the cloth.

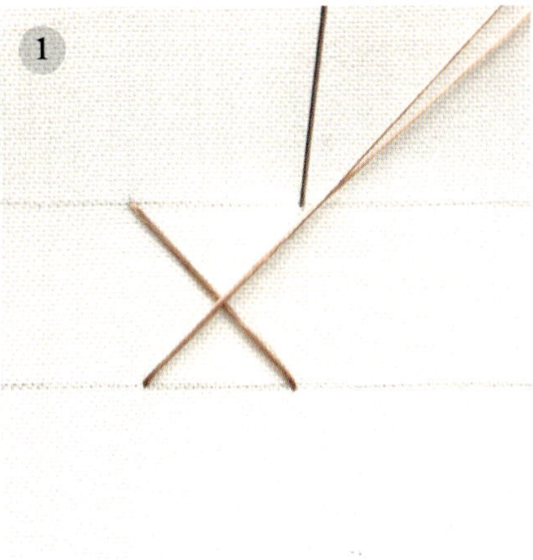
1
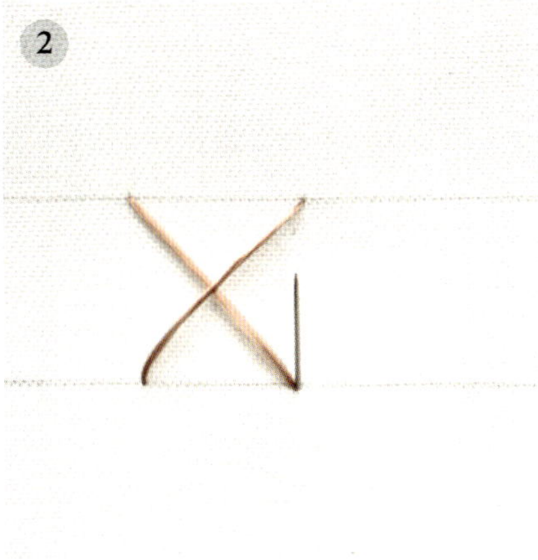
2
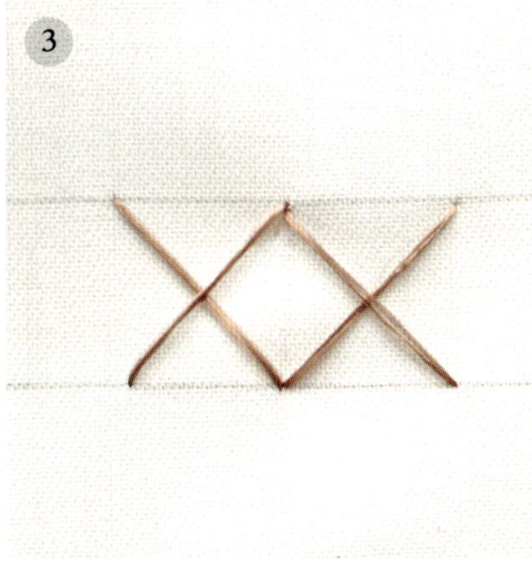
3
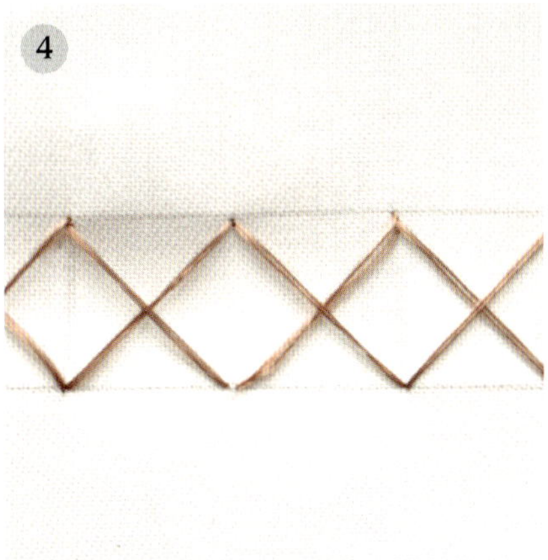
4
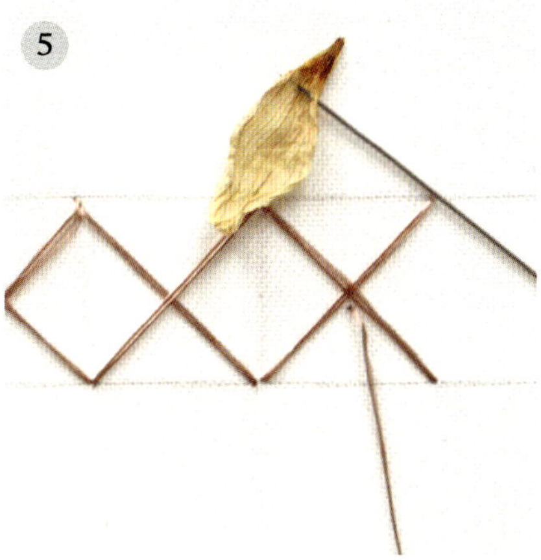
5
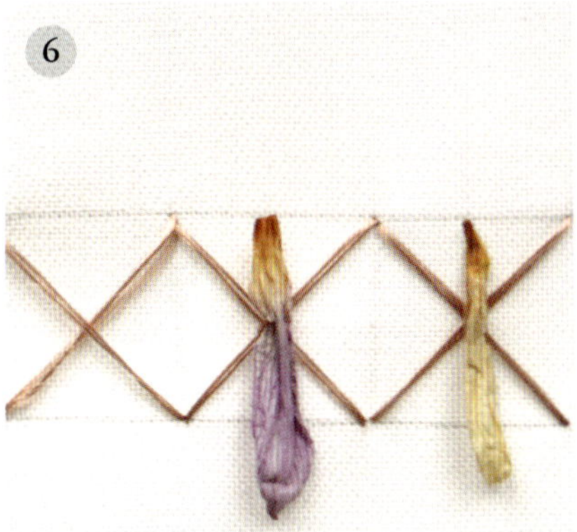
6
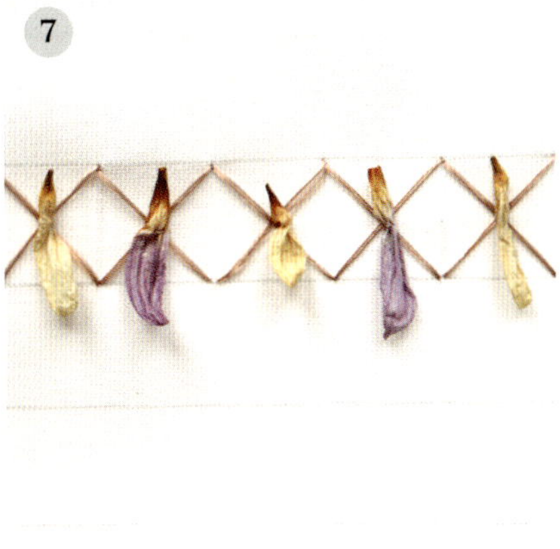
7
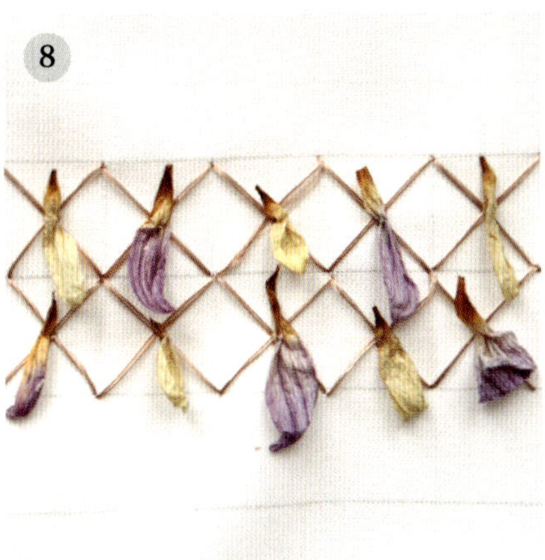
8
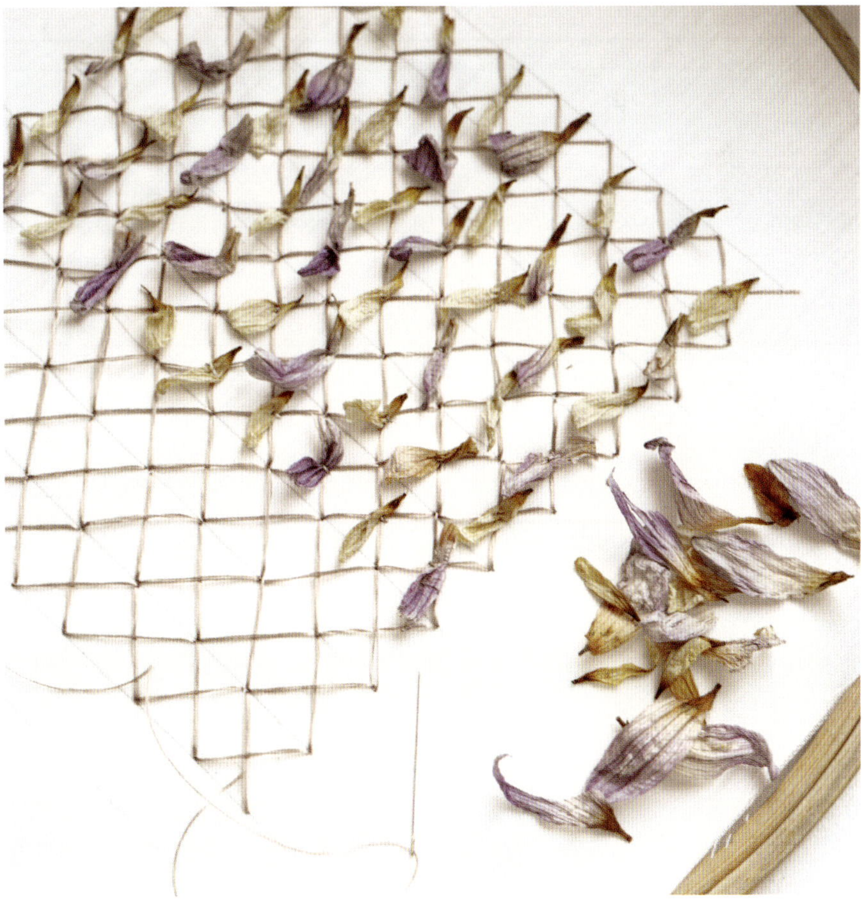

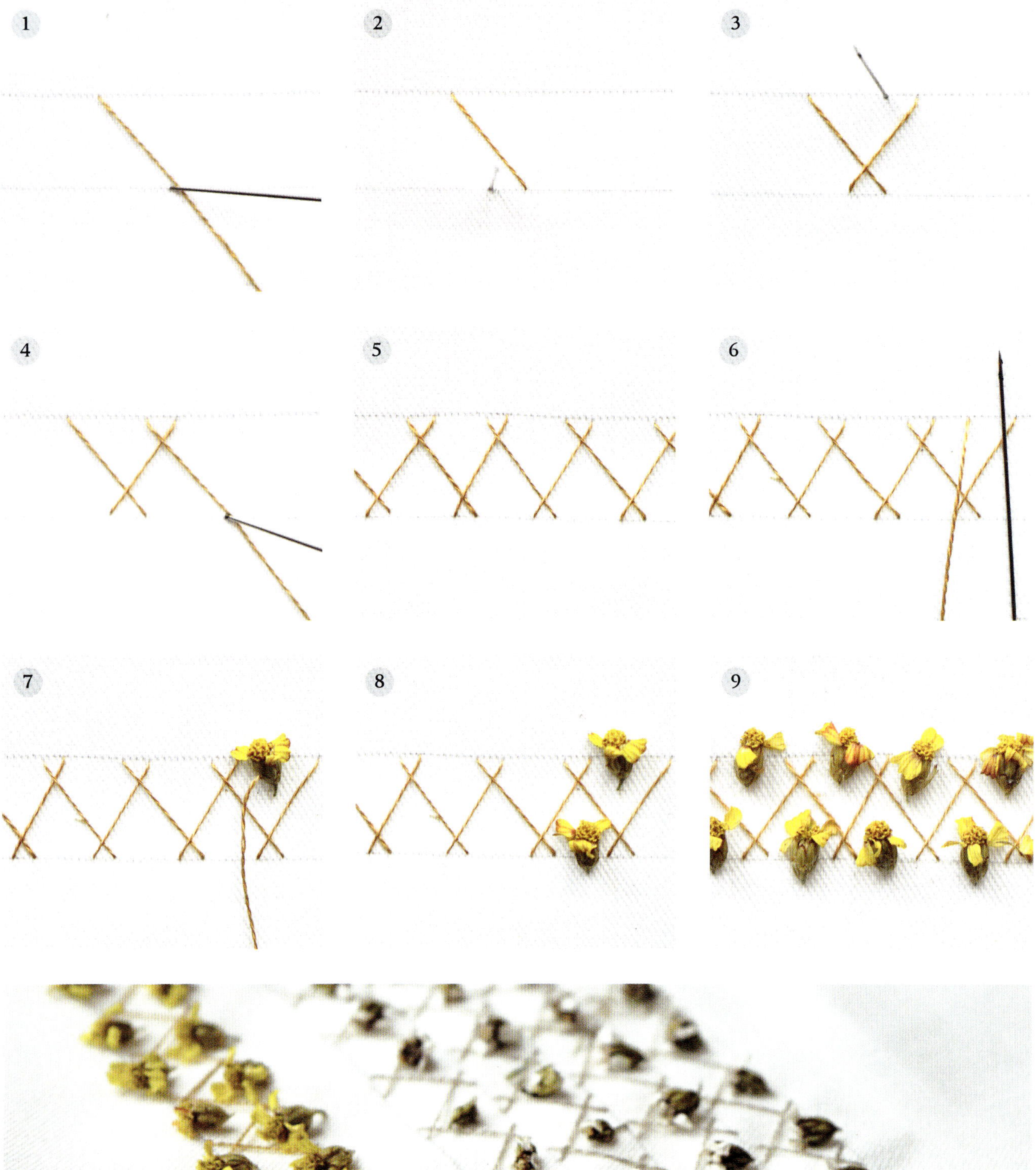
1
2
3
4
5
6
7
8
9

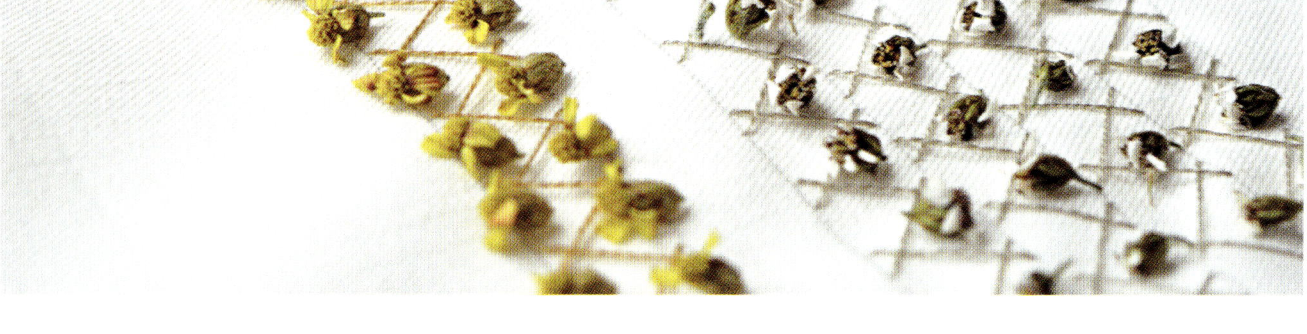

Herringbone

USING ACHILLEA

The herringbone is a classic technique with some similarity to the cross stitch, as it consists of slanted, diagonal, overlapping stitches. Worked in rows, this stitch creates beautiful decorative borders or a trim-like embroidery effect.

STITCH STEPS . . .

1. Mark out two parallel design lines on the cloth. For achillea flowers, leave a gap of 2cm (3/4in) between each line. Take your needle up the back of the cloth and through at the left edge of your first line. Take your needle down through the cloth on your second line at a slant to create your first diagonal stitch.

2. Bring the needle up 2mm (1/12in) back from where you made your diagonal stitch point on your second line. Take the needle diagonally across the top of your first stitch, then down through the cloth. This stitch should be the exact same length as your first stitch. This will form the first herringbone stitch.

3. Bring the needle up 2mm (1/12in) back from the top right corner of your first herringbone stitch.

4. Take your needle across at a slant diagonally to meet your second line and create your second herringbone stitch.

5. Continue these steps until you reach the end of your line.

6. To add the achillea embellishment, starting at the end of your row on the top line, take your needle up through the back of the cloth at the central gap between your last herringbone stitch.

7. Take your needle through the achillea flower and back through the cloth as close to the flower as possible so no thread is visible.

8. Now take your thread up through the central gap of your bottom line and secure another achillea embellishment here.

9. Continue until you have completed adding the embellishments along your row of herringbone stitches.

Further Explorations of the Herringbone Stitch

USING ACHILLEA AND LAVENDER

This stitch can also be worked in rows as a filling stitch to create an embroidered pattern that covers the surface of the cloth.

Advance the herringbone technique by using two contrasting threads and working a second layer of herringbone stitches over your first set to create a double herringbone.

STITCH STEPS . . .

1 Once you have completed stitches 1–6 of the herringbone technique, return to the start of your row, and thread your needle with a different colour thread.

2 Take your needle up through the gap of your first herringbone stitch on your top line. This will become the starting point for your second layer of herringbone stitches.

3 Repeat steps 1–6 down your row, to create another layer of herringbone stitches.

4 Once you reach the end of the row, you can work back down the row, stitching your plant embellishments on top of your herringbone stitches at your desired points.

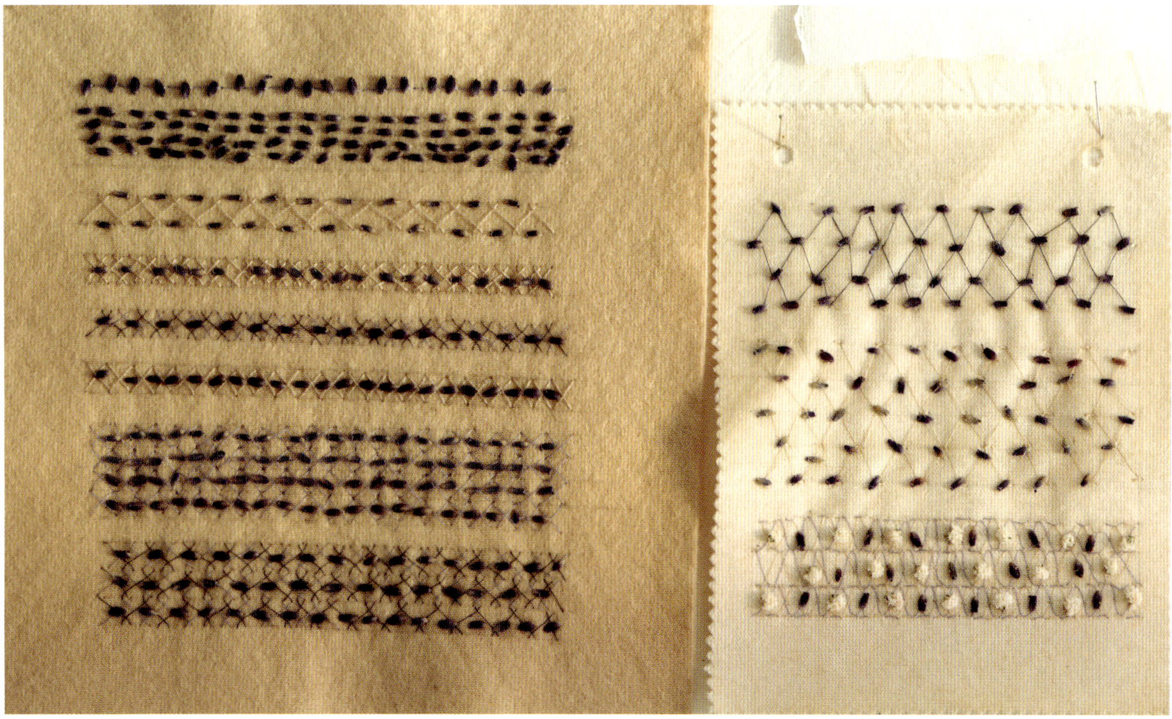

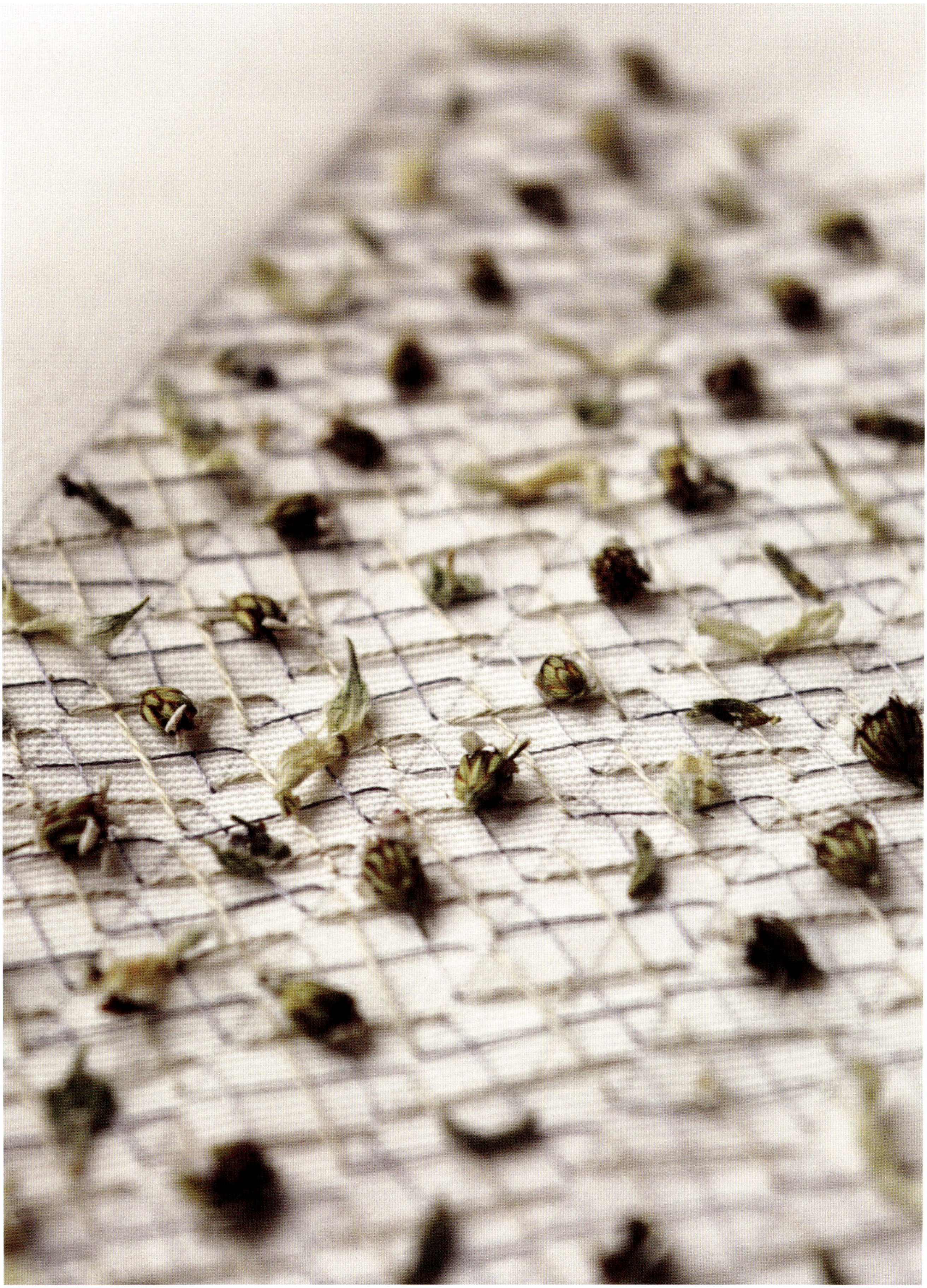

Diamond Interlace

USING LAVENDER SEEDS

Interlace stitches can look elaborate. They allow you to create intricate decorative patterns, but the fundamentals of the stitch are quite simple. You can then make your designs as complex as you desire. Essentially, interlace stitches rely on a set of running stitches on parallel rows that you work your threads between on the surface of the cloth. The interlace stitch is a good introduction to needlelace techniques.

STITCH STEPS . . .

1 Mark out dotted horizontal lines on your cloth. To do this, on your first line mark a dot 0.5cm (3/16in) from the edge, and continue to mark dots at intervals of 1cm (3/8in). On the second line, mark your first dot 1cm (3/8in) from the edge, and then continue with dots at intervals of 1cm (3/8in). You want the dots on line one to be staggered with the dots on line two. Your third row should follow the same pattern as row one; your fourth row should follow row two, and so on. The width in between your lines should depend on the type of petal with which you are embellishing. On your first row, stitch a line of even running stitches that have an equal gap in between each stitch.

2 On your next row, stitch a second line of running stitches that are level with the gaps between your stitches on your first row.

3 Bring your needle up through the first stitch you made on your second row.

4 Take your needle horizontally through a seed of lavender and position the seed so it lies flush on top of the running stitch. Now take your needle behind the seed and underneath the running stitch, but not back through your cloth. The lavender seed will be secured in place, covering your stitch.

5 Now take your needle up to and behind the first stitch on your top row, again not going through the cloth, but only through the running stitch.

6 Secure a lavender seed embellishment over this stitch, repeating the process of step 4.

7 Continue working between your two lines of running stitches until you reach the end row.

8 Now you will follow the same process but working between lines two and three: line two will already have the embellishment, so you will just be adding the lavender seed to line three. This is where you will start to see the diamond shape take form.

9 Continue working between lines two and three until you reach the end of the row. You will then have created your first set of diamond interlace stitches.

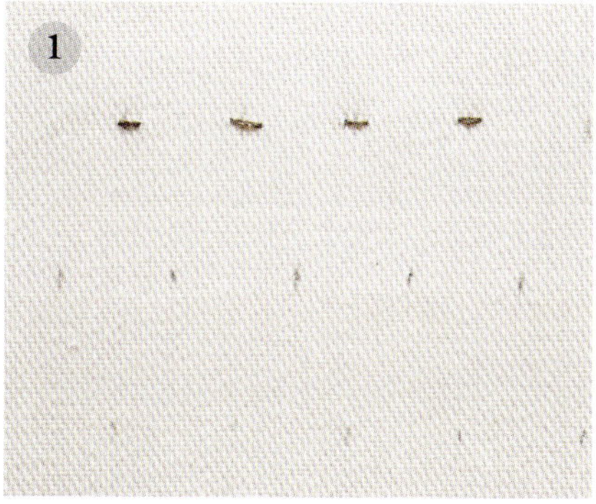
1

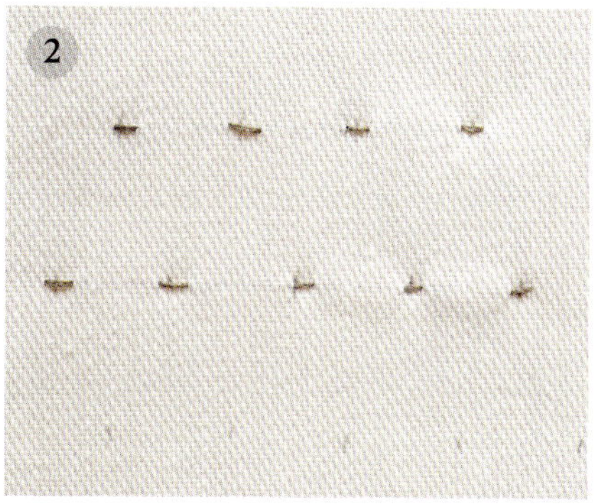
2

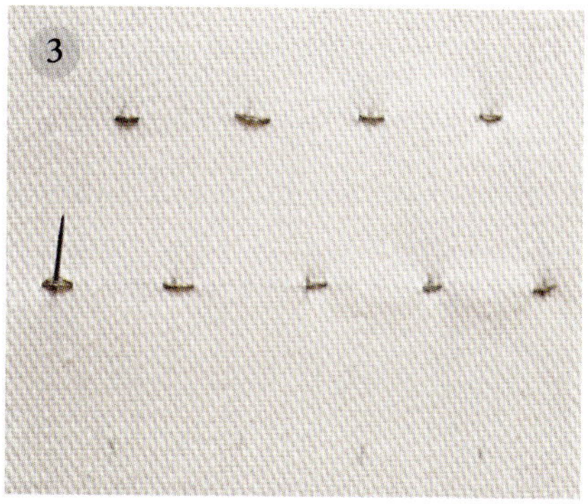
3

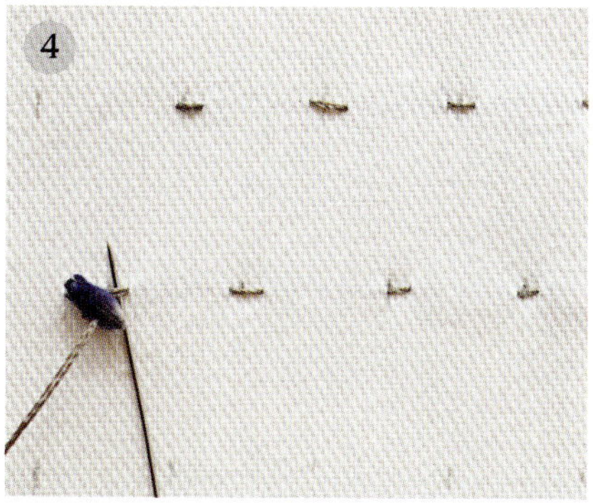
4

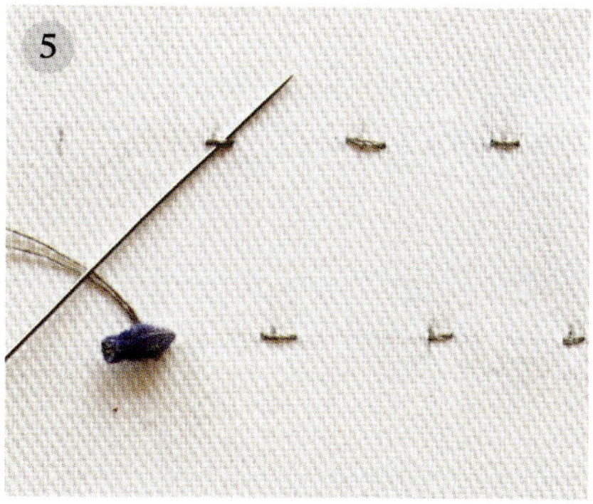
5

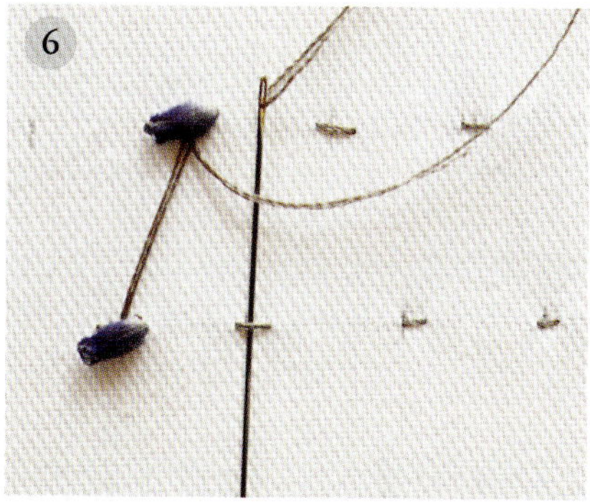
6

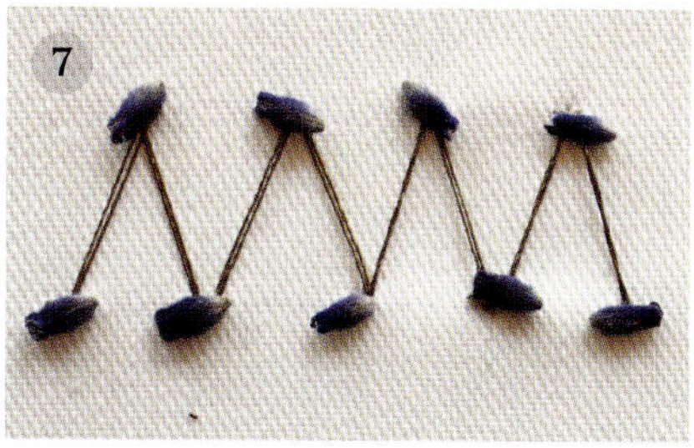
7

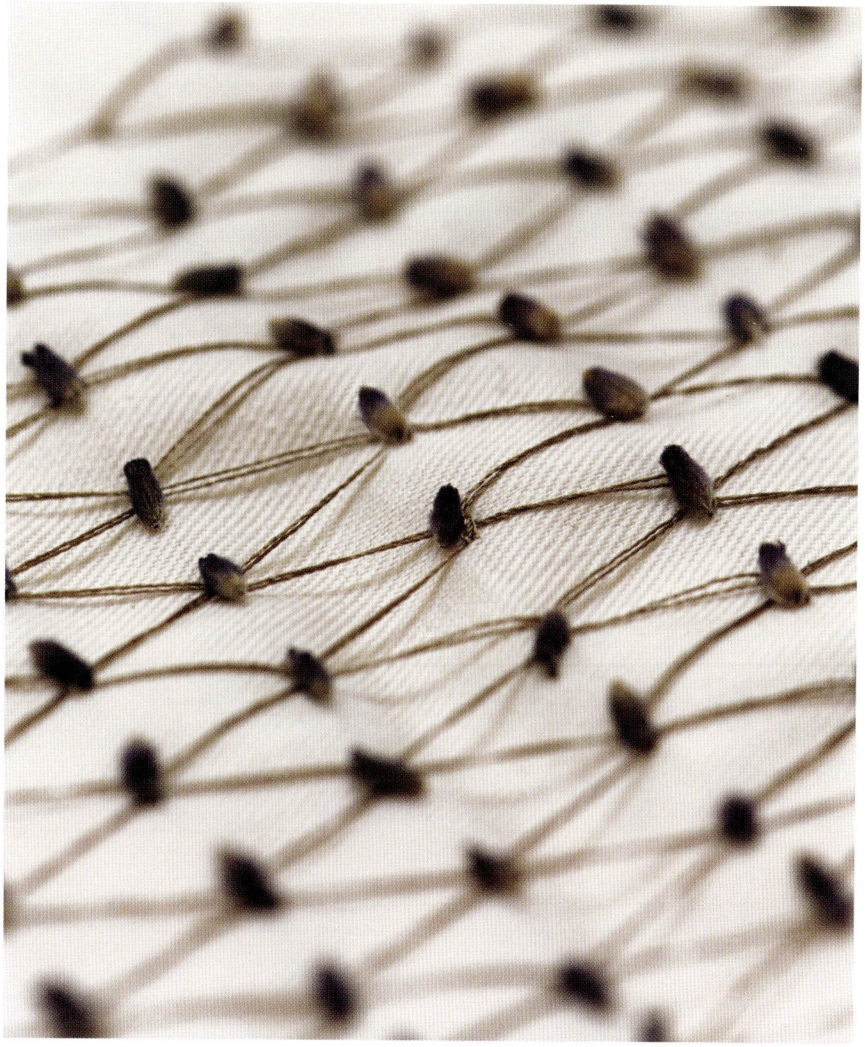

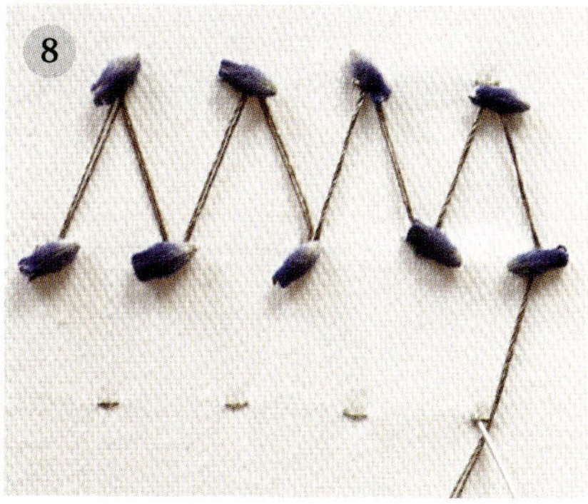
8

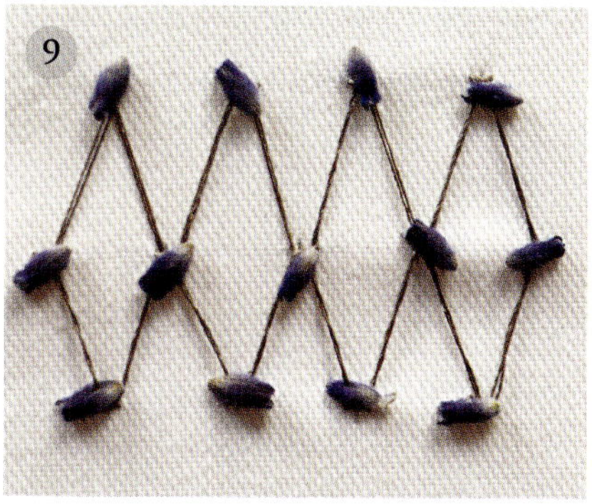
9

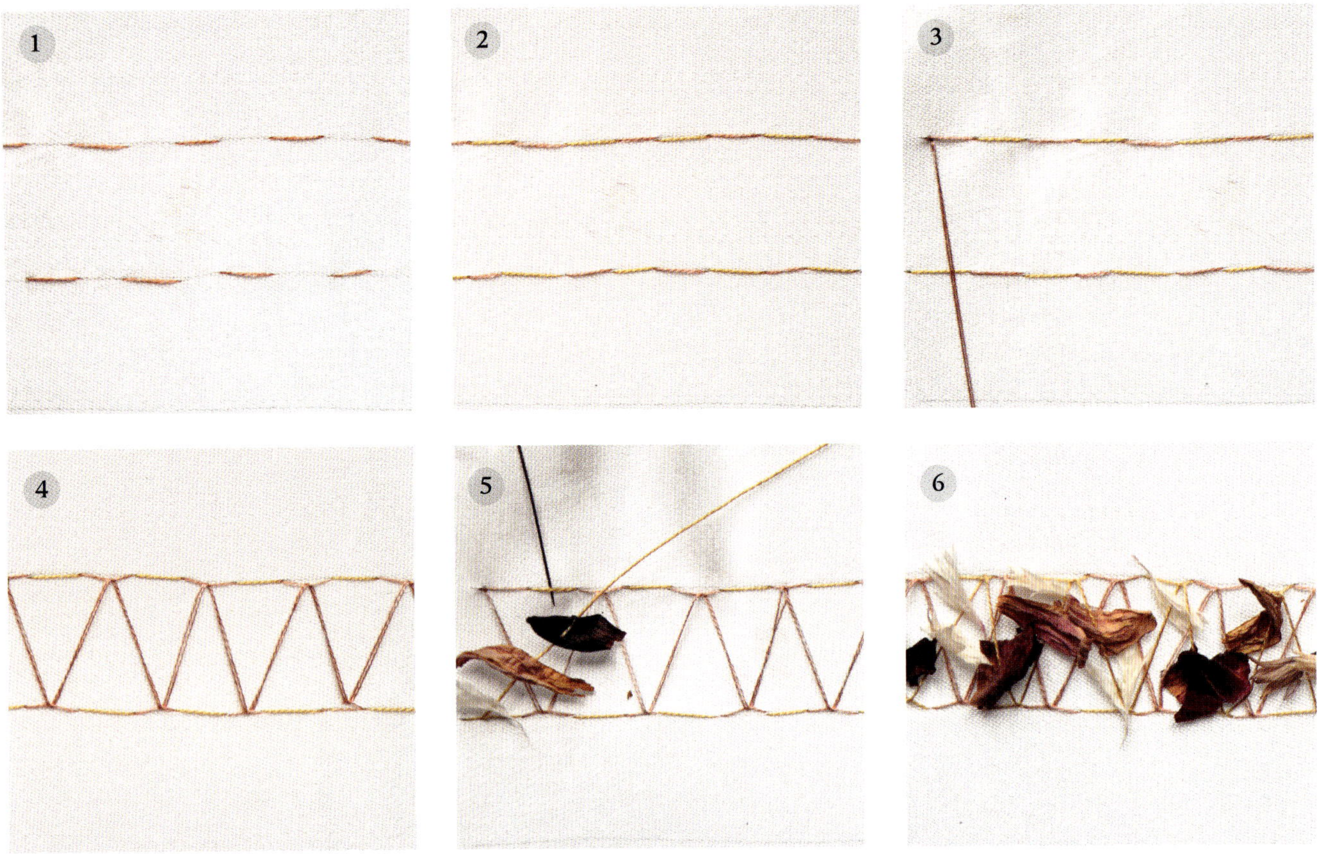
1
2
3
4
5
6

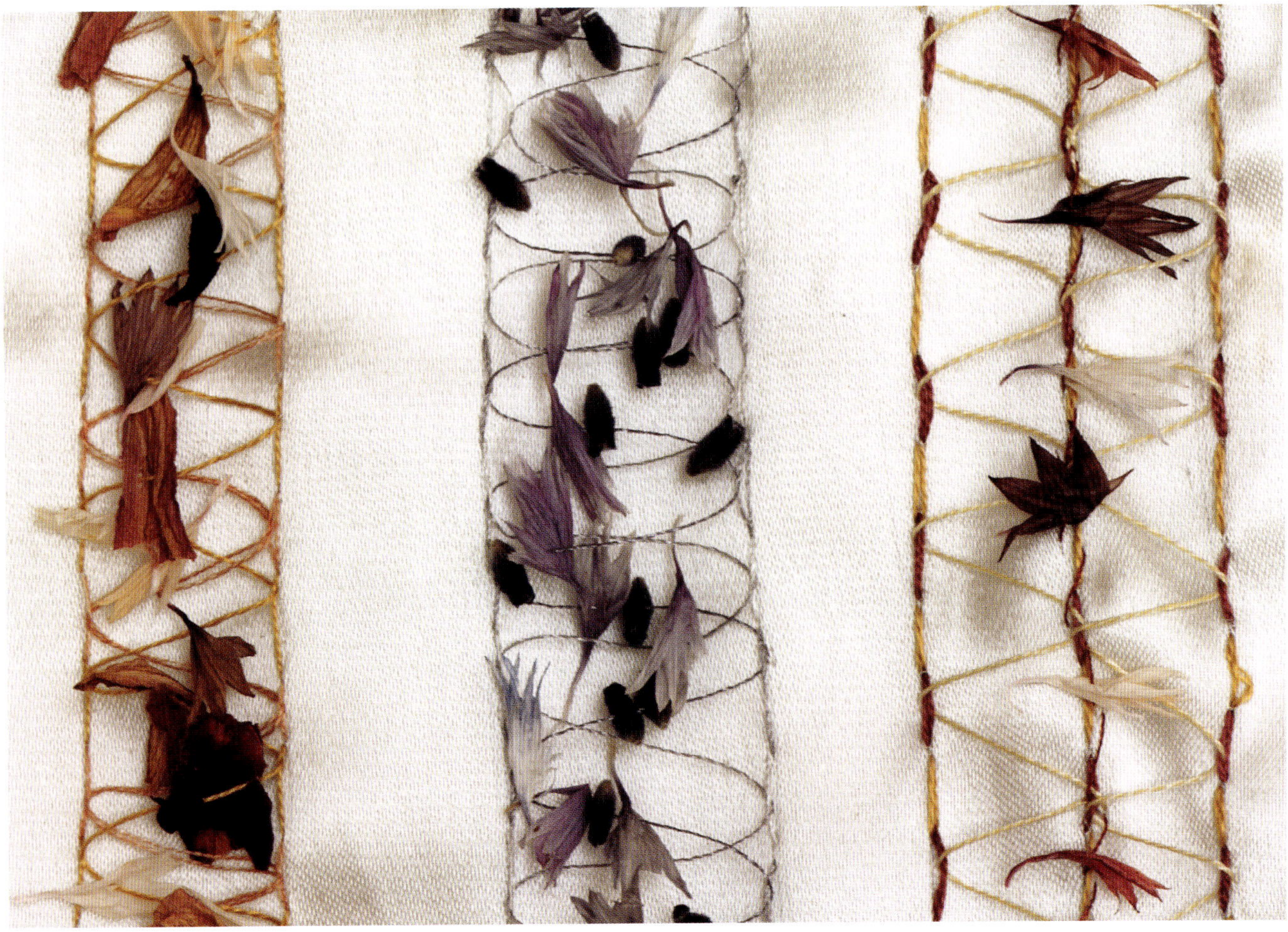

Woven Interlace

USING A MIX OF PETALS

You can also use the interlace stitch to create a free-flowing pattern where threads criss-cross and interweave between each other. This process allows you to work more intuitively, adding your floral embellishments as you wish.

STITCH STEPS . . .

1. Pick two contrasting colour threads. With your first colour, stitch two staggered lines of running stitches, with even gaps between the stitches.
2. Switch to your second colour thread and fill the gaps between your first set of running stitches with stitches in your contrasting thread.
3. Return to your first colour thread and take your needle through the back of the cloth on the left-hand side of your first running stitch in colour one.
4. Then weave in and out between the running stitches in this same colour on lines one and two – not going back through the cloth, only weaving behind the stitches.
5. Now, using your second colour thread, go back to the start of line two and take your needle up through the back of the cloth, through the centre of your first running stitch in this same colour.
6. You will now repeat the process of weaving in and out of the same colour running stitches along your two lines, but this time adding your petal embellishments as you go so they are woven along the line of thread.

Now you have the techniques, you're not limited to using just these materials. Allow your curious mind to wander – gather and explore plant materials that you find enticing and start to form your own library of embroidered floral embellishments.

BELOW *Holding a Garden in My Hands* (2023). Dried flora embroidered on silk organza dyed with chamomile.

OPPOSITE A detail in Katerina's studio, embroidery samples and dried flowers pinned at her desk.

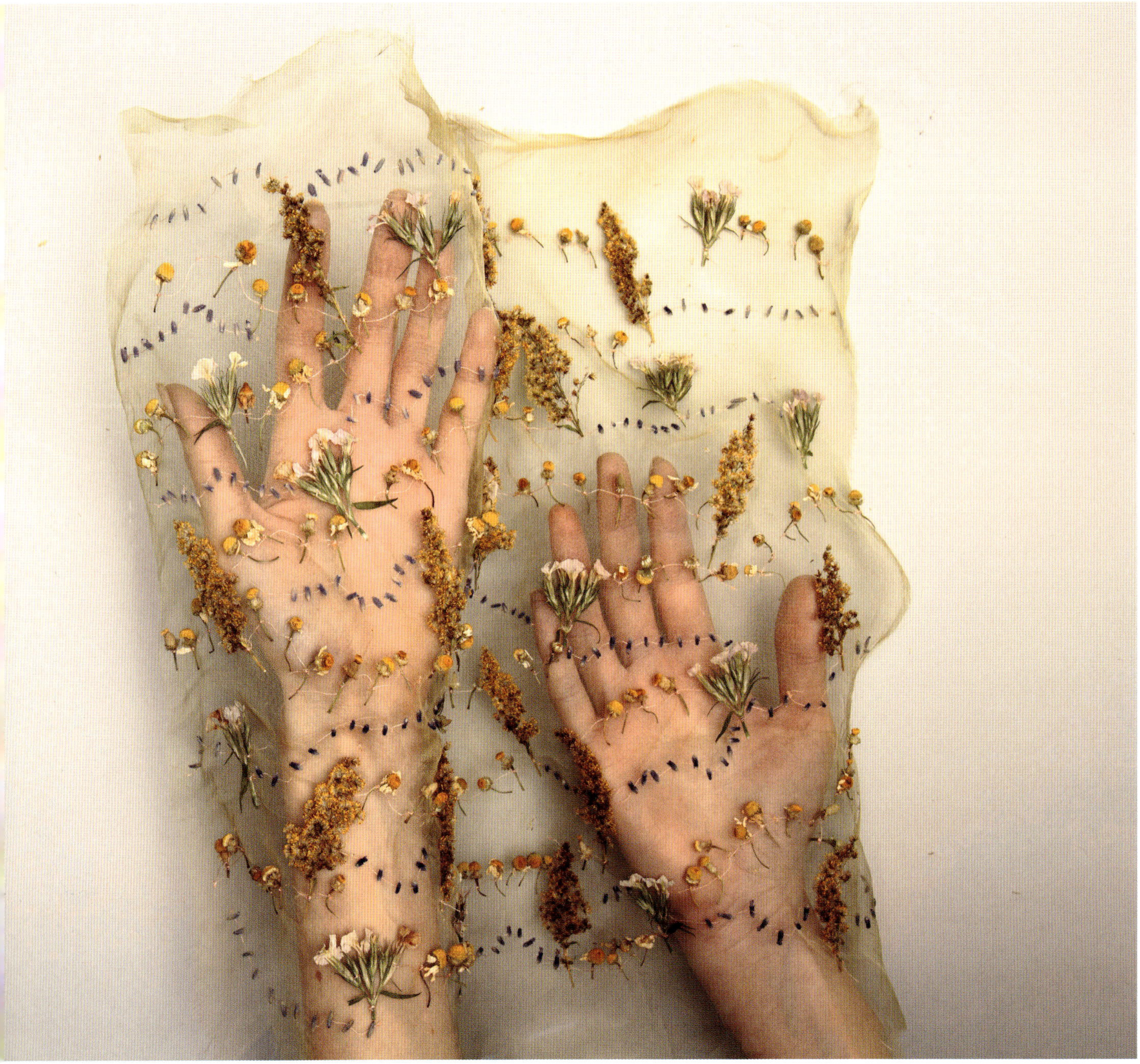

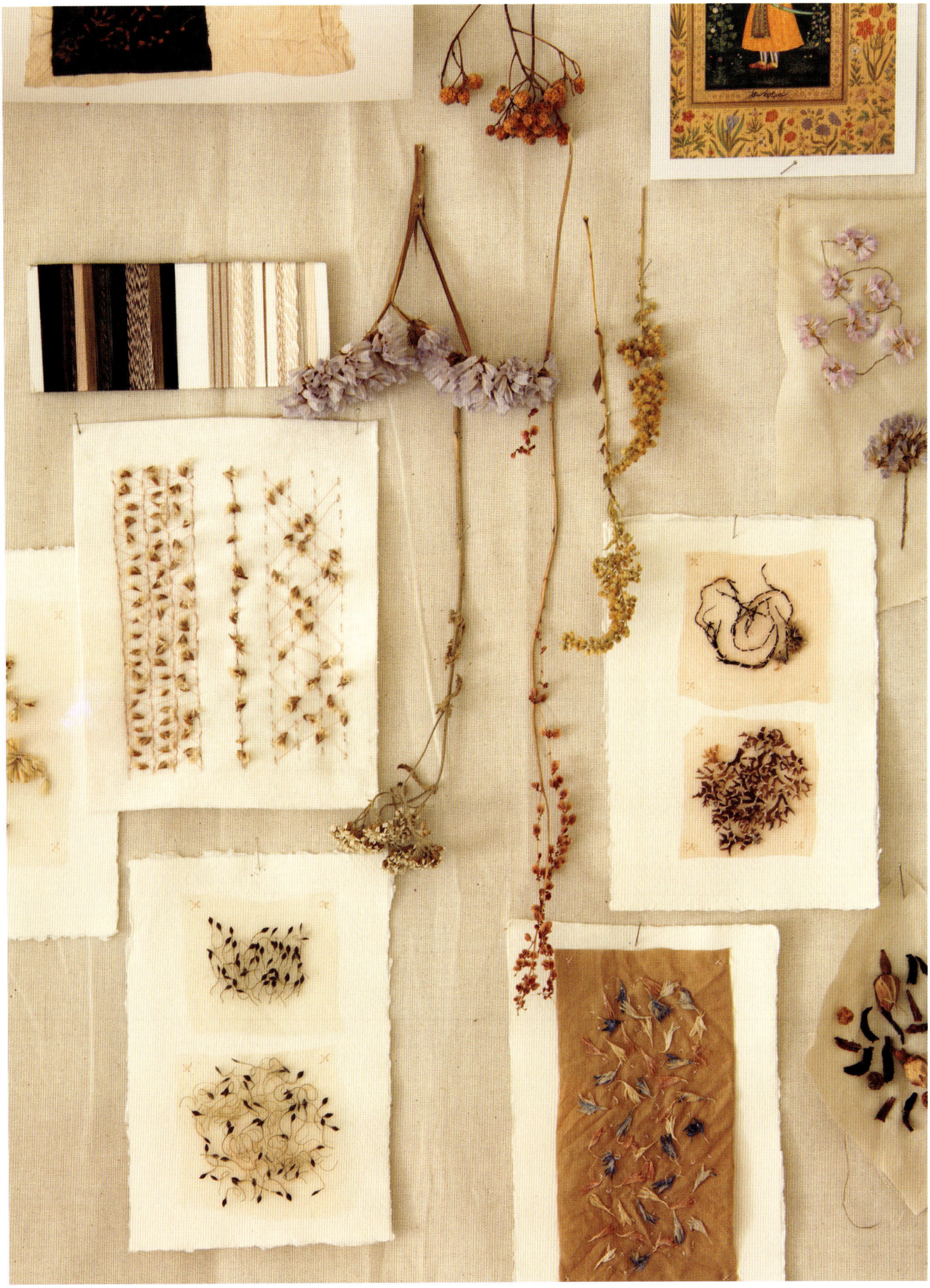

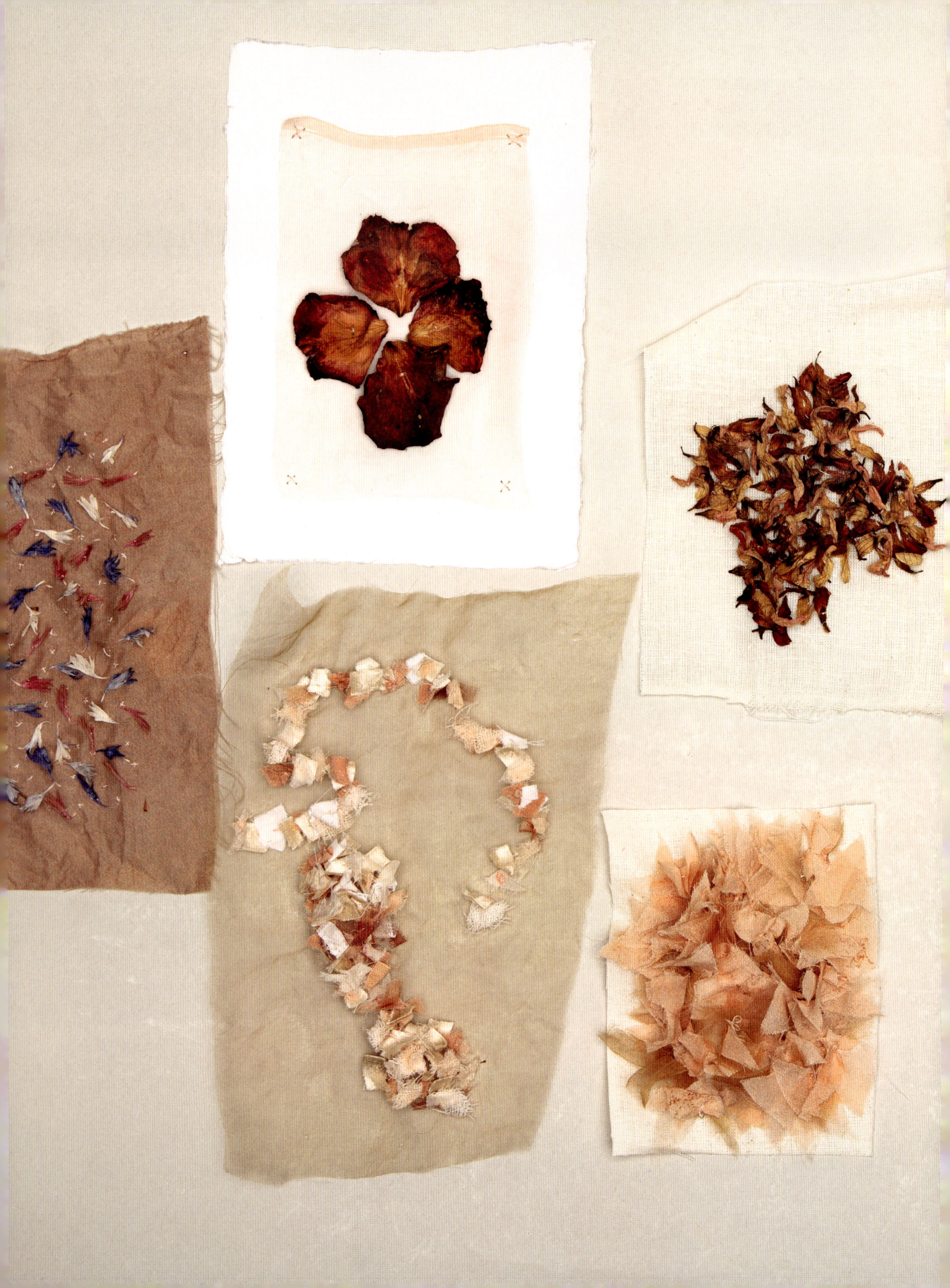

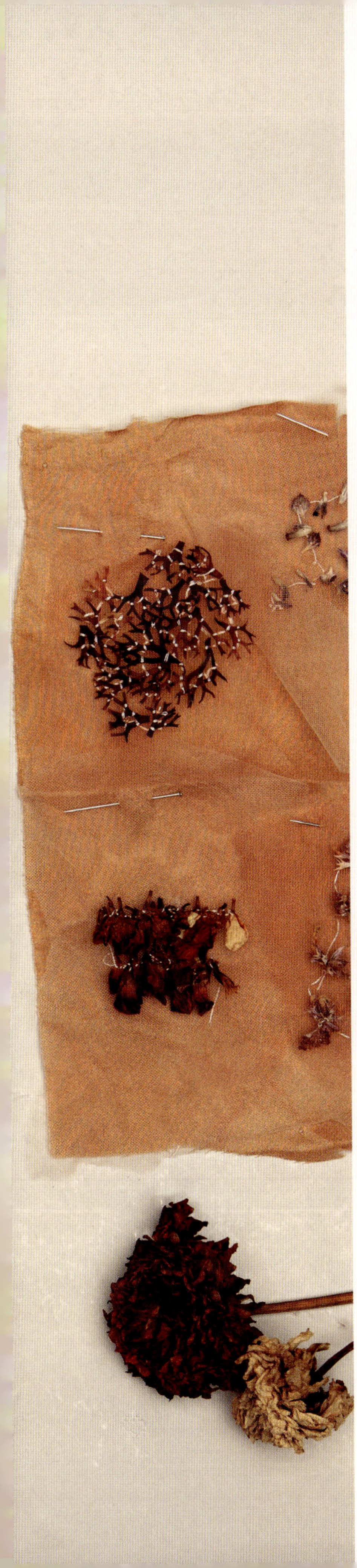

DYEING WITH PLANTS

'The value of living colour is to appreciate and treasure the inherent uniqueness of nature.'

JASON LOGAN

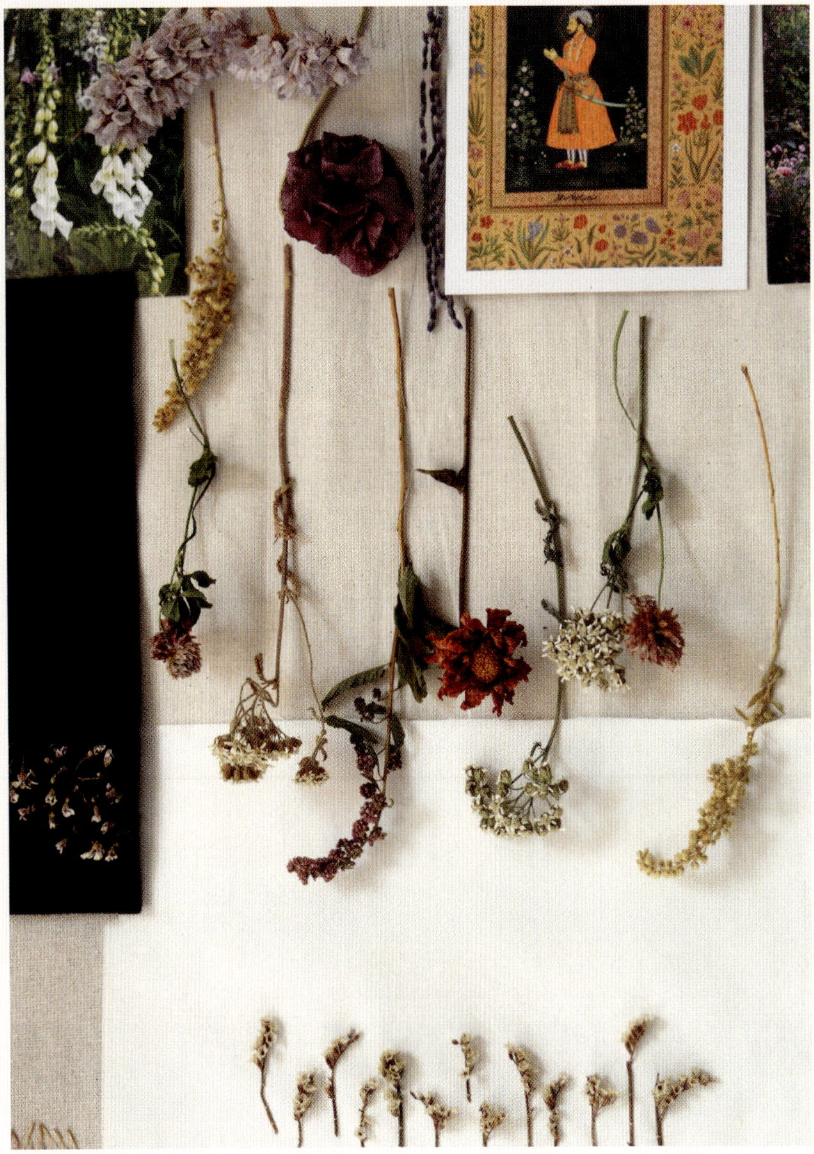

The plants referenced in this book, or those that you can forage for locally, not only will provide you with interesting embellishments but also offer natural dyes to colour your own threads and fabrics. Once you have mastered the stitch techniques, you can then progress to dyeing or eco-printing your own base cloths to then embroider onto.

I enjoy exploring natural colour through an artistic and experimental approach. Rather than aiming for precise or repeatable shades, I embrace the unpredictability of the process. I love throwing my materials in the dye pot and seeing what happens and what colour I achieve.

It is important that you ensure your textiles – cloths and yarns – are only natural fibres. I personally like to work with silk for stitching. Silk takes dye very well and you are able to achieve a rich depth of shade which can be more difficult with other fibres. Cotton and wool also dye well. Linen is notably harder to dye, so you would find it works best to select a natural dye material with a strong colour, such as indigo.

When selecting my dye materials, I try to always look for those that are available to me at that season – blackberries in mid-summer for a cool purple, pine in late autumn for a rich ochre, for example. But you can also store many dye materials for use later in the year by keeping them in your freezer. This works well for plant materials such as berries and rhubarb leaves.

Natural dyeing is sensorial, as we experience the plants not only with our eyes but through our other senses too. The dyeing process unlocks the rich aromas of the plants and so we start to see, smell, touch and connect with these materials in a more intimate way. My personal favourite dyes to work with are the herbal plants that I grow – lavender, rosemary, chamomile – they offer a soothing scent while simmering away and result in subtle, calm tones that can range from pale yellows to deeper purples.

When dyeing with plants it is important to remember the colour you achieve can often differ each time. This can be affected by a number of things, such as the variety of the plant, the soil conditions it has grown in, the level of exposure the plant had to the sun, the time of year you harvest the material, and whether you dye with your plant material fresh or dried.

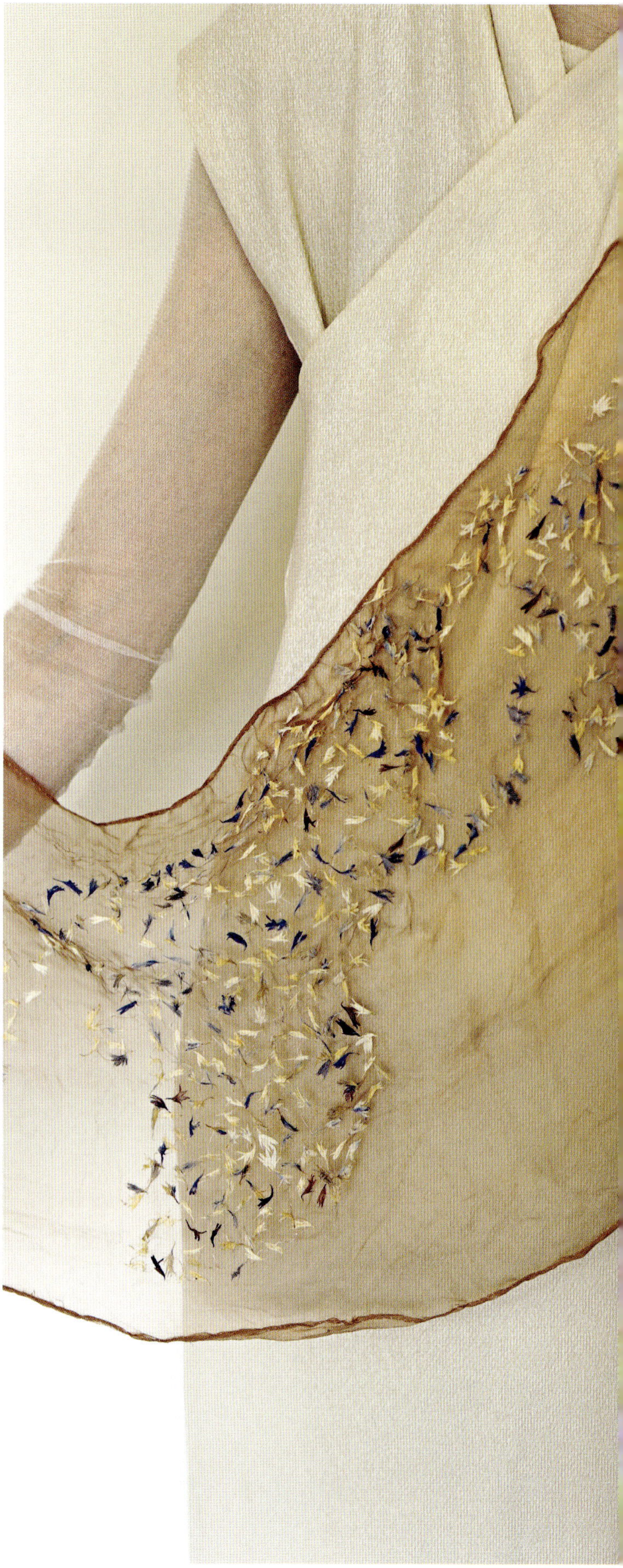

RIGHT *Cornflower Scarf* (2023). Hand-embroidered cornflower petals on silk organza dyed with hibiscus.

Dye Preparation: Mordanting

Before beginning the natural dyeing or eco-printing process, your threads and fabrics need some preparation. Natural dyes fall into two main categories: adjective dyes and substantive dyes. Adjective dyes are those that require a mordant (fixative) because the dye molecule is not strong enough to chemically bond the colour from the natural material to the textile. These include dyes such as marigold and roses. Substantive dyes on the other hand do not require a binding agent, their chemical composition is strong enough and they can be used without a mordant. Examples of substantive dyes are indigo and acorns.

Thus, for adjective dyes, you will need to prepare your cloth and yarn through mordanting. Mordanting is the process of treating your fibres so that they bond more successfully with natural dyes, resulting in long-lasting, vivid colour. The following example dye bath and eco-printing process use rosemary, marigold and roses, which are adjective dyes and require a mordant.

The most popular and widely used mordant is alum, because it is proven to yield the best results. However, alum is a chemical, and I prefer to keep my dyeing and printing processes chemical-free. Some examples of natural, chemical-free mordants are green tea leaves, rhubarb leaves and soya milk. In the following natural dye and eco-printing techniques, I will be using pre-mordanted threads and cloths treated with soya milk.

Mordanting with Soya Milk

YOU WILL NEED . . .

- Pot
- Measuring jug
- Yarn and cloths to dye. I dyed 5 pieces of silk and two pieces of cotton, each approximately 21 x 30cm (8¼ x 12in) and 4 skeins of silk embroidery thread, each 8m (26¼ft) long.
- Soya milk

STEPS . . .

1. Begin by soaking your yarn then scouring your cloth or yarn in a warm bowl of water with a neutral soap. The scouring process removes any coatings on the cloth.

2. Prepare your soya milk mordant bath using a ratio of 1:4, one part soya milk to four parts water. The amount of liquid you need will depend on your quantity of cloth; the cloth should be fully submerged, if it is not, simply make up a larger quantity. Then transfer the cloth or yarn to the soya milk bath and leave for 12 hours. After that time you can remove the materials, wring out and leave flat to dry.

TIP: *For the best dye results, complete the mordant process one week prior to dyeing, as the activation process continues to deepen as the cloth dries out.*

Dyeing with Rosemary

Dyeing with rosemary will fill your kitchen with an intoxicating aroma. I find the herbal, evergreen notes of this plant immediately soothe my mind. It is a magical process. Sometimes I have achieved rich purples, sometimes earthy greens – the unexpected results always surprise me.

YOU WILL NEED . . .

- Rosemary (250g/9oz)
- Dye pot (3-litre/5¼-pint saucepan)
- Measuring jug
- Rainwater (2 litres/ 3½ pints)
- Heat source (hob)
- Muslin cloth (to be used as a strainer)
- Salt (150g/5½oz)
- Pre-mordanted yarn and cloths to dye (I will be adding my 5 pieces of silk and 4 skeins of silk embroidery thread)
- Wooden dowel for stirring
- Clean pot
- Neutral soap

STEPS . . .

1. Cut your sprigs of rosemary. The more you add to the dye bath, the more intense the colour will be, but around 250g (9oz) for this 2-litre (3½-pint) dye bath will suffice. You can also use dried rosemary you have harvested previously.

2. Add the rosemary to your dye pot and cover it with your rainwater. Leave this for 12 hours to soak to slowly soften the leaves and draw out the colour.

3. You may need to add some more water to ensure that the rosemary is fully submerged. Place your pot onto your heat source – in this case I am using a hob. Turn on your hob to a medium heat. The key is to gently heat the rosemary, slower, for longer, rather than boiling it. Once the dye bath is gently bubbling, turn down the heat. Cover the dye pot and leave to simmer for two hours.

4. After two hours, remove the rosemary and use the muslin cloth to strain the leaves and release as much water/colour back into the dye pot as you can.

5. Add the salt and gently stir until it has completely dissolved.

6. You are now ready to add your textiles. Soak your materials first so they are already wet when they enter the dye bath. Submerge in the bath and keep gently stirring with your wooden dowel for 15 minutes.

7. Your choice of material and preference of colour intensity will determine the length of time in the dye bath. I dye fine silk threads and silk organza cloth. Silk takes colour quickly, so 15–30 minutes in a dye bath can often be enough to achieve my desired tone. Cottons, linens and wool will take longer. Remember, the shade you see when wet will dry two shades lighter.

8. Transfer your materials to a clean pot, and wash thoroughly with neutral soap in cool water. Once the water runs clean, then wash in warm water. You might wish to add some fabric softener here to give the cloth a nice, softer handle. Wring out and leave to air dry out of direct sunlight.

TIP: *If you can, leave a bucket or trough in your garden and collect rainwater. This can be used for the mordanting and natural dye processes.*

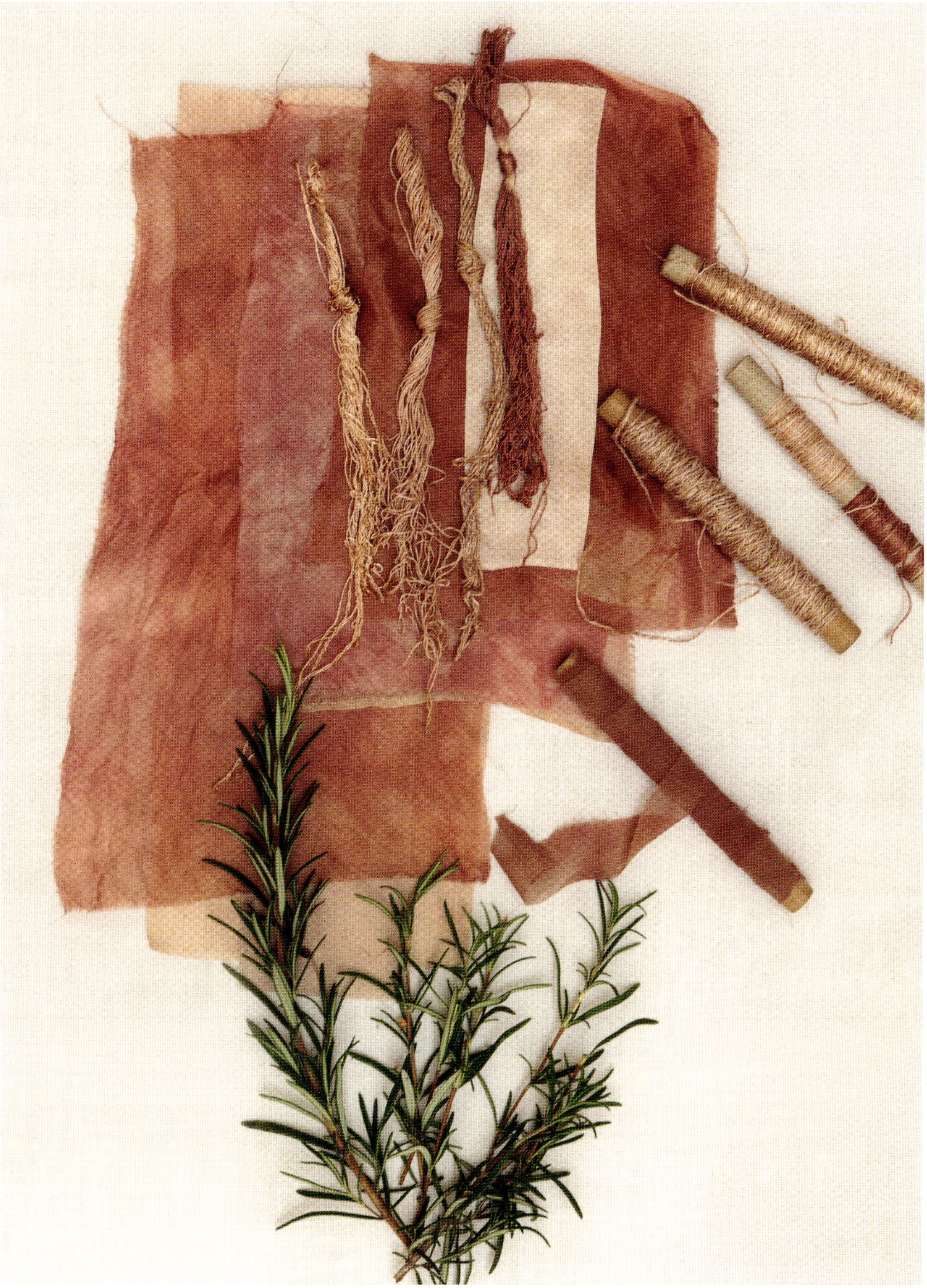

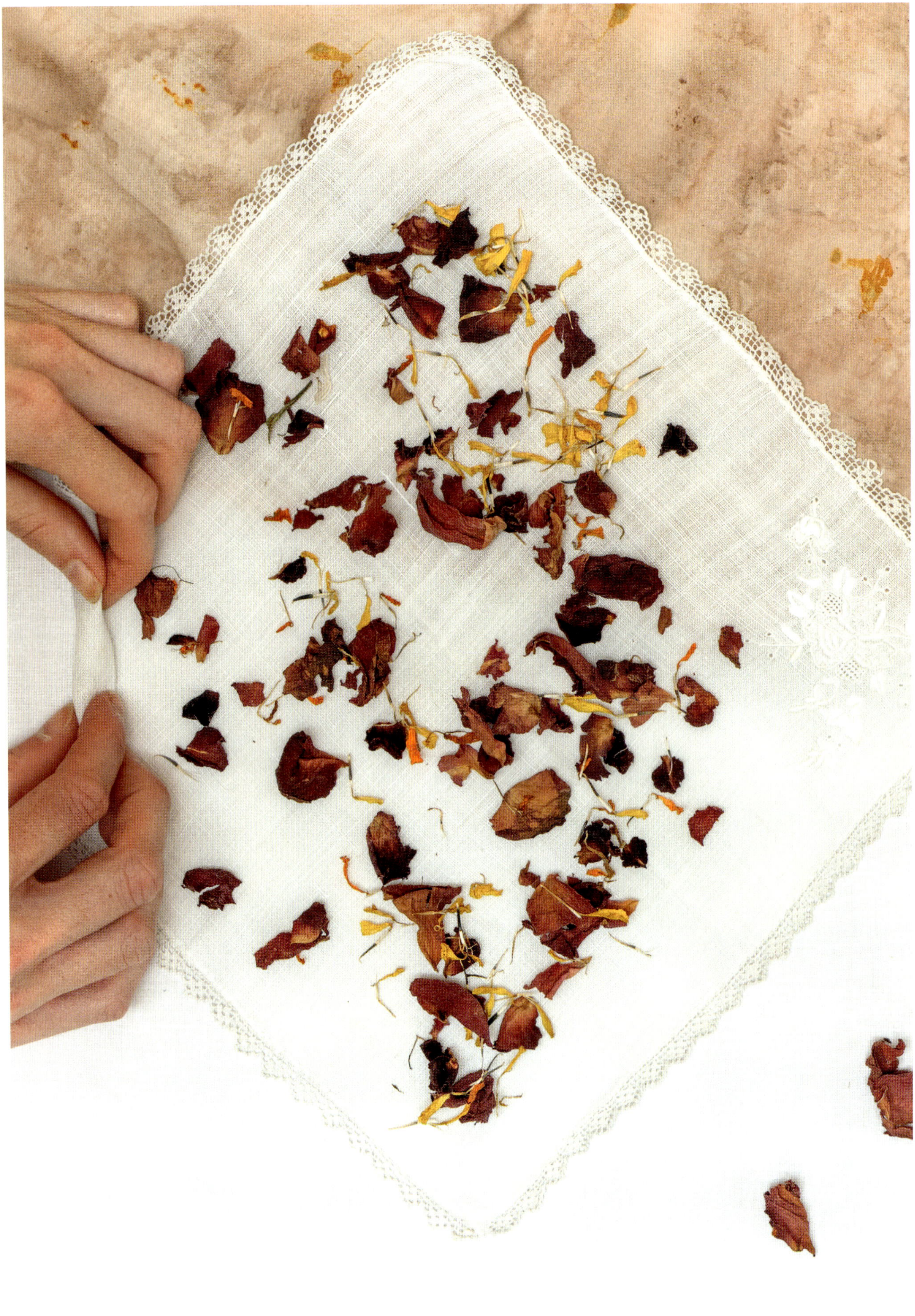

Printing with Plants

USING ROSE AND MARIGOLD PETALS

Eco-printing is the process of transferring colour directly from a flower or plant to a textile through steam. If you take a walk during summer around your local park or even just down the street, you will find fallen petals from flowers such as roses, dahlias and hollyhocks. Gathering these fallen petals will provide you with an excellent array of materials and natural colour to explore with this technique. For this process you can work either with fresh or dried petals.

YOU WILL NEED . . .

- Pot
- White vinegar
- Fabric (pre-mordanted)
- Flowers or leaves
- Dowel rod
- Cotton string or bandage
- Steamer
- Heat source (hob)
- Neutral soap

STEPS . . .

1. Soak your mordanted fabrics in diluted white vinegar (use one part vinegar to four parts water) for an hour prior to dyeing. This will work as a fixative to help set the colour.
2. Remove your fabric from the vinegar solution and wring as much excess moisture out as possible. Lay the fabric on a flat surface and smooth out any wrinkles.
3. Cover your cloth with your petals.
4. Starting at the bottom, roll your pile around the dowel as tightly as possible. Bundles can be rolled without a dowel but expect the prints to be a bit messier.
5. Wrap your bundle. To achieve clean prints, you can wrap a bandage around the bundle. However, you can also secure it simply with cotton string.
6. Now it's time to steam your bundle. Place it in a steamer and heat for anywhere from 15 minutes to 2 hours; this will depend on the intensity of shade you desire.
7. Wash with a small amount of neutral soap. At this point, the dye from the flowers has formed a bond with the mordant in the fabric so any dye that washes away is excess.

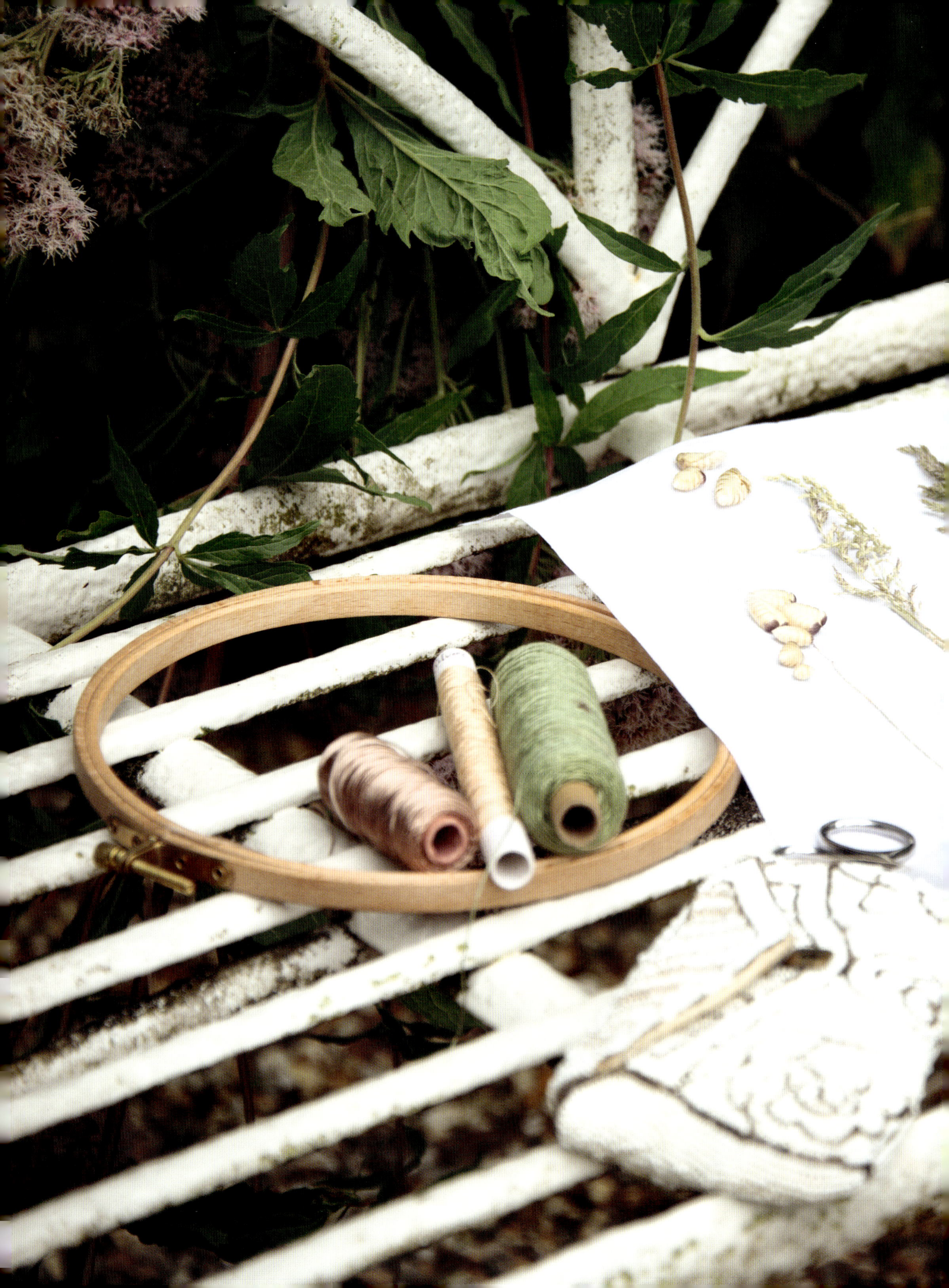

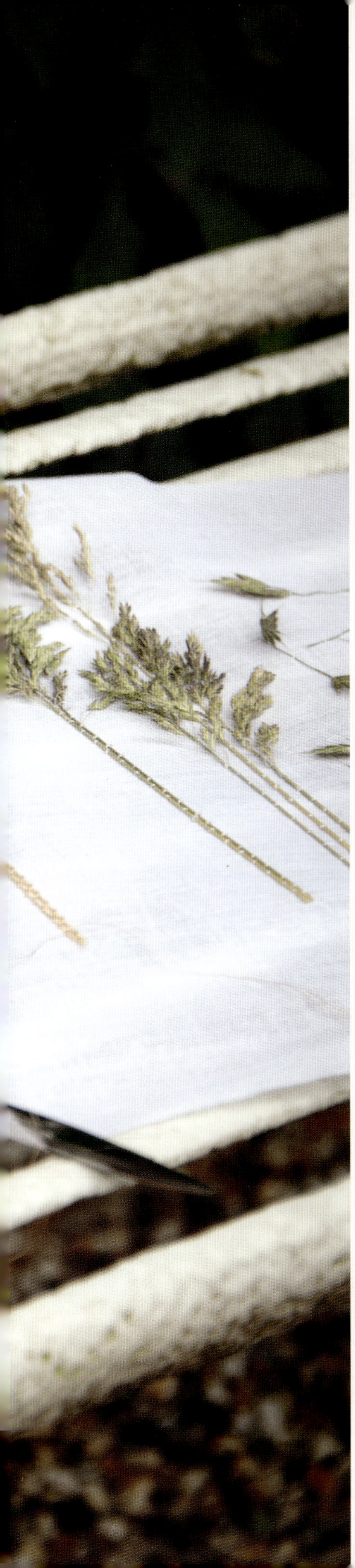

FINDING INSPIRATION

Once you have mastered the delicate hand required in stitching with plant materials and the technical stitches with which they can be incorporated, you will be ready to let your creative individuality flourish. Begin combining plant materials and stitches, exploring new base cloths and threads, working on a larger scale, and maybe even developing a sacred story for your pieces. There are many ways in which you can find inspiration.

'In this moment, I'm aware, living as I do in the world, that I am an atom in the universe, possessing infinite possibilities of development. And I want to explore these possibilities.'

HILMA AF KLINT

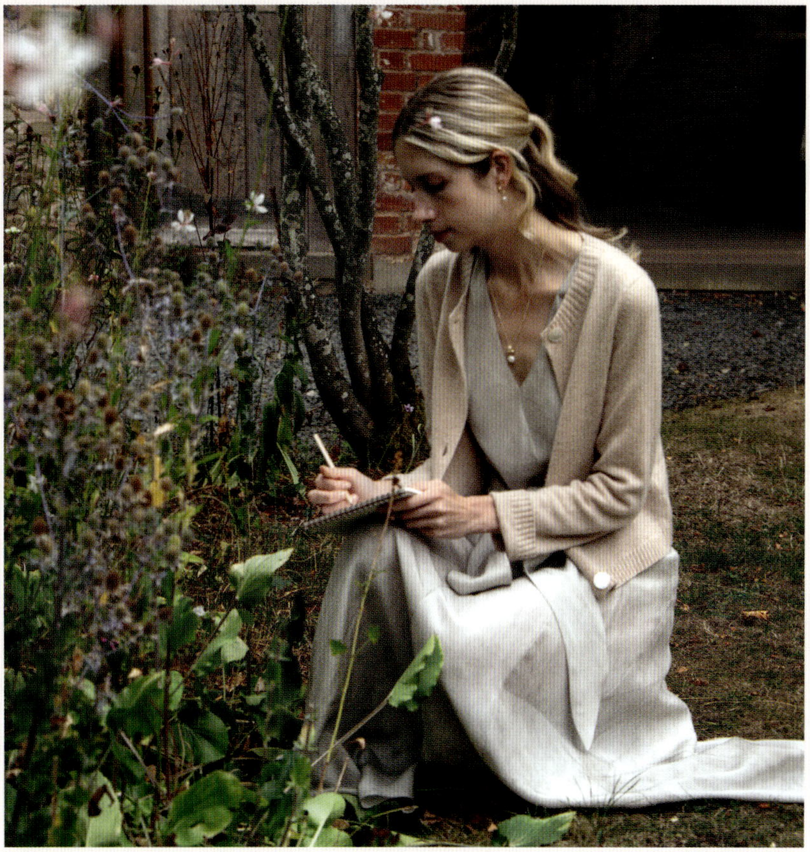

Working Intuitively

I always work intuitively. I may have a vague idea in mind, knowing what materials I want to work with and combine together, and what cloth and threads I will use, but I do not often plan the placement of the materials. I allow the process to guide me, to come together gradually and evolve organically into a precious piece of art that captures nature's instinct.

Summer Days Won't Last Forever (2025) is an example of just this process. I embroidered peach achillea flowers, cornflower petals in pink and white, and soft green-white lavender seeds with cream and rose silk thread onto silk georgette. I hand-stitched using the double darning technique. The flow of lines was not planned; I simply knew that I wanted the petals to cascade from one corner and gradually disperse down the cloth.

This piece was created in the early days of August. For me, August is a time when a sense of melancholy sets in. The flowers are still blooming but the signs of the last weeks of summer come through, the light levels begin to drop, and the wildflower meadows have come to an end. Stitching this piece was a way to remind me to be present in the last moments of enjoying my flowers, but not to hold on to them too tightly. Flowers will blossom again next year, so it is time to let go and embrace the new season coming.

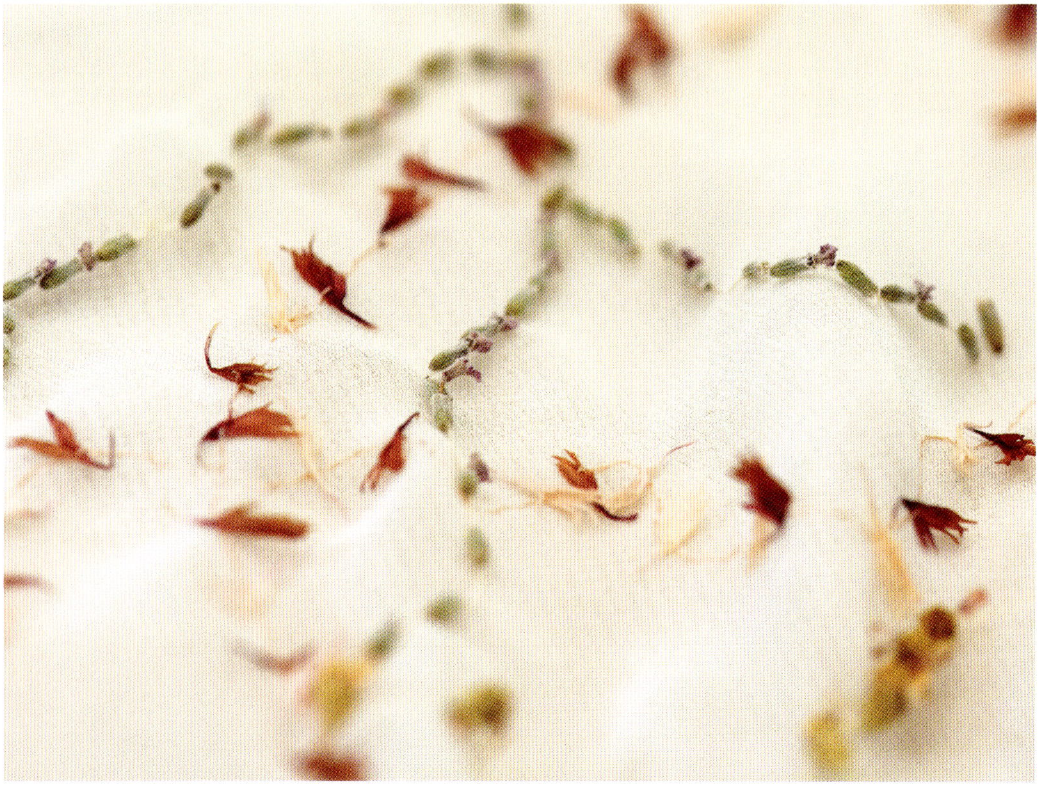

LEFT AND OPPOSITE
Summer Days Won't Last Forever (2025). Lavender, cornflowers and achillea, hand-embroidered with silk thread on silk georgette.

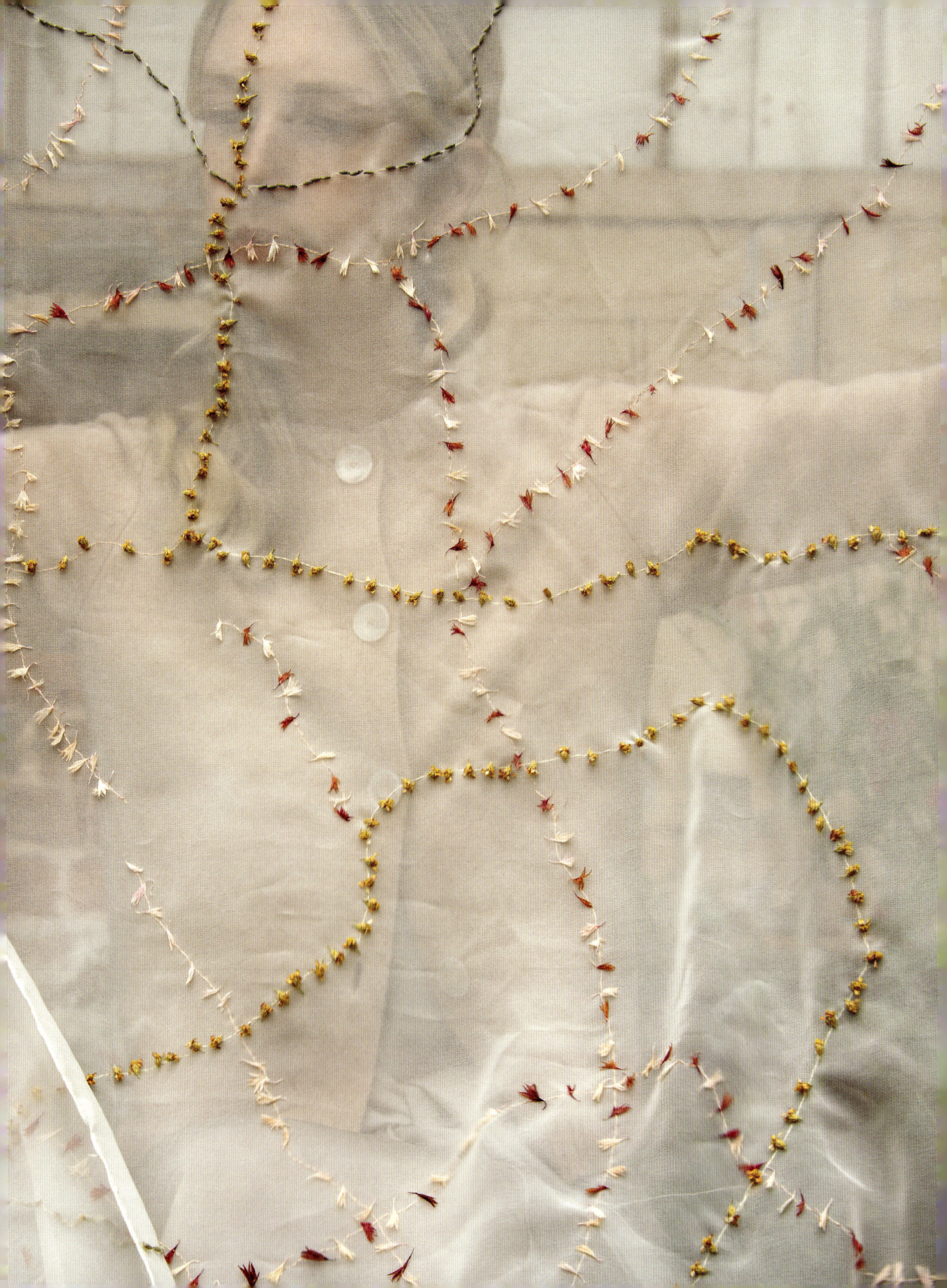

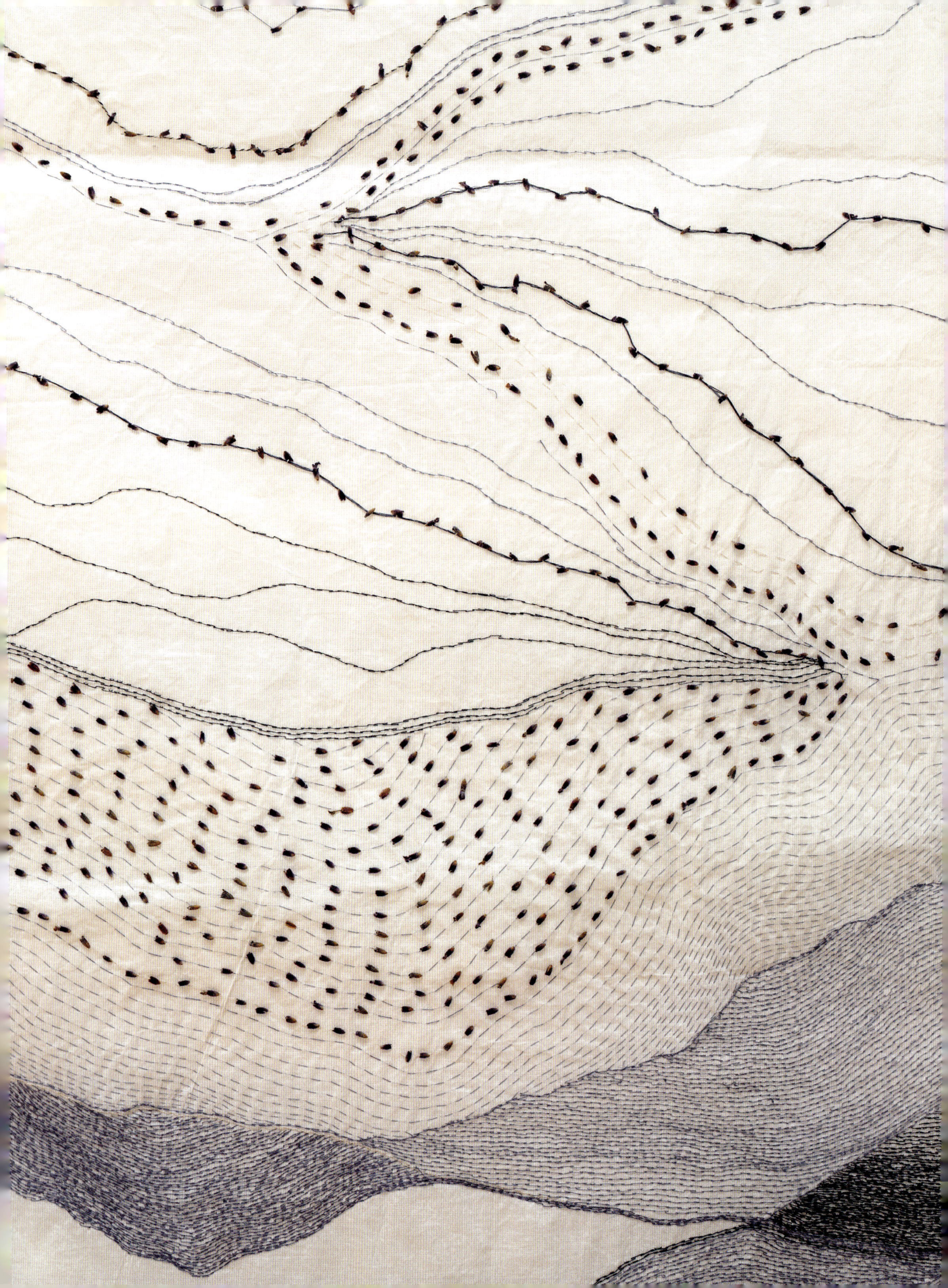

Working on Commissions

For me, working on commissions or exhibition pieces is a way of working through thoughts about ecological conversations and our responsibilities to act as stewards of our Earth and the precious natural resources it gifts us.

Lavender on the Floodlines (2024) was made specially for the group exhibition *Subtle Connections: Water and the Space in Between*, at Ruup & Form Gallery in London. The exhibition responded to water as a symbol of life, renewal, migration and survival, offering reflections on its role in human and ecological contexts.

For this piece, I explored my recent relocation to the countryside and learning about my new landscape. This is an area rich with sacred, untouched beauty, but the rising river levels and extreme flooding in Worcestershire have presented great concerns to the land. Lavender is a plant that is known to grow successfully in a dry Mediterranean climate; thus the damp, wet soil of this region presented an unlikely environment for this plant to thrive in. Yet still, on the floodlines of Worcestershire, my seeds of lavender bloomed.

Through acts of *metta* (a Buddhist teaching and Pali for 'loving kindness'), gentle nurturing and compassion, I put my faith in nature, and patiently waited in hope, and nature rewarded me with the soothing seeds and small blue gems of lavender. But nature is warning us, with waves and water beyond what our land can endure. This work is a calling for kindness, to touch our Earth with tenderness.

In this piece, homegrown seeds of English lavender, grown, harvested and dried in Worcestershire in 2024, were hand-stitched using the interlacing technique on cotton organdie. The piece was completed with heavy kantha stitching to represent the Malvern Hills.

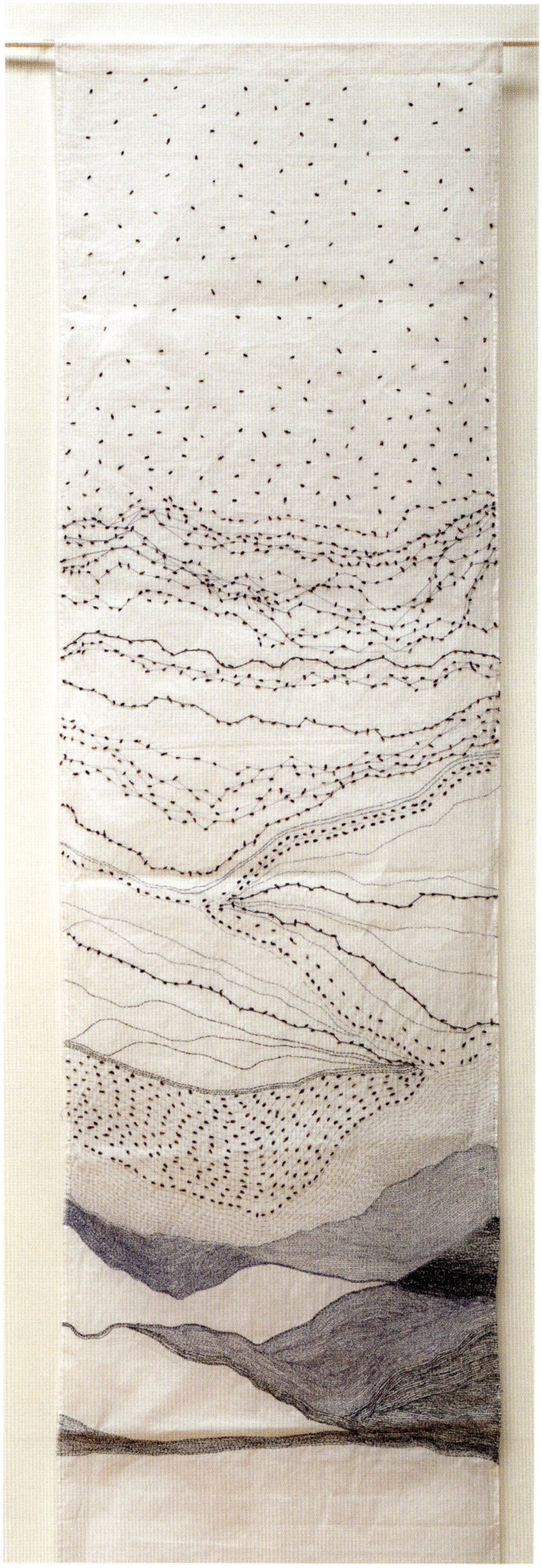

ABOVE AND OPPOSITE
Lavender on the Floodlines (2024). Lavender seeds, hand-embroidered kantha stitching with linen thread on cotton organdie.

Inspiration from Foraged Textiles

Foraging isn't just something I do to gather plants; it's also how I source many of the textile materials I work with. I am always on the lookout for fabrics, threads and yarns to work with, and flea markets and antique fairs are often where I find the most interesting one-of-a-kind textiles. In Malvern, the Three Counties Flea & Collectors Fair is a gem, and the largest flea fair in the UK.

I can always find threads and fabrics that each have their own unique story, with signs of wear and age that offer individuality to each piece I create. Some threads might only have less than a metre remaining, and their finite nature makes them that much more precious. Others may have faded ombré qualities to parts of the fabric; this effect of exposure to natural light imbues them with a sense of age and life.

There's something deeply satisfying about uncovering haberdashery items tucked away in forgotten boxes. I encourage you to seek out your local flea markets and see what hidden treasures you might find.

RIGHT Collection of silk threads and dried floral materials at Katerina's desk.

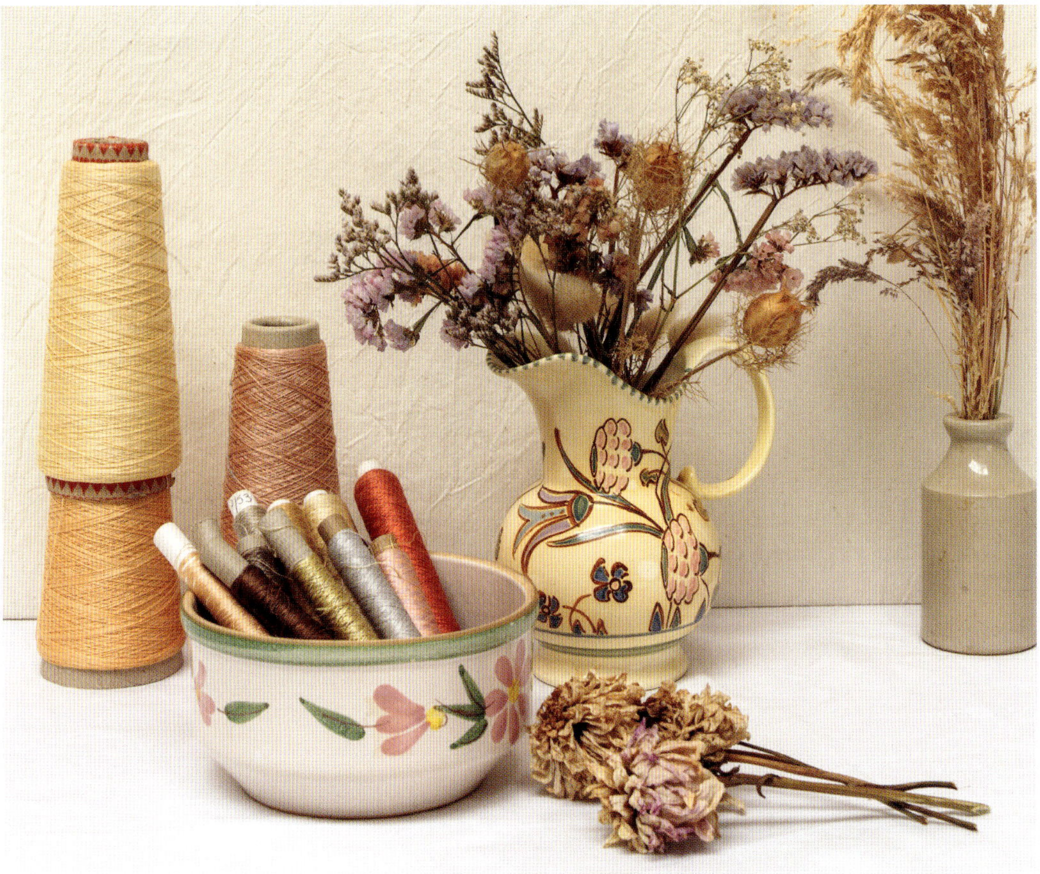

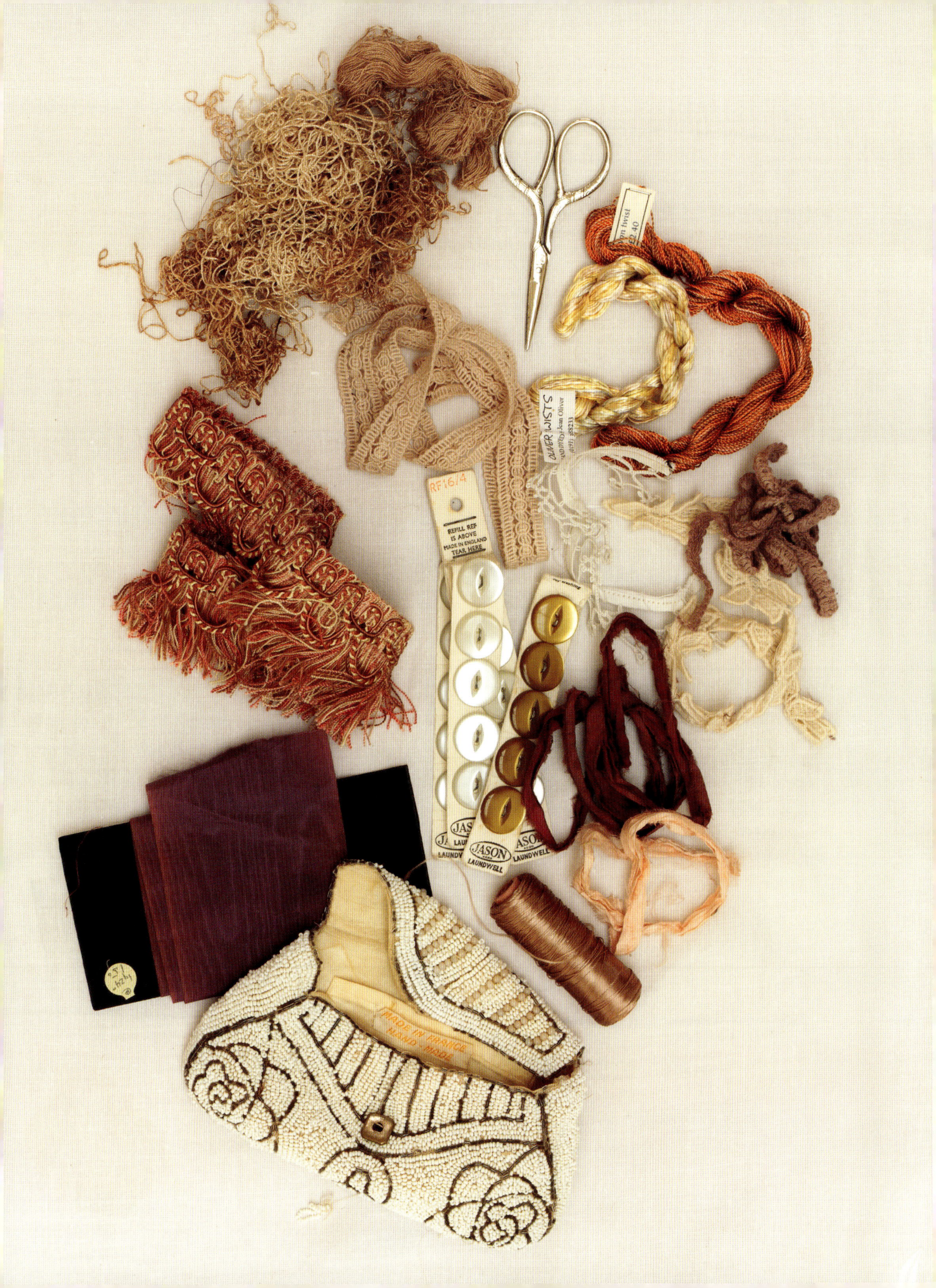
RF16/4
REFILL REF
IS ABOVE
MADE IN ENGLAND
TEAR HERE
OLIVER TWISTS
JASON
LAUNDWELL
JASON
LAUNDWELL
MADE IN FRANCE
HAND-MADE

Inspiration for Colour Palettes

Inspiration for the colour palette of a new work will often come to me when I am not actively searching for it. While I'm taking my daily walk, a wild flower or a single leaf might glisten in the distance and catch my eye, so I will return to my studio desk and pin it to my board. When you select an individual flower or plant, remove it from its context and set it against a neutral and quiet backdrop, you will discover the wealth of tones within that one tiny part of nature.

From my training as a textile designer, I learned to observe colour closely. Try sitting with a paintbrush or threads in one hand and your object of study (in this case your plant) in the other, concentrating on tonality, light, dark, shade, quality of colour. Is it matte? Shiny? Coarse? And what material might reflect this? Cotton? Silk? Linen? And what are the proportions of colour in the plant? Considering your colours in this way will allow you to set a colour palette for your design so you can pair together pleasing tones of threads, cloths and floral materials.

Making a thread wrap is a simple exercise for planning your colour palette. It allows you to carefully consider and plan out your thread colours before you begin a piece of work. The repetitive action of wrapping threads around a piece of card and twisting threads together to achieve subtle tones is incredibly pleasing.

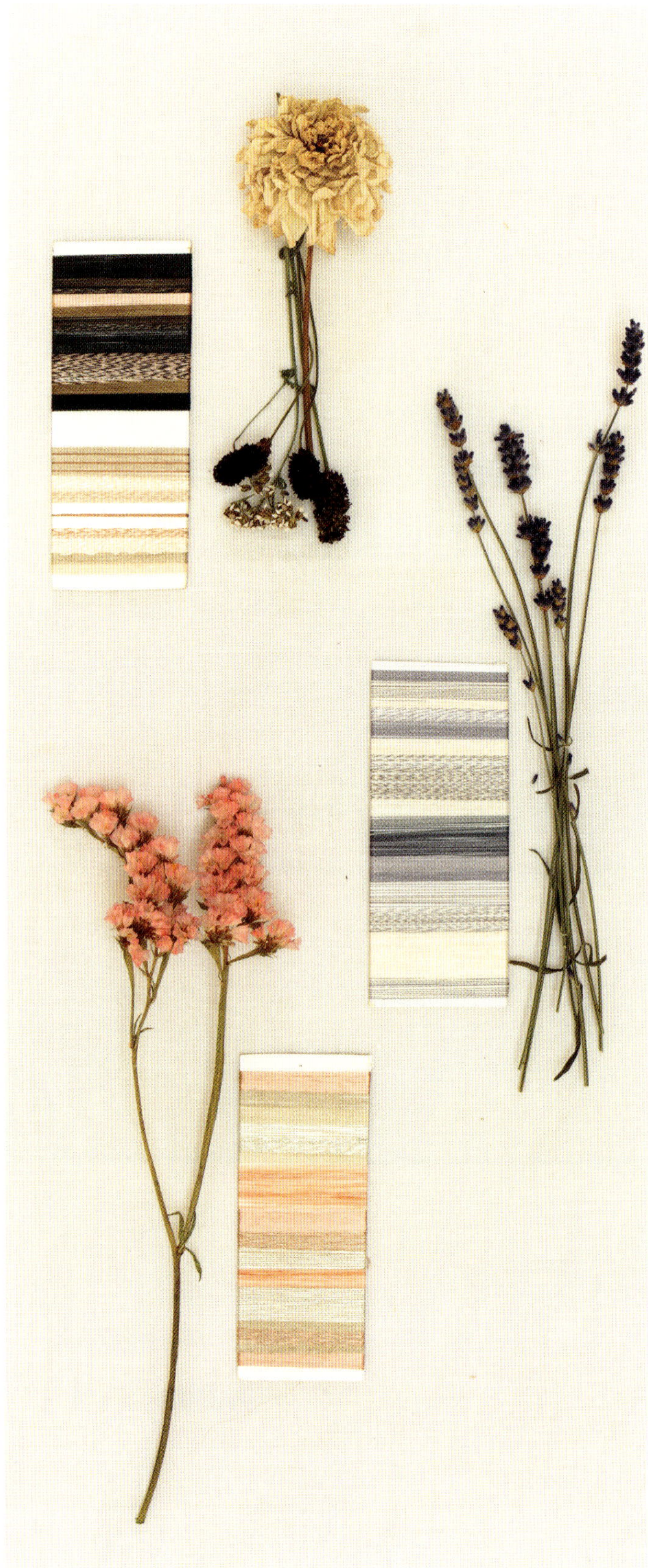

YOU WILL NEED . . .

- Rectangular strip of thick card (rigid enough so it won't bend)
- Selection of threads
- Flower
- Masking tape
- Snips

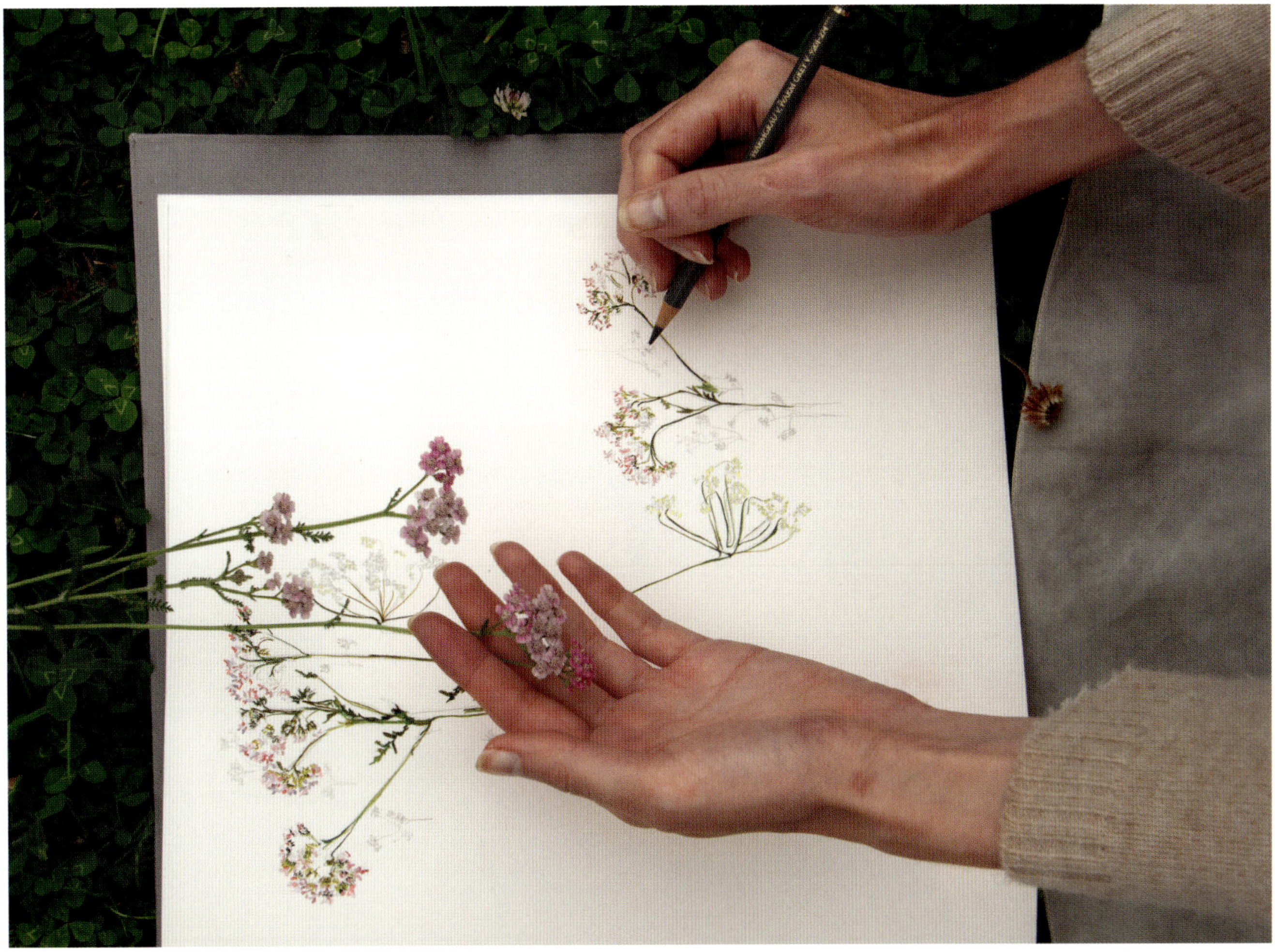

Close Observation for Inspiration

OPPOSITE Silk thread wraps inspired by dried florals.

ABOVE Sketching in the garden at Hellens Manor, Herefordshire.

Spending time observing plants, how they grow, and the organic structures they create can offer inspiration for your embroidery compositions.

Take sweet peas, for example: a sweet pea is a climbing plant; they require the support of a trellis and use their tendrils to wrap around this structure. The delicate stems growing around a rigid bamboo cane with cascading silky flowerheads makes me think of a fine silk green thread wrapped around a thick linen cord with bright pink petals sporadically weaving between the threads.

Time spent in gardens or natural spaces, noticing these small details in both plants and the landscape will provide you with a wealth of creative inspiration to work from. Carry a sketchbook with you wherever you go, recording your thoughts and ideas as they emerge. Make small sketches to document details to later inspire your designs.

Inspiring Locations

Living in the countryside, I am spoiled for choice with beautiful gardens to visit to find inspiration. Here are a couple of my most treasured places.

HELLENS MANOR

Located in the village of Much Marcle in Herefordshire, this is a Tudor mansion surrounded by rural grounds and exquisite gardens. Spring is particularly magical here, after the winter season, when the landscape starts to come alive again with daffodils, orchids, anemones and bluebells, all set against sweeping views of the Malvern Hills and Herefordshire.

What I especially love about this place is the Long Garden, which in June and July is abundant with a rich variety of roses. The contrast between Hellens' structured garden areas and the untamed beauty of the surrounding wildflower meadows reflects a harmonious collaboration with nature. It is a place where beauty can be carefully crafted to create areas of thought-out planting, yet leave room for the wild to thrive, offering us moments of unexpected, untouched wonder. This is a garden I often frequent for slow Sundays, gathering thoughts and planning new ideas to be explored when I return to the studio.

WINTERBOURNE HOUSE AND GARDENS

This peaceful haven sits on the edge of Birmingham city centre and is just minutes from the city's vibrant energy. This early 20th-century suburban villa and garden is a prime example of the Arts and Crafts movement, reflected throughout both the house and garden. Built in 1903, it was once home to John and Margaret Nettlefold. Margaret, inspired by the influence of British horticulturist and garden designer Gertrude Jekyll (1843–1932), created the original garden design.

In 2021, I was the Artist in Residence at Winterbourne. I spent summer days drawing, painting and observing the garden, which offers a vast amount of visual pleasure to explore, including secret passageways leading to hideaways to seek moments of peace and solitude. The gardeners' clever use of colour borders and areas such as the White Garden create a feeling of calm order. Margaret Nettlefold's inspiration from Jekyll's theories on colour drifts within a garden are still apparent at Winterbourne today.

I would find secluded spaces to position myself. While I worked, I would overhear snippets of conversation from passersby, children playing games and running free, and the sounds of wildlife. Working in the garden was an immersive sensory experience. It is these sacred intimate moments between humans and nature that I try to embed within each work I make.

OTHER INSPIRING GARDENS TO VISIT IN THE UK

- **For roses** – Kiftsgate Court, Chipping Campden, Gloucestershire
- **For a walled garden wonder** – Cambo, St Andrews, Scotland
- **For tranquillity and craftsmanship** – Sculpture by the Lakes, Dorchester, Dorset
- **For aroma** – FARMERS' Welsh Lavender, Builth Wells, Wales
- **For ancient topiary** – Levens Hall, Kendal, Cumbria
- **For healing** – Chelsea Physic Garden, London
- **For art and nature combined** – Jupiter Artland, Edinburgh, Scotland
- **For a classic English cottage garden** – New Forest Lavender Garden, Landford, Salisbury

OPPOSITE View from the pergola at Winterbourne House and Garden, Birmingham.

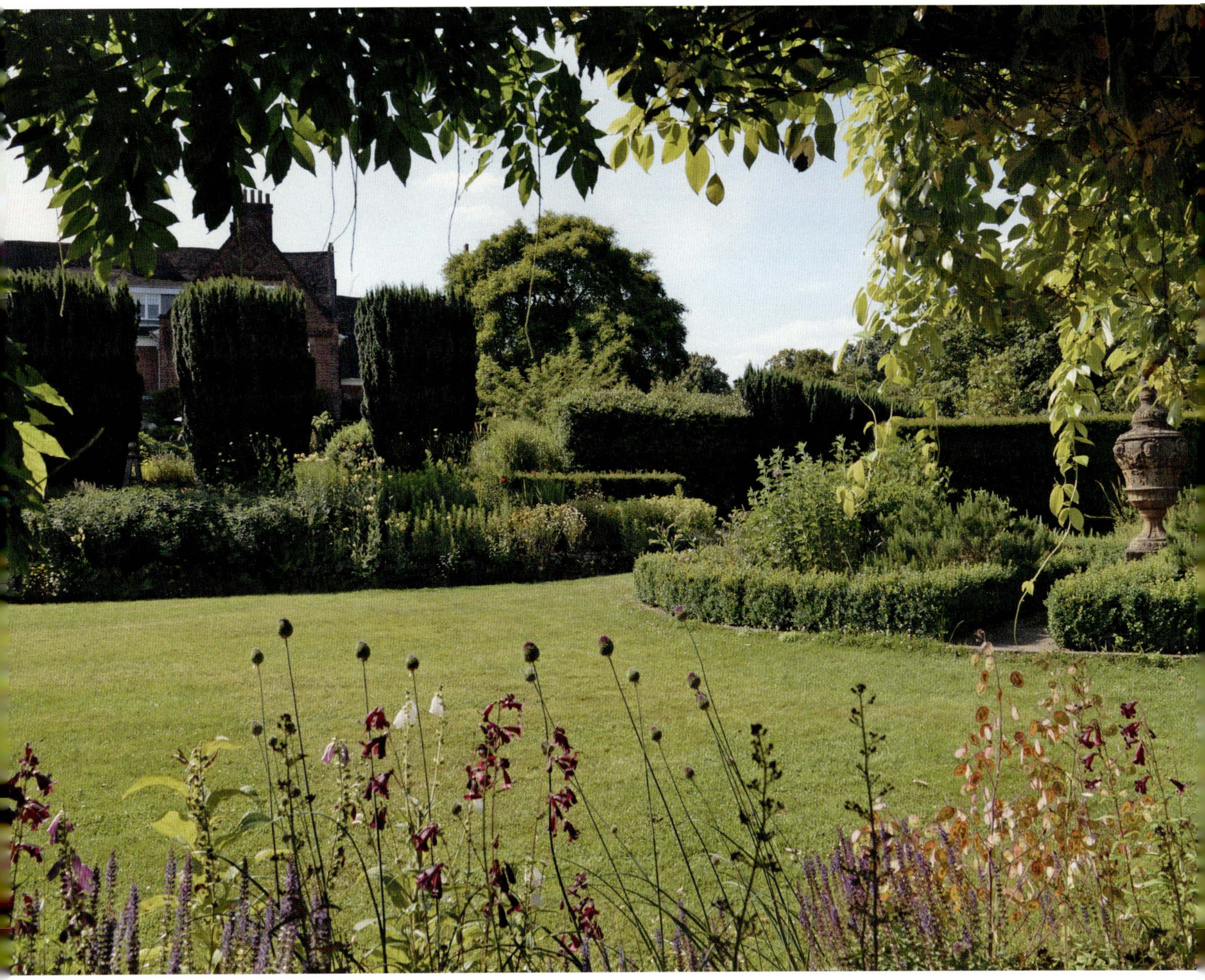

Where Else you Might Find Inspiration from Nature

Nature can offer inspiration all year round, but sometimes, on rainy grey days or in the harshness of winter, our bodies tell us they do not want to go outside. In these moments when the weather is dreary, I like to imagine a garden on a warm summer's day, flowers in bloom, and I get excited about the new growing season to come. Archives, libraries and herbariums can provide excellent sources of inspiration too.

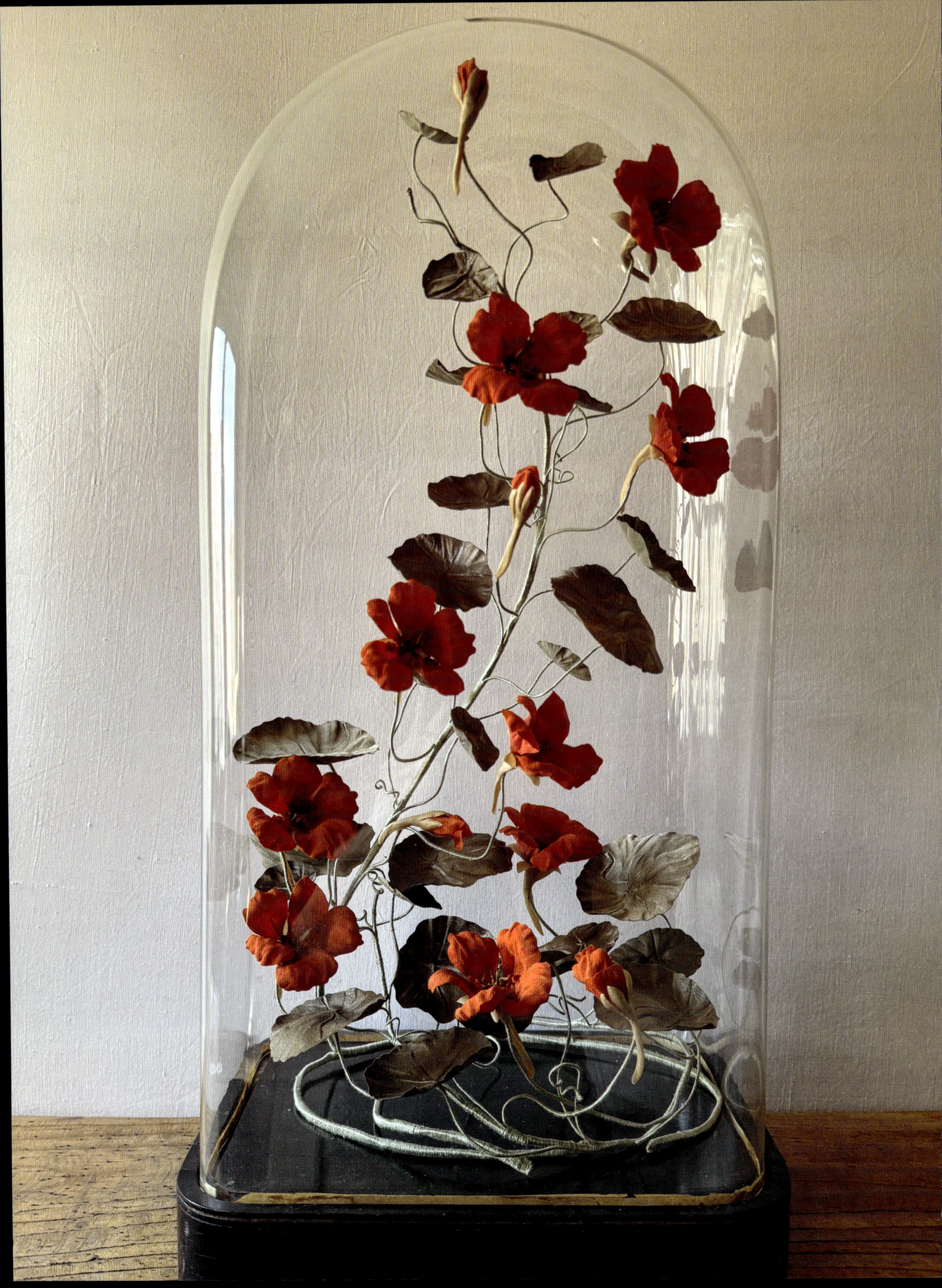

Ana Lamata

'For me, crafting flowers is certainly an invitation to pay closer attention to the delicacy and wonder of nature.'

In the heart of Madrid, just moments from the Royal Palace and the sculpted Jardines de Sabatini, with its neatly trimmed hedges, intricately carved fountains and rose gardens, is the home of hat-maker and silk flower master Ana Lamata.

OPPOSITE *Tropaeolum majus* (2024). Flowers made in crêpe silk dyed with madder root and red wood; stamens, style and ovary painted with rhubarb, weld and indigo. Leaves made in satin silk, and silk ribbon to wrap the stems, all dyed with logwood and weld.

BELOW Hat in beaver felt with silk lining, ribbons and thread all botanically dyed with madder root, 2024.

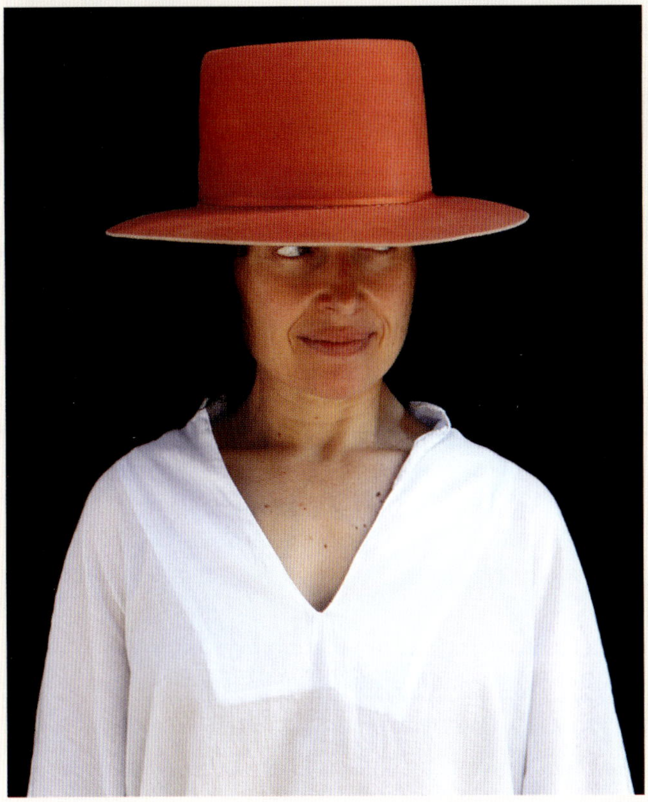

From her city apartment, Ana's life and craft are seamlessly interwoven. Her cookery kitchen also functions as her apothecary kitchen, where shelves are lined with plant dye powders arranged in a rich spectrum of colours. And in her guest suite above the bed, shelves display traditional wooden hat blocks, hand-carved by Paris-based Italian master hat-block carver Lorenzo Re. Ana's home is a representation of a maker who is truly enmeshed with her art.

While pursuing a PhD in Contemporary Art History at the Complutense University of Madrid, Ana started to accumulate a collection of hats. Fascinated by their construction, her curiosity grew until it led her to London, where she trained in hat-making under one of the best – Rose Cory. Later, returning to Madrid in 2014, Ana was equipped with the skills in fine hat-making from finishing, to lining, to blocking to draping.

Her hats are undoubtedly works of art – yet it is her more recent transition into the world of silk flower-making for gallery artefacts that captivated me when I met her for the first time at XTANT in 2024 – a world textile fair curated by Kavita Parmar, held each May at Can Vivot in Palma, Mallorca.

But where did this infatuation with flowers stem from?

As a child, Ana would spend her summers at her grandmother's house in the mountains, 50km (30 miles) north-west of Madrid, in Collado Mediano. The journey was magical. The house was a natural oasis – the garden in full bloom, butterflies fluttering, and grasshoppers leaping from flower to flower. 'Everything was so special,' Ana recalls, smiling as she remembers the thrill of jumping the garden fence and running into the forest with her older brother and cousin.

Her grandmother's garden had a walkway lined with fragrant roses, but it was one flower in particular – the gum rockrose (*Cistus ladanifer*) – that left a lasting impression. With its white petals and creamy golden centre, the flower has a sweet and intense smell.

With such personal fond memories of flowers locked in her mind, it's no surprise, then, that Ana found her way into silk flower-making – a traditional millinery art that she picked up intuitively. She furthered her skills by taking classes with English silk flower master Anne Tomlin.

'Flowers provide an endless source of inspiration,' says Ana. 'It doesn't matter how many times you look at one, you always discover something new.' She often walks the streets of Madrid with her sketchbook, documenting the shape, size and petal count of any bloom that catches her eye. Each flowerhead is carefully drafted before being brought to life.

Once a pattern is mapped out, Ana translates this onto cloth, working predominantly with silks she has pre-dyed – organza, crepe, chiffon and velvet. Ana relies on a trusty set of Japanese and French tools to achieve the petals' form.

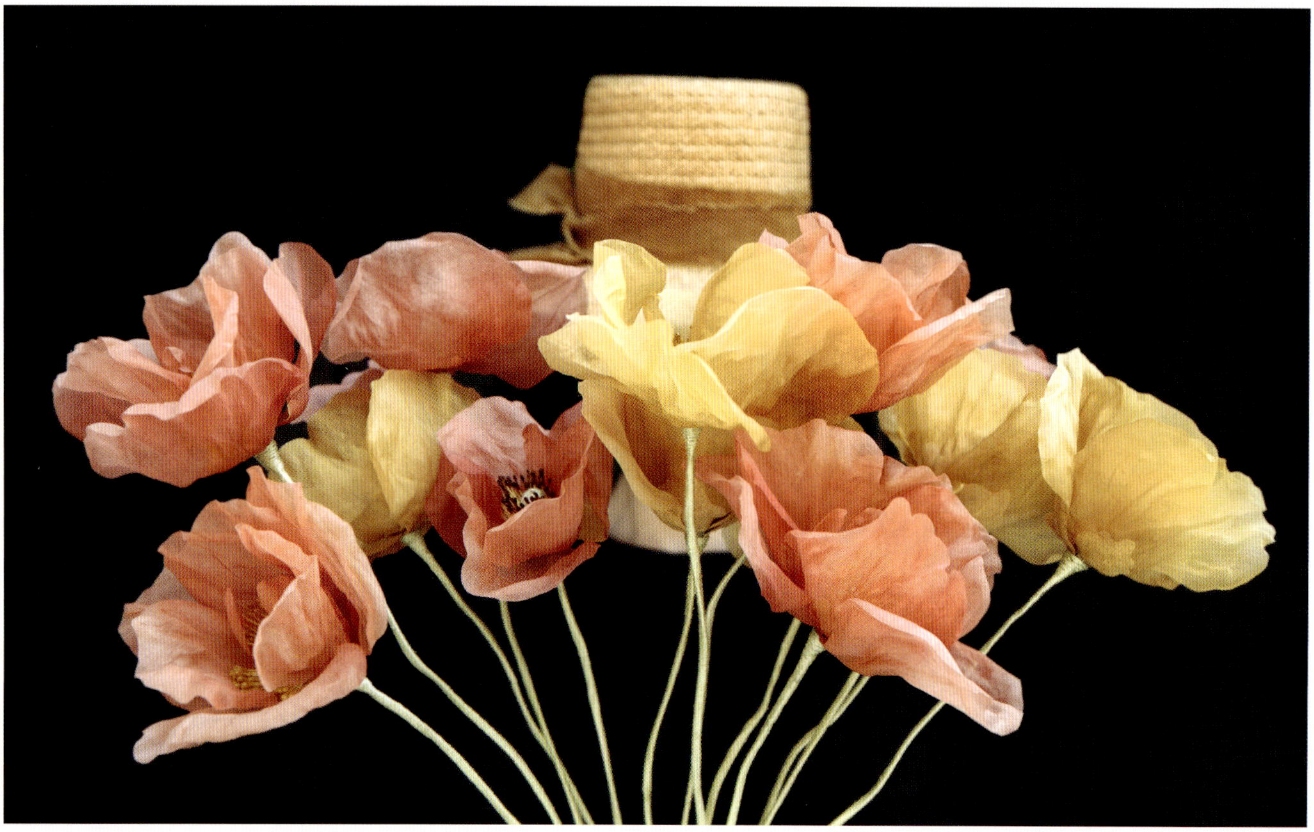

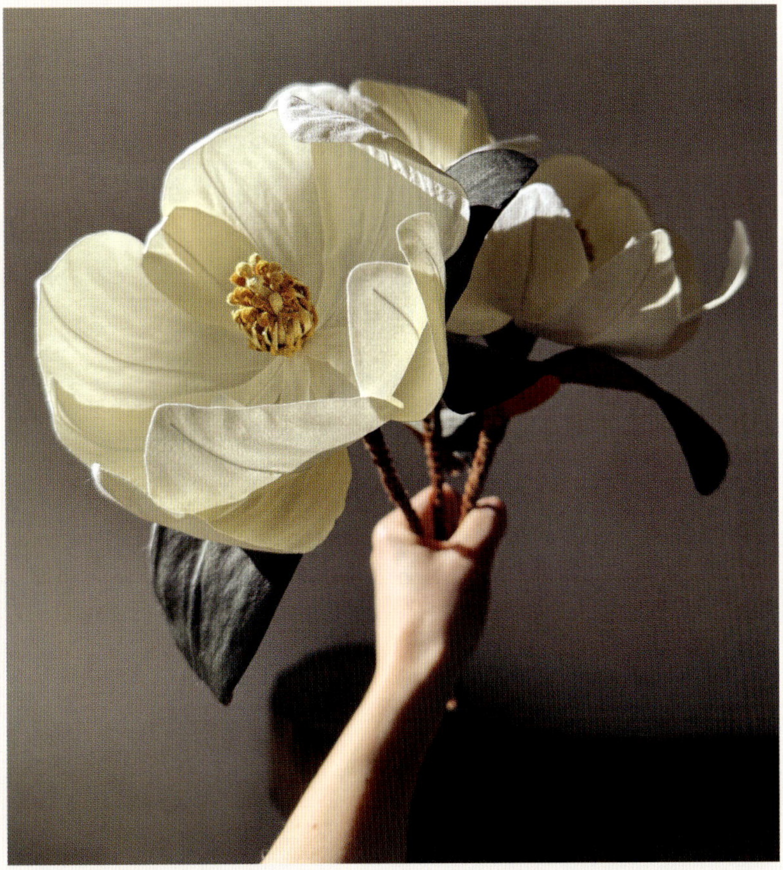

'I've made ranunculus, tulips, peonies, magnolias, cornflowers, poppies ...'

ABOVE *Magnolia grandiflora* (2024). Silk crêpe; branch dyed with myrobalan; petals dyed with cochineal; silk velvet dyed with rhubarb, weld, myrobalan and cochineal for the composite centre; and satin silk dyed with weld and indigo for the leaves.

OPPOSITE *Papaver nudicaule* (2021). Made in satin organza silk, dyed with madder root and rhubarb root. Silk velvet dyed with rhubarb for the pistil and silk thread for the stamens. Silk thread to wrap the stems dyed with myrobalan and iron acetate.

She dampens the silk and uses heat tools to delicately mould each petal into shape.

Initially, Ana made silk flowers as bridal headpieces and corsages. 'I still make them,' she says, 'but they're so delicate, they crush easily.' That changed when a friend, who is a woodworker, gifted her oak bases made from dying trees. These natural plinths became the perfect foundation for her more sculptural, gallery-focused pieces.

Ana was invited to exhibit in the Spanish Pavilion at the Venice Biennale 2024, where she presented two silk flower specimens encased in antique glass domes. She made two migrant plants brought to the Iberian Peninsula in the 16th century – garden nasturtium (*Tropaeolum majus*) and passion flower (*Passiflora caerulea*). In the domes they look like true museum artefacts, merging the realms of science, art and craft.

'For me, crafting flowers is certainly an invitation to pay closer attention to the delicacy and wonder of nature. My hope is by putting them in another context, by making them in silk, you may pay more attention to it as well.'

Ana's attention to detail is like no other; she notices minute details which the normal eye might miss. 'Take the lily of the valley. You may think, Oh yeah, it's just a flower then. No, no, in fact there is a little leaf between the span of each of the flowers.'

Working exclusively with natural fibres for both her hats and her flowers, Ana's development into natural dyeing felt inevitable. During lockdown, she had the time to explore the process. Guided by the teachings of Michel Garcia, Ana began experimenting. 'Natural dyes have a vibrancy and richness that synthetic colours simply can't match,' she says.

'This one is for a mother of the bride,' she tells me, holding a nearly finished flower. 'The statement petals are dyed with indigo. The centre is cochineal – a silk velvet dyed in deep red – and the buds are silk velvet dyed with logwood and weld to get a bright green.' Ana always keeps a stash of dyed silks at the ready.

'I've made ranunculus, tulips, peonies, magnolias, cornflowers, poppies ...' Ana's list goes on.

So what's next? Could it be the flowers from her grandmother's garden, I ask?

'I have the pattern ready and waiting,' says Ana.

Thoughts to Leave You With

I doubt that I will ever run out of inspiration year after year, as nature never looks how it did the year before. In gardening there is always more to learn, more to discover, and it is the same with textiles too. I am always learning new stitches or variations on a technique that might be similar yet different from one culture to the next.

It is this constant discovery and wonder that breathes fresh life into my work. It keeps my work gently moving, flowing and evolving, but always akin with the rhythms of nature.

I see each piece I create as an artistic maker on the ongoing journey I am committed to in developing a deeper connection between myself and our Earth.

While the pieces I make won't last forever, this book documents this precious way of making.

While writing this book, we sadly lost one of my greatest inspirations, the Buddhist scholar and environmental activist, Joanna Macy. So I leave you with her words:

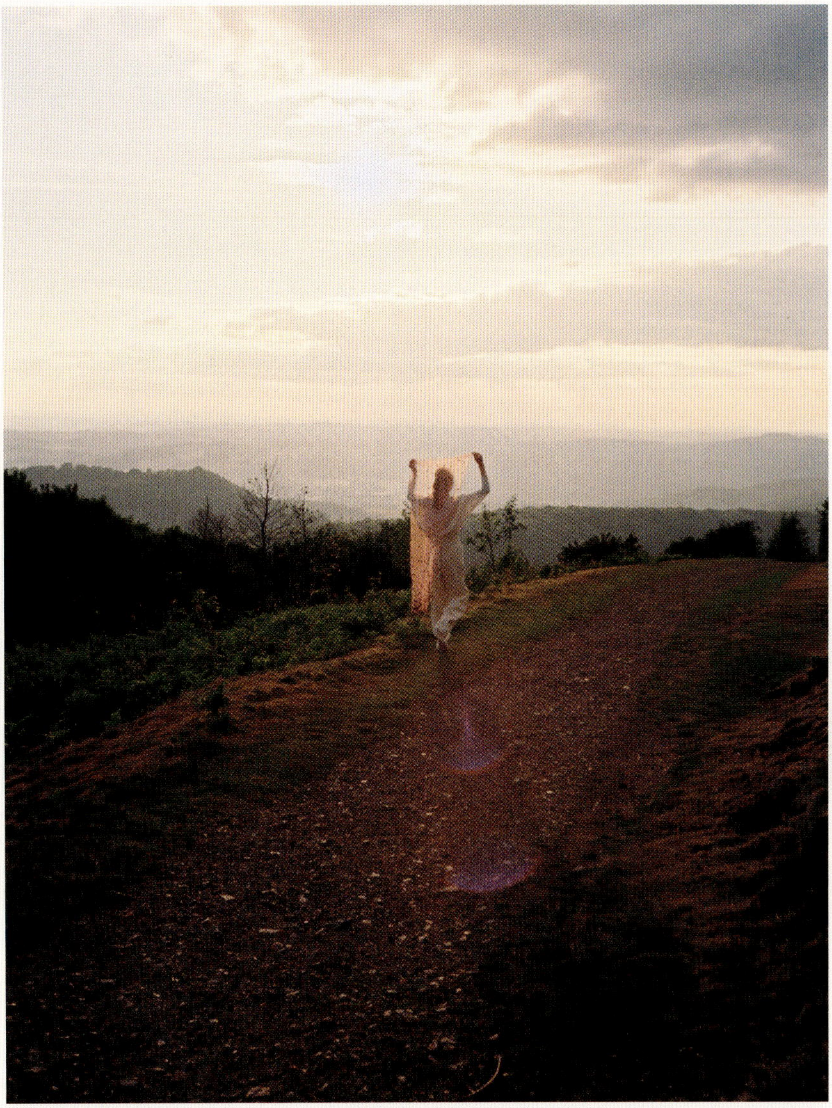

'To be alive in this beautiful, self-organizing universe is to participate in the dance of life with senses to perceive it, lungs that breathe it, organs that draw nourishment from it – it is a wonder beyond words.'

JOANNA MACY (1929–2025)

Resources

BOOKS

Almqvist, Kurt and Belfrage, Louise, *Hilma af Klint: Visionary* (Stolpe Publishing, 2019)
Austin, David, *The Breathing Earth* (Enitharmon Press, 2014)
Blackie, Sharon, *If Women Rose Rooted* (September, 2019)
Celant, Germano, *Louise Bourgeois: The Fabric Works* (Skira Editore, 2010)
Chanin, Natalie, *Geometry of Hand Sewing* (Abrams, 2017)
Fletcher, Kate, *Design and Nature: A Partnership* (Taylor & Francis Group, 2019)
Hunter, Clare, *Threads of Life: A History of the World Through the Eye of a Needle* (Sceptre, 2020)
Jekyll, Gertrude, *Gertrude Jekyll's Colour Schemes for the Flower Garden* (Country Life, 1911)
Kaul, Ekta, *Kantha: Sustainable Textiles and Mindful Making* (Herbert Press, 2024)
Kumar, Satish, *Earth Pilgrim: Conversations with Satish Kumar* (Green Books, 2009)
Kumar, Satish, *Spiritual Compass: The Three Qualities of Life* (Green Books, 2007)
Logan, Jason, *Make Ink: A Forager's Guide to Natural Inkmaking* (Abrams, 2018)
Macy, Joanna, and Johnstone, Chris, *Coming Back to Life* (New Society Publishers, 2014)
Vincent, Alice, *Why Women Grow* (Canongate Books, 2024)
Vuong, Ocean, *On Earth We're Briefly Gorgeous* (Johnathan Cape, 2019)
Wall Kimmerer, Robin, *Braiding Sweetgrass* (Penguin, 2020)

WEBSITES

Bright Earth Buddhist Temple
brightearth.org

Joanna Macy: Work That Reconnects Network
workthatreconnects.org

The Resurgence Trust
resurgence.org

RHS: Plant Library
rhs.org.uk/plants

RSN Stitchbank
rsnstitchbank.org

FEATURED ARTISTS

Shannon Clegg
shannonclegg.co.uk

Rachna Garodia
rachnagarodia.com

Ana Lamata
analamata.com

Jasmine Linington
jasminelinington.com

Index

Acknowledgements

Firstly, thank you to Amanda for saying yes to coming on this journey with me, capturing my vision so perfectly through your lens – this book has marked the start of a wonderful creative partnership and blossoming friendship.

Thank you to the team at Batsford Books for finding resonance in my story, and providing me with the joy of being able to slowly craft this book.

Thank you to the sangha at Bright Earth Buddhist Temple, and Ravavani, for welcoming me into your garden and offering me a sacred space to grow my flowers.

My practice *Stitching with Nature* started while completing my Masters at RCA, so thank you to my tutor Seetal Solanki, for your gentle nurturing guidance. Thank you to my RCA friends and fellow artists – especially Isabel, Line and Penelope – for your trusting critique and encouragement.

Thank you to my sister, my best friend, Tanisha, who is always by my side. You inspire the ambition within me.

But most of all, thank you to my parents, for your eternal support and love. You are always keeping your eyes open, with secateurs in hand, foraging and gathering from your garden, thinking of me. The day you took on the allotment, without knowing it, you didn't just give me a place to learn to grow, you gave me a place to find myself – and to find kindness, contentment and healing.

PICTURE CREDITS

Photography by Amanda Jackson, with the exception of:

Page 2: Leonie Sinden for *The Lissome* magazine
Pages 9, 102 and 125: Claire O'Keefe for Cortana
Pages 10, 12, 13, 17 (bottom), 18, 36, 37, 40, 42, 43, 45, 51, 52, 56, 77, 80–90, 93–98, 100, 119: Katerina Knight
Pages 46, 48 and 49: Yeshen Venema
Page 47: Alice Poole
Pages 58, 59, 60 (bottom) and 61: Shannon Clegg
Page 60 (top): Anna Olszewska
Pages 66 and 68: Jasmine Linington
Page 67: Alex McIntosh
Pages 120 and 123: Ana Lamata
Pages 121 and 122: Miguel Cocera